The Adolescent Criminal

The Adolescent Criminal
An Examination of Today's Juvenile Offender

by
R. Barri Flowers

McFarland & Company, Inc., Publishers
Jefferson, North Carolina, and London

British Library Cataloguing-in-Publication data are available

Library of Congress Cataloguing-in-Publication Data

Flowers, Ronald B.
    The adolescent criminal: an examination of today's juvenile
offender / by R. Barri Flowers.
      p. cm.
    [Includes index.]
    Includes bibliographical references.
    ISBN 0-89950-479-5 (lib. bdg. : 50# alk. paper) ∞
    1. Juvenile delinquency — United States. 2. Juvenile justice,
Administration of — United States. I. Title.
HV9104.F63 1990
364.3'6'0973 — dc20   89-13429
                                          CIP

364.36
F644

Manufactured in the United States of America

McFarland & Company, Inc., Publishers
  Box 611, Jefferson, North Carolina 28640

In devotion to my darling wife, Loraine, indeed a rare gem among mere mortals, who captured my heart so long ago and who continues to redefine what it means to be beautiful and in love. May the future continue to be ours to pursue our personal and professional aspirations together.

In earnest presentation as well to my wonderful parents, Johnnie Henry Flowers, Sr., and Marjah Aljean Flowers. Mother dear, you believed in me well before I ever did. Thank you for your love, support, and faith. Dad, do know that my ascent into the worlds of criminology and criminal justice and striving to fulfill my objectives in life are but a reflection on you.

Contents

**Part IV   Further Issues in Delinquency,
Trends, and Implications for the Future**

Preface

ADOLESCENCE IS A TIME in our lives when our behavioral patterns are most susceptible to influence. These transitional years are often accompanied by new wants and desires, sexual and drug experimentation, loss of respect for authority, peer pressure, recognition of differences in opportunity among our contemporaries, frustrations of various kinds, a yearning for adventure, loneliness—a search for one's identity. The pressures of adolescence today are intensified in a society characterized by high mobility, fragmented families, sexual and physical abuse, inconsistent child disciplinary practices, social changes, high-crime neighborhoods, double standards, racial prejudices, affluence, and poverty. Given that most juveniles must confront some combination of these elements during their teenage years, it is reasonable to suggest that, for many, delinquent behavior is inevitable. In fact, if delinquency is taken in its broadest context, which includes status offenses such as talking back to one's parents or incorrigibility, it is highly likely that each of us has at one time qualified as being an "adolescent delinquent."

This book is about the explanations put forth in attempting to understand adolescent crime and delinquency; the role of the juvenile justice system in creating "delinquency" and trying to combat it; trends in juvenile delinquency prevention; and implications for controlling adolescent criminality in the future. But what this book is most about are the adolescent offenders themselves: who they are, the nature and extent of their crimes and delinquencies, what makes them tick, and what has been and is being done to come face to face with the issues surrounding the adolescent offender.

This study of juvenile delinquency is primarily concerned with the adolescent years of youth where delinquency behavior is most pronounced. Unlike most criminology books that rely on a sociological perspective in examining crime and delinquency, this work has taken a multicontextual, multidisciplinary approach to exploring the adolescent criminal. The advantage in this is that it takes into consideration the contributions, strengths and weaknesses of the various schools of thought with respect to

ix

the delinquency of adolescents—sociological, psychological, biological, familial, demographical, legal, and international, and their implications for the future—in order to present the reader with a greater overall perspective and knowledge of the dynamics of adolescent crime today.

The Adolescent Criminal has been written for undergraduate and graduate students of criminology, criminal justice, sociology, psychology, law and related disciplines. The book is also relevant to law enforcement and juvenile justice officials, legislators, sociologists, and other professional audiences, as well as a general readership of intelligent citizens wishing to be more enlightened on the deeper ramifications of juvenile delinquency in America.

I would like to express my gratitude toward my parents, Johnnie and Jean Flowers, whose vision propelled me into a career as a criminology writer. I owe all the thanks in the world to my strong support system, administrative secretary, typist, and beautiful wife, H. Loraine, who wonderfully recreated my many tables in type form, painstakingly translated my rough draft into a very readable manuscript, and lovingly kept the pressure on me to see this project through to completion.

R. Barri Flowers
Winter, 1990

Introduction

ADOLESCENT ANTISOCIAL BEHAVIOR is one of the most important and debatable issues we face as a nation in the 1990s. Despite indications that juvenile delinquency is decreasing, a closer look at the picture gives much cause for concern. Adolescent crime has become increasingly more sophisticated, violent and heterogeneous, and its participants younger. Gang violence has spread out from urban centers into suburbia, and gang members have become more organized in their activities. Juvenile prostitution has shown little sign of abating despite the new presence of the deadly disease AIDS. Drug and alcohol use among adolescents has reached epidemic proportions, as have running away from home and pettier acts of delinquency.

One obvious subfacet of the predicament of adolescent misbehavior is how best to solve it. The juvenile justice system was once thought to be the answer. However, in recent years the justice system has come under attack from at least two quarters: from those who feel the system is incapable of responding to the serious, adult-like adolescent offender; and from others who believe that the juvenile justice system has no business defining and governing behavior of juveniles that, even if not always acceptable, would not be legal offenses were the perpetrators of adult age. Then there are charges that sexual and racial discrimination are employed in juvenile justice practices. The police are caught in the middle, as they must often fight a losing battle on the front line against juvenile crime, decide whom to pull into the justice system and whom not to, and at the same time honor the rights of juveniles and protect themselves and the community.

At the root of the issue of adolescent deviance are the various causes that are theorized and proposed by experts from various disciplines. Unfortunately in many cases such propositions produce more questions than answers.

In *The Adolescent Criminal* we will examine the most important issues, components, and trends concerning adolescent misconduct from the vantage point of the end of the 1980s, and will concern ourselves with what to look for in the future. The book has been divided into four parts.

1

Part One explores the various dimensions of adolescent crime. Chapter 1 defines adolescent criminality, examines the major means for measuring juvenile crime, and analyzes its general scope and characteristics. Chapter 2 investigates the dynamics of the violent adolescent offender. In Chapter 3, magnitude and diversity of adolescent property crime is probed. The controversies and dimensions of the status offender are explored in Chapter 4. An in-depth investigation of adolescent prostitution and child pornography is presented in Chapter 5. Chapter 6 looks at key issues surrounding the delinquency of females. In Chapter 7, the ramifications of adolescent use and abuse of drugs and alcohol are closely examined. The problem of adolescent gang delinquency is focused on in Chapter 8.

Part Two addresses theoretical insight and explanations concerning adolescent deviant behavior. Chapter 9 explores biological approaches to delinquency. Chapter 10 discusses the psychological perspective on adolescent antisocial behavior. Chapter 11 reviews the sociological contribution to understanding juvenile delinquency. In Chapter 12, the role of family determinants in adolescent delinquent conduct is explored.

Part Three examines the juvenile justice system. The role of law enforcement in adolescent-police encounters is addressed in Chapter 13. Various issues in the juvenile court system such as its history, juvenile rights, and the court process are analyzed in Chapter 14. In Chapter 15, the features of juvenile correctional institutions and inmates are analyzed. Chapter 16 looks at noninstitutional, community-based corrections for young offenders.

Part Four addresses further issues in adolescent crime, delinquency prevention, and future implications. Chapter 17 examines adolescent delinquency and crime in other countries. Chapter 18 discusses trends in delinquency prevention and control and ways in which we might better be able to deal with the problem and prevention of adolescent misbehavior in the future.

1. The Measurement and Characteristics of Adolescent Crime

FEW PEOPLE WOULD ARGUE that crime and delinquency among our youth is one of the nation's most pressing problems. How we come to grips with the issues surrounding juvenile delinquency in the future may well hinge on our basic understanding today of the dynamics of adolescent criminality. As we begin our examination into the adolescent criminal, our first step will be to define juvenile criminality, its scope and how it is recorded and the built-in shortcomings of such indicators, and to establish some perspective on the magnitude and range of adolescent antisocial behavior.

Defining Adolescent Criminality

There has never been a uniform definition of adolescent antisocial behavior, and it figures that there never will be. This is largely because the adolescent or juvenile is in a unique position regarding how they are viewed by the rest of us. They can be labeled antisocial both for acts of criminality and for other behavior that is considered legal and even acceptable by adults. Even then such definition is subject to interpretation, variation, and subjectiveness. Generally, definitions of adolescent misbehavior follow two distinct lines: legalistic and nonlegalistic.

Legalistic Definitions

Legalistic definitions of delinquency are primarily derived from cases decided in state and federal courts and state statutes. In the strictest legal sense, an adolescent is considered a juvenile delinquent when he or she has been officially processed by the juvenile court and adjudged by the court to be delinquent. However, legal definitions of delinquency do not stop or, for that matter, even begin there. Typically, the legality of juvenile offenders is broken down into those who are referred to as delinquents and

3

those termed status offenders. For the most part, a delinquent is anyone who has broken a criminal law, while a status offender is a juvenile who has violated a law applicable only to juveniles. Generally, whether it is for status or criminal law violations, juveniles are subject to juvenile court jurisdiction.

The legal differences between the juvenile delinquent and the juvenile status offender can be seen clearly in, for instance, the California laws which govern juvenile behavior. Although the wording may vary from state to state, the basic premise of juvenile laws is the same in every state. The California statute falls under the Welfare and Institution Code, of which Sections 601 and 602 summarize the state's legal definitions of juveniles and delinquents.

> Section 601 defines the status offender as any person under the age of 18 years who persistently or habitually refuses to obey the reasonable and proper orders or directions of his [or her] parents, guardian, custodian, or school authorities, or who is beyond the control of such person, or any person who is a habitual truant from school within the meaning of any law of this state, or who from any cause is in danger of leading an idle, dissolute, lewd or immoral life, is within the jurisdiction of the juvenile court which may adjudge such person to be a ward of the court.[1]

This broad definition of a status offender makes it possible for juveniles to be arrested and labeled for any number of behavioral patterns. Status offenders may be adolescents who consistently talk back to their parents or youths who run away from an abusive home. In either case, the conduct would not be considered an offense were it committed by an adult.

Section 602 groups together all remaining possible offenses of juveniles in defining the juvenile delinquent as

> any person who is under the age of 18 years when he [or she] violates any law of this state or of the United States or any ordinance of any city or county of this state defining crime or who, after having been found by the juvenile court to be a person described by Section 601, fails to obey any lawful order of the juvenile court, is within the jurisdiction of the juvenile court, which may adjudge such person to be a ward of the court.[2]

All juveniles who commit any criminal offenses in California are charged under Section 602, whether the crime is murder or shoplifting.

Although technically all criminal laws apply to both juveniles and adults, how the laws are applied to juveniles (if at all) varies with their age and the state in which the offense occurs. Currently only six states have established a minimum age for a juvenile to be referred to the juvenile court, with four of these states making such an age to be 10 years old.[3] Under common law, it is presumed that criminal liability can not be affixed to a person younger than the age of 7; however, there are no state statutes to this effect.

The maximum age for which the juvenile court has original jurisdiction is inconsistent in state and federal codes. In 38 states, the District of Columbia, and federal codes, the highest age over which the juvenile court has original jurisdiction is 17; in eight states the age is 16; and in four states the maximum age of juvenile court jurisdiction is 15.[4] Hence, a person 18 or under who breaks the law could be referred to the juvenile or adult court, depending upon the state the crime was committed in.

In certain instances, juveniles may be tried as adults in criminal courts even if their age and the state puts them under the original jurisdiction of the juvenile court. One way this occurs is when the state juvenile code specifies that when a juvenile is accused of a serious crime (i.e., murder) or has a long history of crime, regardless of age, the juvenile court has no jurisdiction in the case. Juvenile offenders may also come under adult court jurisdiction in cases of "concurrent jurisdiction," or instances when the prosecutor has at his/her discretion the choice of filing charges against the juvenile in either the adult criminal or juvenile court. The typical means in which cases concerning juveniles comes before adult criminal courts is through judicial waiver, which refers to the transfer from the original jurisdiction of the juvenile court. In ten states there is no minimum age limit in which juvenile cases may be waived to adult criminal courts. For those states that have such a limit, the age usually ranges from 14 to 16.[5]

In rare instances, a person over the age of 18 can be tried by the juvenile court.[6] Predominantly, however, the "legal age" in a given state determines whether the person will fall under the juvenile or adult court jurisdiction.

Nonlegalistic Definitions

Nonlegalistic definitions of delinquency are generally formed from studies on adolescent behavioral patterns, interpretations of the law, social trends, prejudices, and misconceptions. The nonlegal definition of a delinquent youth can vary drastically from person to person and, as illustrated below, from profession to profession:

> Sociologists define the juvenile delinquent as a person who not only commits a delinquent act, but who is also labeled by the way society reacts to it. Psychiatrists' definitions emphasize the emotional tones and attitudes involved and any mental pathology. Psychologists view the delinquent not only by the act of delinquency, but by the way the juvenile thinks about it.[7]

Defining who is delinquent and who is not is largely a matter not simply of individual tastes, but of the norms and culture of the society we live in. What may be deemed as a delinquent act in the United States may well be acceptable behavior in another part of the world. As we shall see later in this book, even in this country the same activity could be viewed differently depending upon the perspective of the labeler. For example, minority youths are often disproportionately labeled delinquents for activities in which middle class white youths are seen as merely "sowing their oats."

For purposes of this study, the adolescent offender shall be defined as a person who falls within the legal age range of a juvenile in any given state or the federal codes, who, under that definition, commits an act that violates the norms of that state, federal codes, or society, which by law would be construed as criminal, deviant, or a status offense.

The Boundaries of Adolescent Offenses

The depth of adolescent behavior that falls within the definition of delinquency varies from the least serious (status offense) to the most serious criminal violations of the law. Adolescents who commit offenses applicable only to juveniles such as running away, incorrigibility and truancy are labeled juvenile status offenders. The juvenile status offense is the broadest and most frequent category of adolescent criminality for which youths are arrested.

Petty offenses are the most frequent juvenile violation of criminal laws. Such offenses include substance abuse/misuse, shoplifting, and malicious mischief. The majority of these crimes go undetected; those that are discovered rarely result in the arrest of the offender.[8] Some criminologists estimate that petty crimes represent as much as 90 percent of all juvenile criminality.[9]

Serious crimes, or felonies, such as murder, rape, assault, auto theft, and robbery are the least common yet most noticed and publicized types of adolescent antisocial behavior. Violent crimes account for roughly 10 percent of all juvenile arrests. It is estimated that between 5 and 10 percent of all serious delinquent offenses fall into this category.[10] The most common types of juvenile felonies are property offenses, such as auto theft, burglary, and grand larceny, where no violence is used.

Assessing Adolescent Criminality

There is no foolproof method for recording accurately the incidence of delinquency. This is not surprising when one considers the heterogeneity of adolescent behavior that classifies as delinquency, the nonuniformity of methodology in gathering data, the subjectiveness of labeling, and the unknown delinquency. Yet the importance of gathering data on the magnitude, characteristics, and frequency of juvenile delinquency can not be overstated, for before we can effectively fight criminality we need a heightened perspective on its dimensions.

There are three primary sources in which the bulk of what we know about the scope and nature of adolescent antisocial behavior is gathered and tabulated: official statistics, self-report surveys, and victimization surveys.

The predominant means of compiling and recording official statistics on juvenile delinquency is the Federal Bureau of Investigations' *Uniform Crime Reports* UCR. Beginning with its 1964 edition, this annual has presented various offender, arrest and incarceration data on juveniles as provided by the police, courts, and corrections departments in the United States. Offenses are dichotomized into two categories: Type I (Crime Index) and Type II (nonindex). Type I consists of eight offenses believed to comprise the most serious crimes reported to law enforcement: violent crimes — murder/nonnegligent manslaughter, forcible rape, robbery and aggravated assault; and property crimes — burglary, larceny, motor vehicle theft, and arson. Type II refers to less serious offenses including forgery and counterfeiting, embezzlement, prostitution and commercialized vice, sex offenses, and drug abuse violations.

Self-report surveys offer a second means of gathering information on the frequency and distribution of delinquent activities. This data consists of asking the youths themselves if they committed acts that led (or could have) to arrest or referral to the juvenile court.

The third significant source of information on juvenile criminality is crime victimization surveys. These surveys rely on random victim respondents to describe the type and nature of the offense perpetrated against them, and estimate the age of the offender.

Each of these sources have major flaws that limit their reliability. These will be explored later in the chapter.

Official Statistics on Delinquency

Law enforcement tracks two kinds of delinquency statistics based on arrest. One of these focuses on the offenses cleared or solved by the arrest of at least one person, the charge with commission of the crime (where applicable), and an appearance in court. In 1986, persons under age 18 accounted for 19.1 percent of the Crime Index clearances in the United States (see Table 1-1). The clearance rate for violent crime was 9 percent, compared to 22.6 percent for property crimes. The highest percentage of clearances was for arson cases, whereas the lowest clearance rate of juvenile participation was for murder.

Table 1-1. Offenses Cleared by Arrest[a] of Persons Under 18 Years of Age, 1986 (1986 estimated population)

Offense	Total All Agencies: 13,461 Agencies; Population 223,695,000	
	Total Clearances	Percent Under 18
Crime Index total	2,600,384	19.1
Modified Crime Index total[b]	2,616,652	19.2
Violent crime[c]	657,297	9.0
Property crime[d]	1,943,087	22.6
Murder & nonnegligent manslaughter	13,619	4.6
Forcible rape[e]	42,808	9.6
Robbery	130,010	11.2
Aggravated assault	470,860	8.4
Burglary	416,708	20.9
Larceny-theft	1,354,885	23.4
Motor vehicle theft	171,494	20.2
Arson[b]	16,268	35.4

[a]Includes offenses cleared by exceptional means.
[b]The number of agency reports used in arson clearance rates is less than used in compiling clearance rates for other Crime Index offenses.
[c]Violent crimes are offenses of murder, forcible rape, robbery, and aggravated assault.
[d]Property crimes are offenses of burglary, larceny-theft, and motor vehicle theft. Data are not included for the property crime of arson.
[e]Forcible rape figures furnished by the state-level Uniform Crime Reporting (UCR) Program administered by the Illinois Department of State Police were not in accordance with national UCR guidelines and were excluded from the Forcible rape, Violent crime, Crime Index total, and Modified Crime Index total categories.
Source: U.S. Federal Bureau of Investigation, Crime in the United States 1986 (Washington, D.C.: Government Printing Office, 1987), pp. 161-162.

The other statistical data recorded by police agencies is the number of persons arrested for a certain crime. These figures do not measure the number of individuals taken into custody, since a person may be arrested more than once during a particular year for the same or different offenses. As seen in Table 1-2, persons under 18 accounted for 16.8 percent of all arrests in 1986, with those under age 15 making up 5.2 percent of the total arrests. These percentages rise dramatically for Crime Index offenses.

Table 1-2. Total Arrests of Persons Under 15 and 18 Years of Age, 1986 (10,743 agencies; 1986 estimated population 198,488,000)

	Total All Ages	Number of Persons Arrested		% of Total All Ages	
		Under 15	Under 18	Under 15	Under 18
TOTAL	10,392,177	536,609	1,747,675	5.2	16.8
Murder & nonnegligent manslaughter	16,066	156	1,396	1.0	8.7
Forcible rape	31,128	1,514	4,798	4.9	15.4
Robbery	124,245	6,615	27,987	5.3	22.5
Aggravated assault	293,952	10,816	37,528	3.7	12.8
Burglary	375,544	47,080	134,823	12.5	35.9
Larceny-theft	1,182,099	156,033	378,283	13.2	32.0
Motor vehicle theft	128,514	11,961	50,319	9.3	39.2
Arson	15,523	3,837	6,271	24.7	40.4
Violent crime[a]	465,391	19,101	71,709	4.1	15.4
Property crime[b]	1,701,680	218,911	569,696	12.9	33.5
Crime Index total[c]	2,167,071	238,012	641,405	11.0	29.6
Other assaults	593,902	30,411	85,905	5.1	14.5
Forgery & counterfeiting	76,546	1,101	7,234	1.4	9.5
Fraud	284,790	6,722	17,727	2.4	6.2
Embezzlement	10,500	52	696	0.5	6.6
Stolen property; buying, receiving, possessing	114,105	7,613	28,739	6.7	25.2
Vandalism	223,231	45,247	95,479	20.3	42.8
Weapons; carrying, possessing, etc.	160,204	6,394	25,170	4.0	15.7
Prostitution & commercialized vice	96,882	247	2,192	0.3	2.3
Sex offenses (except forcible rape & prostitution)	83,934	6,110	13,753	7.3	16.4
Drug abuse violations	691,882	9,374	68,351	1.4	9.9
Gambling	25,839	105	610	0.4	2.4
Offenses against family & children	47,327	1,255	2,521	2.7	5.3
Driving under the influence	1,458,531	456	22,749	(d)	1.6
Liquor laws	490,436	10,163	132,335	2.1	27.0
Drunkenness	777,866	3,283	26,589	0.4	3.4
Disorderly conduct	564,882	22,517	82,986	4.0	14.7
Vagrancy	32,992	539	2,500	1.6	7.7
All other offenses (except traffic)	2,272,589	70,918	276,876	3.1	12.2

	Total All Ages	Number of Persons Arrested		% of Total All Ages	
		Under 15	Under 18	Under 15	Under 18
Suspicion	7,455	846	2,595	11.3	34.8
Curfew & loitering law violations	72,627	19,260	72,627	26.5	100.0
Runaways	138,586	55,984	138,586	40.4	100.0

[a]*Violent crimes are offenses of murder, forcible rape, robbery, and aggravated assault.*
[b]*Property crimes are offenses of burglary, larceny-theft, motor vehicle theft, and arson.*
[c]*Includes arson.*
[d]*Less than one-tenth of one percent.*
    Source: *U.S. Federal Bureau of Investigation,* **Crime in the United States 1986** *(Washington, D.C.: Government Printing Office, 1987), p. 180.*

Nearly 30 percent of the arrestees were under 18; 11 percent under 15. However, the bulk of these arrests were for property crimes as opposed to violent crimes.

The figures show that for nonindex offenses, the crimes in which juveniles were highest represented were all other offenses (except traffic), liquor law violations, vandalism, and other assaults; and the status offenses of runaways and curfew and loitering law violations, both of which comprised of 100 percent persons under the age of 18.

If we look at Table 1–3 and 1–4, we can compare 1986 arrest patterns for males and females under the age of 18. Table 1–3 shows the offenses for which youths were most arrested. The only common rankings by sex were for larceny-theft (rank one), liquor laws (rank four), and drug abuse violations (rank 9). Overall, males tended to be arrested more frequently for criminal violations of the law; whereas female arrestees were more apt to be arrested for status offenses. At the same time, both sexes had the same ten offenses in which they were most frequently arrested.

When examining the offenses that accounted for the least arrests of male and female adolescents in 1986, as shown in Table 1–4, we see that there also is no consistent pattern in the rankings, aside from suspicion (rank six). Gambling ranked in the top two for each sex for least arrests. The same offenses made up 9 of the top 10 least arrests of adolescents of both sexes, differing only in the number 9 ranking of sex offenses for females and forgery and counterfeiting for males.

These comparisons in association with other data give us an important indication of the types and frequency of crime for males and females under the age of 18.

The distribution of adolescent criminality is also broken down by race and ethnic origin. According to the 1986 UCR, whites under the age of 18 accounted for 74.8 percent of the total arrests of juveniles; blacks 23.3

Table 1-3. Most Frequent Arrests of Adolescents,[a] by Sex, 1986

Rank	Male	Rank	Female
1	Larceny-theft	1	Larceny-theft
2	All other offenses (except traffic)	2	Runaways
		3	All other offenses (except traffic)
3	Burglary		
4	Liquor laws	4	Liquor laws
5	Vandalism	5	Other assaults
6	Disorderly conduct	6	Curfew and loitering law violations
7	Other assaults		
8	Runaways	7	Disorderly conduct
9	Drug abuse violations	8	Burglary
10	Curfew and loitering law violations	9	Drug abuse violations
		10	Vandalism

[a]*Persons under the age of 18.*
Source: Compiled from U.S. Federal Bureau of Investigation, **Crime in the United States: Uniform Crime Reports 1986** *(Washington, D.C.: Government Printing Office, 1987), pp. 176, 178.*

Table 1-4. Least Arrests of Adolescents,[a] by Sex, 1986

Rank	Male	Rank	Female
1	Gambling	1	Embezzlement
2	Forcible rape	2	Gambling
3	Murder and nonnegligent manslaughter	3	Prostitution & commercialized vice
4	Embezzlement	4	Murder and nonnegligent manslaughter
5	Vagrancy		
6	Suspicion	5	Offenses against family and children
7	Arson		
8	Offenses against family and children	6	Suspicion
		7	Vagrancy
9	Sex offenses (except forcible rape and prostitution)	8	Forcible rape
		9	Forgery and counterfeiting
10	Prostitution & commercialized vice	10	Arson

[a]*Persons under the age of 18.*
Source: Compiled from U.S. Federal Bureau of Investigation, **Crime in the United States: Uniform Crime Reports 1986** *(Washington, D.C.: Government Printing Office, 1987), pp. 176, 178.*

percent; and other minorities 2 percent. However, black juveniles were arrested more often than whites for violent crime (52.2 percent to 46.5 percent).[11] By comparison, youths of Hispanic origin comprised of 11.8

percent of all juvenile arrests to 88.2 percent non–Hispanic youths.[12] Both blacks and Hispanics were arrested in disproportion to their numbers in the juvenile population.

Other sources in which official data are available on delinquency and juvenile offenders include the Bureau of Justice Statistics' *Children in Custody Reports,* the National Council on Crime and Delinquency's *Uniform Parole Reports,* the National Center for Juvenile Justice's *National Juvenile Court Data Archive* and the *Report of the National Juvenile Justice Assessment Centers* which combines and analyzes data from the sources noted in addition to *Uniform Crime Reports.*

The most useful secondary barometer of official delinquency to the UCR are the youths processed by the juvenile court as tabulated by the National Juvenile Court Data Archive. In 1983, the most recent data year available, an estimated 1,247,000 delinquency and status offense cases were disposed by the nation's juvenile courts. Four-fifths of these cases involved male juveniles. Minority youths are disproportionately likely to be referred to juvenile courts.[13]

Self-Report Surveys

Self-report studies have become an important supplement to official statistics in gauging the dimensions and incidence of juvenile delinquency. By asking juveniles themselves whether they have "ever" or during a particular time frame committed delinquent acts, researchers have been able to gain more insight into adolescent criminality than with only official sources. What has emerged from self-report data is that juvenile misconduct is considerably more widespread than officially recorded.

One recently completed self-reported delinquency survey of 2,000 Canadian youths aged 12 to 18 disclosed that 93 percent had committed at least one offense the preceding year that could have resulted in their referral to juvenile authorities. Eighty-eight percent of the adolescents had committed status offenses (such as truancy), while 82 percent had participated in criminal violations of the law (for example, theft and drug involvement). However, only 9 percent of the youths admitted involvement in serious crimes such as aggravated assault.[14]

The Institute for Juvenile Research conducted one of the most comprehensive surveys of self-reported delinquency. Using a random sample of 2,122 Illinois youths aged 14 to 18, the survey revealed that

> Seventy-four percent reported that they had cheated on examinations, 59 percent had consumed alcoholic beverages without parental permission, 56 percent had made anonymous telephone calls, 51 percent had engaged in petty theft, 47 percent had been involved in fistfights, 46 percent had

shoplifted, 41 percent had driven without a license, 37 percent had used or kept stolen goods, 29 percent had driven too fast or recklessly, 27 percent had intentionally damaged the property of others, 20 percent had carried weapons, and 16 percent had taken part in gang fights.[15]

Other self-report studies have focused on the distribution, nature, and variation of delinquency over time amongst male and female youths. Gary Jensen and Raymond Eve's mid–1960s questionnaire to 4,000 black and white Richmond, California, youths concluded that girls were less delinquent than boys.[16] Martin Gold and David Reimer, who examined self-report data on delinquency among American adolescents 13 to 16 years of age in 1967 and 1972, found that delinquency among girls increased during the time frame, but predominantly for non–Index offenses such as drug and alcohol use.[17]

In a comparison of nationwide self-reported delinquency surveys of 1967, 1972, and 1977, the National Institute of Mental Health found that in each of the years male youths committed significantly more delinquent acts of every type than female youths.[18] However, in 1977 in a survey of 822 midwestern adolescents conducted by Steve Cernkovich and Peggy Giordano, it was contended that although males were found to be most likely involved in delinquent activities, the gap between male and female delinquency was smaller than official data would have us to believe.[19]

Crime Victimization Surveys

The third prominent means for assessing adolescent criminality is through victimization surveys. As opposed to self-report surveys, victim surveys contact randomly selected households and ask respondents if they have been the victims of crime and the nature of such crime, including estimating the age of the perpetrator(s).

The most extensive national victimization research has been conducted annually by the Department of Justice's National Crime Survey Program (NCS) since 1972. The NCS focuses its survey on crimes with specific victims (for example, forcible rape and robbery) and victims who "understand what happened to them and how it happened and who are willing to report what they know." The age range of respondents are 12 and over and the NCS defines a victim as "the recipient of a criminal act, usually used in relation to personal crimes, but also applicable to households and commercial establishments."[20]

A recent NCS involving some 102,000 respondents nationwide reported that approximately one-third of the victims of personal crimes perceived single offenders to be between the ages of 12 and 20, while nearly 40 percent of the offenders in multiple-offender crimes were believed to be in the 12 to 20 age group. For violent single and multiple-offender crimes, roughly two-thirds of the victims under age 20 perceived their perpetrators as falling within the age group of 12 to 20. Offenders in this age category also were believed, by victims age 65 and over, to be responsible for about one-third of the single-offender robberies and the multiple-offender crimes of violence.[21] At the same time, NCS data shows that victims tend to believe that on the whole, "juvenile crime is less serious in terms of weapons use, thefts, financial losses, and injuries than is adult crime."[22]

Trends in Adolescent Criminality

Tracking adolescent criminality over a period of years enables us to better assess its nature and patterns both presently and in the future. Between 1960 and 1980, the total number of juveniles arrested displayed a pattern of increase, reaching a peak in 1974, and leveling off somewhat from 1974 to 1980.[23] The latter reduction in the number of persons arrested can be partly attributed to a decline in the United States of persons aged 10 to 17 after 1974. However, more recent indicators suggest juvenile crime is in fact slowing down.

Table 1-5 reflects the number of persons arrested under 18 years of age between 1977 and 1986. There was a 12.1 percent reduction of all juvenile

Table 1-5. Total Arrest Trends, 1977-1986 (8,494 agencies; 1986 estimated population 180,790,000)

	Number of Persons Arrested Under 18 Years of Age		
Offense Charged	1977	1986	Percent Change
TOTAL	1,824,712	1,603,497	− 12.1
Murder & nonnegligent manslaughter	1,301	1,297	− 0.3
Forcible rape	3,527	4,316	+ 22.4
Robbery	31,661	26,380	− 16.7
Aggravated assault	30,887	34,141	+ 10.5
Burglary	198,132	123,037	− 37.9
Larceny-theft	369,801	347,046	− 6.2
Motor vehicle theft	60,514	45,907	− 24.1
Arson	7,137	5,619	− 21.3

	Number of Persons Arrested Under 18 Years of Age		
Offense Charged	1977	1986	Percent Change
Violent crime[a]	67,376	66,134	− 1.8
Property crime[b]	635,584	521,609	− 17.9
Crime Index total[c]	702,960	587,743	− 16.4
Other assaults	61,726	79,391	+ 28.6
Forgery & counterfeiting	7,510	6,587	− 12.3
Fraud	21,362	17,360	− 18.7
Embezzlement	682	657	− 3.7
Stolen property; buying, receiving, possessing	29,076	26,651	− 8.3
Vandalism	99,842	86,674	− 13.2
Weapons; carrying, possessing, etc.	17,642	23,092	+ 30.9
Prostitution & commercialized vice	2,572	2,106	− 18.1
Sex offenses (except forcible rape & prostitution)	9,435	12,512	+ 32.6
Drug abuse violations	111,945	62,399	− 44.3
Gambling	1,425	559	− 60.8
Offenses against family & children	2,525	2,416	− 4.3
Driving under the influence	20,699	20,147	− 2.7
Liquor laws	101,355	117,748	+ 16.2
Drunkenness	42,439	24,348	− 42.6
Disorderly conduct	90,621	77,446	− 14.5
Vagrancy	5,028	2,313	− 54.0
All other offenses (except traffic)	263,420	259,019	− 1.7
Suspicion	5,305	2,519	− 52.5
Curfew & loitering law violations	75,672	66,757	− 11.8
Runaways	156,776	127,572	− 18.6

[a]*Violent crimes are offenses of murder, forcible rape, robbery, and aggravated assault.*
[b]*Property crimes are offenses of burglary, larceny-theft, motor vehicle theft, and arson.*
[c]*Includes arson.*
Source: *U.S. Federal Bureau of Investigation, Crime in the United States: Uniform Crime Reports 1986 (Washington, D.C.: Government Printing Office, 1987), p. 168.*

arrests, 1.8 percent for violent crime, and a 17.9 percent decline in property crime arrests. The only two Crime Index offenses to show an increase over the period were forcible rape (up 22.4 percent) and aggravated assault (up 10.5 percent). Significant decreases occurred in non–Index crime juvenile arrests for gambling, suspicion, vagrancy, drunkenness, and drug abuse violations. However, there was a marked increase over the ten year period in other assaults (up 28.6 percent), sex offenses (up 32.6 percent), and possession of weapons (up 30.9 percent).

Arrest Trends by Sex

Although males under the age of 18 have consistently far outnumbered female arrestees under 18 years of age for most offenses, females have moved gradually closer to males over the years in total criminality. For instance, in 1960 the total number of male arrestees under 18 was 414,082; compared to 70,925 arrests of females under 18, or a 6 to 1 differential.[24] In 1986, this differential had narrowed to 3.5 to 1.[25]

As we see in Table 1-6, although both males and females under the age of 18 showed declines in total arrests between 1977 and 1986, the female percentage change was 4.1 percent less. In other words, the rate of overall female arrests over the period moved 4.1 percent nearer to male arrests. This narrowing of the gap is particularly noticeable in such crimes as embezzlement, driving under the influence, and forgery and counterfeiting, where female arrests rose during the period while male arrests declined.

Table 1-6. Percent Changes of Arrests, Sex, 1977-1986 (8,494 agencies; 1986 estimated population 180,790,000)

Offense Charged	Male Under 18 Percent Change	Female Under 18 Percent Change
TOTAL	− 13.0	− 8.9
Murder & nonnegligent manslaughter	+ 3.0	− 31.0
Forcible rape	+ 23.5	− 20.7
Robbery	− 16.2	− 22.0
Aggravaged assault	+ 9.7	+ 15.3
Burglary	− 38.9	− 22.9
Larceny-theft	− 3.3	− 13.1
Motor vehicle theft	− 25.6	− 9.6
Arson	− 21.8	− 16.4
Violent crime[a]	− 2.3	+ 1.7
Property crime[b]	− 18.9	− 13.9
Crime Index total[c]	− 17.2	− 13.0
Other assaults	+ 25.7	+ 39.5
Forgery & counterfeiting	− 18.7	+ 4.6
Fraud	− 22.7	− 3.3

Offense Charged	Male Under 18 Percent Change	Female Under 18 Percent Change
Embezzlement	− 27.7	+ 83.1
Stolen property; buying, receiving, possessing	− 9.0	− 1.7
Vandalism	− 14.6	+ 4.1
Weapons; carrying, possessing, etc.	+ 30.5	+ 36.7
Prostitution & commercialized vice	− 15.0	− 19.7
Sex offenses (except forcible rape & prostitution)	+ 35.4	+ 5.1
Drug abuse violations	− 42.8	− 51.6
Gambling	− 61.0	− 58.1
Offenses against family & children	− 3.6	− 3.8
Driving under the influence	− 7.0	+ 38.9
Liquor laws	+ 10.2	+ 37.7
Drunkenness	− 43.5	− 37.2
Disorderly conduct	− 15.3	− 11.1
Vagrancy	− 53.8	− 55.1
All other offenses (except traffic)	− 0.8	− 5.0
Suspicion	− 56.4	− 29.4
Curfew & loitering law violations	− 16.6	+ 6.3
Runaways	− 18.9	− 18.4

[a]*Violent crimes are offenses of murder, forcible rape, robbery, and aggravated assault.*
[b]*Property crimes are offenses of burglary, larceny-theft, motor vehicle theft, and arson.*
[c]*Includes arson.*
Source: *U.S. Federal Bureau of Investigation,* **Crime in the United States: Uniform Crime Reports 1986** *(Washington, D.C.: Government Printing Office, 1987), p. 169.*

The increase in delinquency among females is attributed to a variety of reasons, including greater mobility for girls due to the more relaxed social and sexual mores of today, a breakdown of the traditional family, and the influence of the women's movement. Female delinquency will be examined in greater detail in Chapter 6. It should be pointed out, however, that despite the increase in the criminality of female youths, it is still quite low in comparison to male youth delinquency.

Delinquency Trends of Minority Adolescents

Delinquency trends have consistently shown minority youths, most notably blacks and Hispanics, to be overrepresented in adolescent violations of the law. In the United States Department of Justice's recent *Report to the*

Nation on Crime and Justice, which summarizes the characteristics of serious adolescent offenders, it was noted that along with being predominantly male, offenders tended to be disproportionately black and Hispanic, in relation to their representation in the population.[26] A good example of this overrepresentation can be seen in California's youth inmate population. In 1965, 50 percent of the inmates of California State Youth Authority facilities were white, 28 percent black, and 19.7 percent Hispanic. In 1986 the proportions were 25.3 percent white juvenile inmates, 39 percent were black, and 32 percent Hispanic.[27]

   Arrest figures also demonstrate this glaring disproportion of minority youths (Table 1-7). In 1986, blacks constituted 23.3 percent of all arrests

Table 1-7. Total Arrests of Persons Under 18, Distribution by Race and Ethnic Origin, 1986

| | Percent Distribution: | | | | | | | |
| | By Race[a] | | | | | By Ethnic Origin | | |
Offense Charged	*Total*	*White*	*Black*	*American Indian or Alaskan Native*	*Asian or Pacific Islander*	*Total*	*Hispanic*	*Non-Hispanic*
TOTAL	100.0	74.8	23.3	0.8	1.1	100.0	11.8	88.2
Murder & nonnegligent manslaughter	100.0	49.4	48.1	0.9	1.6	100.0	21.8	78.2
Forcible rape	100.0	45.9	52.9	0.6	0.6	100.0	9.6	90.4
Robbery	100.0	32.9	65.9	0.3	0.8	100.0	14.6	85.4
Aggravated assault	100.0	56.5	42.0	0.7	0.8	100.0	14.8	85.2
Burglary	100.0	75.7	22.6	0.8	0.9	100.0	13.9	86.1
Larceny-theft	100.0	71.7	25.8	1.1	1.4	100.0	10.8	89.2
Motor vehicle theft	100.0	65.2	32.5	1.1	1.3	100.0	14.3	85.7
Arson	100.0	84.6	14.3	0.6	0.5	100.0	8.1	91.9
Violent crime[b]	100.0	46.5	52.2	0.6	0.8	100.0	14.5	85.5
Property crime[c]	100.0	72.2	25.5	1.0	1.3	100.0	11.8	88.2
Crime Index total[d]	100.0	69.3	28.5	1.0	1.2	100.0	12.1	87.9
Other assaults	100.0	65.3	32.7	0.8	1.2	100.0	11.0	89.0
Forgery & counterfeiting	100.0	83.0	15.7	0.6	0.7	100.0	5.9	94.1
Fraud	100.0	50.0	48.3	0.2	1.4	100.0	21.2	78.8
Embezzlement	100.0	74.2	25.3	0.1	0.3	100.0	10.2	89.8
Stolen property; buying, receiving, possessing	100.0	63.4	35.3	0.5	0.8	100.0	14.4	85.6
Vandalism	100.0	83.2	15.1	0.7	0.9	100.0	9.1	90.9

	Percent Distribution:							
	By Race[a]					*By Ethnic Origin*		
Offense Charged	*Total*	*White*	*Black*	*American Indian or Alaskan Native*	*Asian or Pacific Islander*	*Total*	*Hispanic*	*Non-Hispanic*
Weapons; carrying, possessing, etc.	100.0	68.5	30.0	0.5	1.0	100.0	17.6	82.4
Prostitution & commercialized vice	100.0	62.2	35.7	0.9	1.2	100.0	8.7	91.3
Sex offenses (except forcible rape & prostitution)	100.0	73.5	25.2	0.6	0.7	100.0	10.9	89.1
Drug abuse violations	100.0	72.1	26.6	0.4	0.9	100.0	18.9	81.1
Gambling	100.0	32.5	58.2	-	9.3	100.0	10.4	89.6
Offenses against family & children	100.0	73.0	26.1	0.3	0.6	100.0	9.0	91.0
Driving under the influence	100.0	95.9	2.6	1.1	0.4	100.0	12.2	87.8
Liquor laws	100.0	95.5	2.9	1.2	0.5	100.0	5.8	94.2
Drunkenness	100.0	91.7	6.5	1.5	0.2	100.0	25.4	74.6
Disorderly conduct	100.0	74.0	25.0	0.6	0.4	100.0	11.1	88.9
Vagrancy	100.0	86.0	12.5	0.7	0.8	100.0	11.6	88.4
All other offenses (except traffic)	100.0	73.2	24.9	0.6	1.3	100.0	13.4	86.6
Suspicion	100.0	81.7	17.3	0.5	0.5	100.0	10.0	90.0
Curfew & loitering law violations	100.0	75.9	21.9	0.7	1.5	100.0	8.6	91.4
Runaways	100.0	84.3	13.4	1.0	1.4	100.0	8.7	91.3

[a]*Because of rounding, the percentages may not add to total.*
[b]*Violent crimes are offenses of murder, forcible rape, robbery, and aggravated assault.*
[c]*Property crimes are offenses of burglary, larceny-theft, motor vehicle theft, and arson.*
[d]*Includes arson.*
Source: U.S. Federal Bureau of Investigation, Crime in the United States: Uniform Crime Reports 1986 (Washington, D.C.: Government Printing Office, 1987), pp. 183, 186.

for persons under 18, as compared to their approximately 13 percent representation of the juvenile population. The differential was considerably wider for arrests for violent crime (52.2 percent), gambling (58.2 percent), fraud (48.3 percent) and prostitution and commercialized vice (35.7 percent).

Similarly, young people of Hispanic origin comprised of 11.8 percent of the total arrests of persons under age 18 in 1986, in contrast to their approximately 6 percent of the adolescent population. Hispanic youth arrests well exceeded their overall population figures for violent crimes

(14.5 percent), fraud (21.2 percent), drunkenness (25.4 percent), and drug abuse violations (18.9 percent).

The Shortcomings of Adolescent Crime Data

Despite the need for and importance of data on juvenile criminality, there are serious shortcomings in the validity of such information; hence it is flawed in its utilization in the study and understanding of adolescent crime.

Official Statistics

The major weakness of official data is that they are subject to uncontrolled factors. A number of sociologists and criminologists have pointed this out in criticizing such statistics. Charles Shireman and Frederic Reamer argue that the severe limitations of official sources lie in the "unknown relationship between the number of crimes actually committed, the number of those reported to the police, and the number of those so reported actually recorded and reported by the police."[28] In *Criminology,* Edwin Sutherland and Donald Cressey describe the unreliability of official measurement of criminality:

> The statistics about crime and delinquency are probably the most unreliable and most difficult of all statistics. It is impossible to determine with accuracy the amount of crime in any given jurisdiction or any particular time. Some behavior is labeled "delinquent" or "crime" by one observer, but not by another. Obviously a large proportion of all law violations go undetected. Other crimes are detected but not officially recorded.[29]

The most common criticisms leveled against official statistics are as follows:

- Official statistics reflect only offenses law enforcement agencies are aware of.
- Statistics are not compiled for all offenses.
- The reliance on percent changes in the total volume of Crime Index offenses.
- The problem of defining a crime (i.e., arrest, charged, guilty).
- The basis of crime rates.
- An inadequate index of the gravity of the crime.
- The variance of UCR criminal statistics.
- The differential enforcement of criminal statistics.
- Accommodating features of the legal system.
- The voluntary method of gathering criminal statistics.[30]

Self-Report Studies

Self-report data are limited by a number of biases, such as the honesty and accuracy of the respondents. For example, it is virtually impossible to assess the degree of over- or underreporting of the incidence or the nature of the delinquent activities of adolescents. Another weakness can be seen in seeking to verify self-reported data with juvenile court records. By doing this, it would negate the anonymity that the respondents would need if they were to be truthful without worry of punitive actions.

Other biases associated with self-report studies include the variables of sampling, communication problems, and measurement difficulties. The majority of self-report surveys are local rather than national samples, and must depend on both official permission (as in the case of gaining entry to an institution) and individual cooperation.

Victimization Surveys

Victimization surveys are perhaps the least reliable method for tracking and recording the incidence of adolescent criminality. For one, the victim must be willing to discuss his/her victimization (most are not), and must have seen the offender in order to estimate their age, which of course is subject to interpretation and the circumstances of the incident (for example, lighting or the stress involved).

Another prominent weakness of victim data in measuring delinquent activities is the fact that the statistics' main focus is on the victim, not the offender. Also, most victim surveys measure personal victimization of individuals age 12 and over, meaning many younger victims of crime and their perspectives of that crime are not tabulated. Further limitations relate to underreporting, reliability, and communication barriers.

2. The Violent Adolescent Offender

A FEW YEARS AGO, Cindy Collier, 15, and Shirley Wolf, 14, were convicted in the stabbing death of an 85-year-old Northern California woman as well as the burglary of her home. The viciousness of the crime is attested to by the fact that the victim was stabbed 28 times by the girls, one of whom told investigators that they so enjoyed the killing, "we wanted to do another one. . . . We felt good inside. We wanted to go out and celebrate. We were full of laughter . . . it was fun."[1]

It is this frightening spectre of brutal, careless, immoral, violent juveniles that captures our imagination when thinking of the adolescent criminal, and helps, perpetuate our fear of young offenders. However, in truth, such a violent crime as described is the exception in relative terms and not the rule. Moreover, official data indicate that adolescent violent criminality is on the decline.

The Incidence and Characteristics of Violent Adolescent Crime

For all the headlines-making crimes perpetrated by juveniles, most of which are violent acts, violent crimes represent but a small percentage of the overall juvenile criminality. In 1986, only 4.1 percent of the total arrests of persons under age 18 were for crimes of violence.[2] The FBI's *Uniform Crime Reports Program* defines such crimes as murder, forcible rape, robbery, and aggravated assault. The vast majority of adolescent criminality falls under Type II offenses — or those considered of a less serious nature. Nevertheless, this should not be misinterpreted as saying we do not have a problem with adolescent violent criminality. The statistics suggest that we do.

Consider the arrest figures for persons under 18 arrested for violent crimes in 1986, as shown in Table 2–1. More than 71,000 juveniles were arrested during the year for violent crimes. Of this total, 37,528 were arrested for aggravated assault; 27,987 for robbery; 4,798 for forcible rape; and 3,717 for murder. Juveniles were responsible for 15.4 percent of all

Table 2-1. Violent Crime Arrests of Persons Under 18 Years of Age, 1986 (10,743 agencies; 1986 estimated population 198,488,000)

Offense Charged	Number of Persons Arrested Under 18	Percent of Total All Ages Under 18
Murder & nonnegligent manslaughter	1,396	8.7
Forcible rape	4,798	15.4
Robbery	27,987	22.5
Aggravated assault	37,528	12.8
Violent crime[a]	71,709	15.4
Crime Index total[b]	641,405	29.6

[a]*Violent crimes are offenses of murder, forcible rape, robbery, and aggravated assault.*
[b]*Includes property crimes.*
Source: *U.S. Federal Bureau of Investigation,* **Crime in the United States: Uniform Crime Reports 1986** *(Washington, D.C.: Government Printing Office, 1987), p. 180.*

violent crime arrests. The percentage was higher for robbery arrests at 22.5. Persons under age 18 accounted for 9 percent of the violent crimes cleared by law enforcement agencies in 1986.[3] None of these arrest data reflect the vast amount of violent juvenile criminality believed to be unreported.

Age Distribution of Juveniles Arrested for Violent Crime

A further breakdown of juvenile violent crime arrestees is by age-specific arrest data. In Table 2-2, we can see that the bulk of the adolescent arrests

Table 2-2. Juvenile Arrestees for Violent Crimes, Distribution by Age, 1986 (10,743 agencies; 1986 estimated population 198,488,000)

Offense Charged	Age Under 10	10–12	13–14	15	16	17
Murder and nonnegligent manslaughter	7	15	134	245	443	552
Forcible rape	77	297	1,140	982	1,121	1,181
Robbery	199	1,244	5,172	5,792	7,334	8,246
Aggravated assault	781	2,517	7,518	6,934	9,251	10,527
Violent crime[a]	1,064	4,073	13,964	13,953	18,149	20,506
Percent distribution[b]	0.2	0.9	3.0	3.0	3.9	4.4

[a]*Violent crimes are offenses of murder, forcible rape, robbery, and aggravated assault.*
[b]*Because of rounding, the percentages may not add to total.*
Source: *U.S. Federal Bureau of Investigation,* **Crime in the United States 1986** *(Washington, D.C.: Government Printing Office, 1986), p. 174.*

for violent offenses in 1986 are concentrated in the age 15 to 17 group, where there is a ratio of nearly 3 to 1 over arrestees under age 15. The peak age of juvenile arrests is 17, with a decrease in percentage the lower the age except for a leveling off between the ages of 13 and 15.

That very young children are involved in such serious crimes as murder and forcible rape may be surprising to some. However, experts suggest that more and more violent crimes are being perpetrated by younger and younger offenders. As one source put it, as violent crime "becomes more prevalent among younger teenagers, a trickle-down effect among younger children is almost inevitable."[4]

Gender and Violent Juvenile Crime

Male juveniles are much more likely to participate in violent crime than female juveniles. In 1986, males under age 18 were arrested for crimes of violence 8 times as often as females younger than 18.[5] Some contend that such a wide differential is misleading and may be due to more lenient treatment of females by the criminal justice system. We will explore the issue of juvenile female crime more comprehensively in Chapter 6.

Race/Ethnicity and Violent Adolescent Crime

Black youths have received the most attention with respect to violent crime. This is reflected in their overrepresentation in arrest statistics. While blacks under the age of 18 account for approximately 13 percent of the nation's juvenile population, they constituted more than half of the arrests of persons in this age category for violent crimes in 1986. White juveniles made up nearly 47 percent of the persons under 18 arrested for crimes of violence, with other racial minorities accounting for the balance of arrests.[6]

Hispanic adolescents also have a high rate of involvement in violent criminality. Officially categorized as an ethnic rather than racial group, Hispanics comprised of 14.5 percent of the violent crime arrests of persons under age 18 in 1986, more than double their percentage of the juveniles in this country. Non–Hispanics made up 85.5 percent of the juvenile arrestees.[7]

If there is a model city for the impact of adolescent violence, it is the city of Detroit. In recent years, Detroit has felt the brunt of teenage violent crime more than any other city relative to size. A youth was shot there every day on average in 1986; usually the perpetrator was another youth. A typical example of what many consider to be "motiveless" violence among Detroit teenagers is described below:

> Just before spring break ... a 14-year-old student firing a powerful .357 caliber Magnum pistol chased a star football player through the halls of

Murray-Wright High School, past the gymnasium and physics laboratory, as others looked on, helpless and in horror. The football player was killed by a bullet to the head. Two other students were wounded.[8]

City officials have tried a number of fronts to curb the teen violence "which has been spilling over into the hallways of the city's schools with increasing frequency," including mandatory jail sentences for gun violations, tough curfews for adolescents, and student-parent forums. These measures have seemed to do little to stem the tide of violence that in many ways is but a microcosm of an epidemic of teen violence nationwide.

Criminal justice experts are somewhat baffled by Detroit's seemingly unique aimless series of violent acts. Some suggest the Detroit crime is self-perpetuating and that adolescents, who are in their most violent-prone years, are more apt to perpetrate crimes. Says psychology professor Richard Herrnstein, "Seeing other people break the law is disinhibiting." He suggests that teenagers are most vulnerable to criminality when their moral development does not keep pace with their psychological and physical maturity. "They are the people closest to the edge, particularly when they have shallow emotional attachments to people and society."[9]

Trends in Violent Juvenile Crime

Most juvenile justice experts contend that violent crime among adolescents is on the decline, after a period in the 1960s and 70s where it rose dramatically. This decrease in juvenile crime can be seen in the 5- and 10-year arrest trends, as shown in Table 2-3. Total juvenile arrests for violent crimes dropped nearly 2 percent in the 1977 to 1986 period and 2.5 percent

Table 2-3. Trends in Violent Crime Arrests of Juveniles[a]

Offense Charged	Number of Persons Arrested Under 18 Years of Age								
	1977	1986	Percent Change	1982	1986	Percent Change	1985	1986	Percent Change
Murder & nonnegligent manslaughter	1,301	1,297	− 0.3	1,328	1,295	− 2.5	1,243	1,357	+ 9.9
Forcible rape	3,527	4,316	+ 22.4	3,704	4,221	+ 14.0	4,496	4,645	+ 3.3
Robbery	31,661	26,380	− 16.7	31,353	26,245	− 16.3	28,382	27,358	− 3.6
Aggravated assault	30,887	34,141	+ 10.5	30,847	33,757	+ 9.4	33,895	36,197	+ 6.8
Violent crime total	67,376	66,134	− 1.8	67,232	65,518	− 2.5	68,016	69,557	+ 2.3

[a]*Based on different population estimates and agencies for each trend.*
Source: U.S. Federal Bureau of Investigation, **Crime in the United States: Uniform Crime Reports 1986** *(Washington, D.C.: Government Printing Office, 1987), pp. 168, 170, 172.*

between 1982 and 1986. However, in each period arrests for forcible rape and aggravated assault showed a substantial increase. Also, the two-year trend of 1985 to 1986 reflects a slight rise in the percentage of arrestees under age 18 for violent crimes. In 3 of the 4 specific crimes, juvenile arrests climbed during the period. Whether this is indicative of the very short term or a sign of renewed growth in violent juvenile crime remains to be seen.

Who Are the Victims of Adolescent Violent Crime?

Victims of adolescent violence are largely a reflection of adolescent offenders, that is, the majority tend to be young and of the same racial, ethnic, and socioeconomic background. This was found to be true in one of the first national surveys of violent crimes conducted, in 1967, in which victim and offender characteristics were analyzed. Of the four violent crime categories, the study found the closest resemblance between victims and offenders under age 18 to be in robberies.[10] More recently, the Bureau of Justice Statistics *Report to the Nation on Crime and Justice* found that

- Young people have the highest rate of victimization.
- The victim and offender have "uncannily" close characteristics.
- Youthful victims and offenders are of the same race in 3 out of every 4 crimes of violence.
- Both victim and perpetrator tend to be of limited income, employ and education.
- The crime-prone years are under 20.
- Males commit most violent crimes and are most often victimized by such.[11]

Further support of a strong correlation between victim and offender characteristics in violent criminality can be seen through National Crime Survey data (NCS). In 1985, victims age 12 to 19 perceived the age of their offender as being between 12 and 17 in nearly half of the single-offender crimes of violence, with 20 percent of the other offenders believed to be between 18 and 20. Similarly, 61 percent of the violent crime victims under age 20 in multiple-offender victimizations perceived their offenders to be within the age group of 12 to 20. Racial characteristics also heavily favored an intraracial nature to violent crime victimization by youths.[12]

Explanations of Violent Adolescent Behavior

Violent adolescent offenders can be identified as generally one of two types: cold-blooded, ruthless offenders such as the examples to open the chapter; and adolescents who commit acts of violence without giving the consequences forethought. Of the latter type, a Florida public defender posits, "The worst offender just doesn't understand the consequences—not only for himself, but for the victim. Even later on, he'll have trouble empathizing with them."[13]

The question we must ask ourselves is what are the underlying reasons for violent behavior by youths? In later chapters we examine in depth theoretical views of delinquent behavior. However, there are some theories that purport to explain violent juvenile criminality in particular. Let us briefly explore four such perspectives.

Social Learning Perspective

Theorists of the social learning perspective of violent delinquent behavior point toward early childhood experiences as significantly related to later patterns of violent delinquency. Social learning theory views such familial practices as child abuse and spouse abuse as learned behavior that the juvenile considers an appropriate response to problems encountered. A study by Peter Kratcoski of self-reported violent conduct of adolescents revealed that those who had been victimized by parental violence or lived in families typified by weak family functioning were more likely to have engaged in violent behavior than those who were not subjected to such experiences.[14] Other research has supported the association between violent youths and violent family backgrounds.[15] Refer to Chapter 11 for further discussion on the social learning theory.

Subculture of Violence Theory

A subculture of violence perspective of adolescent violence was proposed by Marvin Wolfgang and Franco Ferracuti, who contend that such violence is a reflection of lower class norms and a learned response to the pressures of lower class living.[16] The theorists advance that young males, especially those in households headed by females in socially disadvantaged areas, frustrated by the lack of self-esteem and unequal access to material goods, resort to violence in order to achieve status. Although Wolfgang and Ferracuti acknowledged that some violent youths were "idiopathic" (suffering from a prominent psychological disorder), they believed more than 90 percent were "normatively prescribed violent delinquents" (goal-oriented youths belonging to a subculture of violence).

Stress Theory

Stress theorists regard violent adolescent behavior as a way to cope with intolerable stress, which may transpire when adolescents experience pressure from either a single trauma or the gradual accumulation of several sources of trauma. The resultant acts of violence are often unplanned or intended. Robert Mawson advanced that such violent behavior may be perpetrated upon family members or those within the offender's peer group when the youth experiencing stress wants to continue the intense emotional physical contact with the person victimized, even if such victim is the cause of the stress.[17] Donna Hamparian's research further supports the stress theory perspective of adolescent violence. She found that violent delinquents tend to be characterized by low self-esteem, weak impulse control, lack of empathy toward others, rage, and little tolerance for frustration.[18]

Psychiatric Perspective

Psychiatrists have recently combined traditional psychiatric research with environmental factors in explaining violent delinquent behavior. In a study of homicidally violent children aged 3 to 12, the *American Journal of Psychiatry* linked the behavior with a history of psychomotor seizures, suicidal behavior, psychiatric hospitalization of the mother, and a violent father.[19] Other psychiatric studies of violent youths aged 13 to 19 suggested that the behavior was associated with neurological impairment, psychiatric symptoms, and the victimization or witnessing of severe physical abuse. Notes Jonathan Pincus, a professor of neurology, "We know now that there are three correlates that characterize the repeatedly violent child: neurological impairment, psychiatric symptoms, and the history of having been abused. We're not certain that they are causative factors of violence, but we strongly suspect that this is so."[20]

Adolescent Violent Crime in the Familial Setting

Most of our knowledge of violence among adolescents is that perpetrated outside the home. Much less attention has been devoted to familial youth violence. Only in recent years have we begun to examine the implications of violent adolescent crime in the family setting. Part of this may be attributed to the seemingly more common occurrence of late of parricide, or the killing of one's parent. Two recent examples illustrate the typical pattern of such killings:

- One evening, 16-year-old Richard Jahnke, armed with a 12-gauge shotgun, waited inside the garage of the family's Wyoming home as his father emerged from his Volkswagen Beetle. The youth fired six shots, four of them hitting his father's upper torso.

• Less than a month later in Florida, George Burns, Jr., 17, approached his father from the rear as the elder Burns sat watching television in the living room, and without uttering a word, unloaded six bullets from a .357 magnum revolver into the elder Burns' chest and back.

A number of researchers have studied adolescent familial homicide. The most common explanation is that the murder was triggered by an extremely abusive victim, such as the two examples noted, or identification on the part of the perpetrator with aggressive patterns of family behavior. D. Sargeant hypothesized, in his study of children who kill, that in some cases the child is the unwitting "lethal agent" of a parent who unconsciously incites the child to kill so that the adult can vicariously enjoy the benefits of the act.[21] L. Bender and F. Curran associated adolescent homicide or attempted homicide with "the child's tendency to identify himself with aggressive parents, and pattern after their behavior."[22] C. King cited the case of nine adolescent murderers, each of whom had been subjected to severe parental abuse.[23]

Adolescent Violence Against Parents

A much more prevalent form of adolescent violence aimed at parents than murder is physical battering. The magnitude of parental abuse has recently led Richard Gelles to suggest: "This is the next layer of family violence to be exposed. And if we were talking about some communicable disease, we'd be talking in terms of an epidemic."[24]

It is estimated that 2.5 million parents are battered by their children annually. Some 900,000 are believed to be the victims of extreme violence, with many attacks involving the use of knives and guns. The typical batterers are teenage sons.[25]

Carol Warren, who studied violent youths in a psychiatric setting, identifies three major reasons for adolescent violence against parents: violence in response to the victim's abuse of alcohol, violence in the frustration-theory model (violence as a result of one's goals being blocked), and violence as a resource to be used as status or money might be.[26] Other researchers regard parent-abusing youths as recipients of poor models of social behavior and highly stressful social situations, either or both of which causes them to strike out as they have been directed or in the only way they can.[27]

Sibling Violence

The most common, yet least researched, form of adolescent familial violence is that involving siblings. Suzanne Steinmetz conducted the first major empirical study of sibling physical aggression in the late 1970s. She found that 70 percent used physical violence to resolve sibling conflicts.[28] A study by Murray Straus and associates found that 75 percent of the families with children aged 3 to 17 reported the incidence of physical violence between siblings. Based on "ever happened," the findings estimated that 8.3 million children nationwide have been the victims of sibling violence, while 2.3 million adolescents have at one time or another attacked their sibling with a gun or knife.[29]

Clearly sibling violence may be the last barrier of adolescent violence to be broken down. More study is needed to establish the implications of violence between siblings with respect to other violent behavior of adolescents.

Getting Tough with Violent Adolescent Offenders

What to do with youths who commit heinous crimes of violence has been the subject of debate for many years now. A growing number of criminal justice employees, criminologists, and the citizens of this country have become disenchanted with the juvenile justice system and its inability to adequately penalize violent and chronic adolescent offenders. Explains one criminologist, "Most prosecutors and judges don't want to deal with kids, who end up getting band-aid treatment."[30]

The result of this disenchantment has been a greater shift toward treating violent juveniles as adults, or persons morally and legally accountable for their actions. In fact, most states have long allowed for a waiver of cases to adult criminal courts where persons under 18 were charged with particularly violent crimes.

Recent years have seen the passage of laws in a number of states lowering the age limit for waiver of youths to adult courts, expanding the offenses for which juveniles can be transferred, making sentences mandatory for certain crimes (if convicted), and classifying juvenile offenses in the same manner as *Uniform Crime Reports* classification of adult offenses rather than as delinquent acts.

One advocate of trying adolescents as adults sums up the feeling of many: "Juveniles who commit adult crimes should be tried as adults. The kids who commit rape and murder are past help. . . . The fact that a kid was under 18 doesn't make a heck of a lot of difference to the victim."[31]

Yet there remain those who subscribe to the original concept behind the juvenile court, such as Harvard criminal justice professor Mark Moore who contends that juvenile offenders perpetrating the same crime as an adult cannot be held responsible to the same degree because they do not have the same intent. "Their values are still changing. They are more easily influenced by circumstance. They should be held less accountable."[32]

Hence the argument persists. More detailed treatment on the implication of the juvenile and adult courts with respect to juvenile crime and delinquency can be found in Chapter 14.

3. The Adolescent Property Crime Offender

Property crimes account for the vast majority of adolescent criminal violations of the law. Crimes against property can be divided into two types: felony or Crime Index offenses (burglary, larceny-theft, motor vehicle theft, and arson) and petty or Type II offenses (such as fraud, vandalism, and stolen property). Evidence suggests that a high percentage of all juveniles engage in some form of property crime during their adolescent years, with the rate of such crimes declining considerably as they near adulthood. Most juvenile property crime is believed to be done for "kicks," "fun," or "flirting with danger," as opposed to gain; and most juvenile property offenders tend to operate in groups, which provides a generating force not available for a single offender.[1] For many adolescents, property crime serves as a training ground for more serious crimes and adult criminality.

The Dimensions of Adolescent Property Crime

Assuming that most youths participate in committing property offenses during their adolescence, we can only speculate on its actual incidence. However, even when relying largely on various official data, it becomes clear that juveniles figure significantly in the commission of crimes against property.

Cases Disposed by Juvenile Courts

One way to measure the incidence and range of adolescent property crime is by those cases referred to and disposed by the country's juvenile courts. According to the National Center for Juvenile Justice, of 1,247,000 total cases processed by juvenile courts in 1983, 591,000 or 47 percent involved

32

property offenses.[2] The majority of these cases were referred for Index property crimes as shown below:

* Burglary   11.6 percent
* Larceny-theft   21.6 percent
* Motor vehicle theft   2.5 percent
* Arson   0.4 percent
* Index property crimes   36.2 percent

Nearly half of all property crime referrals of delinquency cases are for larceny-theft.

Two Adolescent Property Offenders

It would be an oversimplification to suggest that adolescent property crime offenders can be easily characterized by such factors as race and social class. On the contrary, studies indicate that most youths, regardless of their demographic or socioeconomic characteristics, at one time or another perpetrate an act that could legally fall under the broad classification of property crime. However, career adolescent property offenders do tend to have some predictable patterns even when background variables are different, as seen in the profiles below of Jake, a white youth, and Evan, a black adolescent.

Jake, age 13, came from a broken working class home. After committing his first crime — bicycle theft — at age 8, he graduated to such property crimes as burglary, motor vehicle theft, and shoplifting, as well as drug use. He described his neighborhood as being crime-ridden and his years growing up as "shaky." The latter included his failure in school, rejection of parental authority, and running away from home several times. He reported that most of his friends participated in property and other criminal offenses. He sometimes acted as an accomplice voluntarily and other times under coercion. When interviewed, Jake was in a detention facility serving 12 to 18 months for motor vehicle theft, while awaiting sentence on other charges, including burglary.[3]

Evan grew up in middle class surroundings and a stable family. At age 8, he committed his first offense — stealing candy from a store. By age 16 he had, usually in the company of friends, participated in shoplifting, vandalism, and burglary. After dropping out of school in the tenth grade, his relationship with his parents deteriorated. His first run-in with the law came after being caught trying to steal money from a phone booth. Subsequent crimes took him in and out of juvenile detention facilities. As of this writing, a 28-year-old Evan was doing time in a state prison for grand larceny.[4]

Arrest Statistics

Official arrest data provides us with a telling portrayal of the dimensions of adolescent involvement in property crimes. Table 3–1 presents juvenile arrest statistics for property crimes in 1986. Juveniles were responsible for

Table 3–1. Property Crime Arrests of Persons Under 18 Years of Age, 1986

Offense Charged	Number of Persons Arrested	Percent of Juvenile Property Crime Arrests	Percent of all Juvenile Arrests	Percent of Total Property Crime Arrests
Burglary	134,823	18.7	7.7	35.9
Larceny-theft	378,283	52.6	21.6	32.0
Motor vehicle theft	50,319	7.0	2.9	39.2
Arson	6,271	0.9	0.4	40.4
Index Property Crime Total	569,696	79.2	32.6	33.5
Forgery & counterfeiting	7,234	1.0	0.4	9.5
Fraud	17,727	2.5	1.0	6.2
Embezzlement	696	0.1	*	6.6
Stolen property; buying, receiving, possessing	28,739	4.0	1.6	25.2
Vandalism	95,479	13.3	5.5	42.8
Total Property Crime Arrests	719,571	100.0	41.2	29.8

*Less than one-tenth of one percent.
Source: U.S. Federal Bureau of Investigation, Crime in the United States: Uniform Crime Reports 1986 (Washington, D.C.: Government Printing Office, 1987), p. 180.

719,571 of the arrests for crimes against property. More than half of these arrests were for larceny-theft offenses. When considering total property crime arrests, persons under the age of 18 accounted for 33.5 percent of the felony property arrests and 29.8 percent of all property crime arrests. Among Crime Index property offenses, the juvenile percentage of total arrests was highest for arson at 40.4 percent and motor vehicle theft at 39.2 percent. For non–Index property crimes, the juvenile representation was highest for vandalism arrests, accounting for 42.8 percent of the total.

The strong relationship between crimes against property and juvenile delinquency, specifically larceny-theft, can be better realized when looking at the property crime percentages of all juvenile arrests and the percentage breakdown of individual property crimes in which persons under 18 were arrested. We can see in Table 3–1 that all property crimes accounted for over 40 percent of the total juvenile arrests; 32.6 percent of these arrests were for felony property crimes and 21.6 percent for larceny-theft. Nearly 80 percent of all juvenile arrests for property crimes fell into the category of Index property crimes. Fifty-two percent of these arrests were for larceny-theft, illustrating the primary criminal activity most juvenile delinquents are involved in. Burglary and vandalism account for most of the other adolescent property crime arrests.

A further indicator of the prevalence of juvenile property crime can be seen in police clearances. In 1986, approximately one-fourth of the property crime cleared by law enforcement agencies involved only persons under the age of 18.

Age Distribution of Juvenile Property Crime Arrestees

Table 3-2 reflects the distribution of juvenile property crime arrestees by age in 1986. Much of all juvenile arrests for crimes against property occur

Table 3-2. Juvenile Arrestees for Property Crimes, Distribution by Age, 1986. (10,743 agencies; 1986 estimated population 198,488,000)

Offense Charged	Age					
	Under 10	10–12	13–14	15	16	17
Burglary	4,201	11,727	31,152	27,367	30,032	30,344
Larceny-theft	15,238	45,210	95,585	70,640	77,171	74,439
Motor vehicle theft	193	1,360	10,408	12,278	13,797	12,283
Arson	1,028	1,113	1,696	954	784	696
Property crime[a]	20,660	59,410	138,841	111,239	121,784	117,762
Percent distribution[b]	1.2	3.5	8.2	6.5	7.2	6.9
Forgery & counterfeiting	39	206	856	1,204	1,937	2,992
Fraud	178	1,398	5,146	6,028	1,958	3,019
Embezzlement	1	9	42	61	205	378
Stolen property; buying, receiving, possessing	327	1,412	5,874	5,915	7,191	8,020
Vandalism	7,156	13,872	24,219	16,654	17,145	16,433

[a]*Property crimes are offenses of burglary, larceny-theft, motor vehicle theft, and arson.*
[b]*Because of rounding, the percentages may not add to total.*
*Source: U.S. Federal Bureau of Investigation, **Crime in the United States 1986** (Washington, D.C.: Government Printing Office, 1987), p. 174.*

during the ages of 15 to 17, with arrests peaking at age 16. Because some of the breakdowns are combined ages, it is difficult to be able to adequately evaluate all ages. However, the figures indicate that in each age category, larceny-theft was the property offense most frequently arrested for. The second most common offense of arrest varies with age. For those ages 13 and up, burglary constitutes the second highest total of property crime arrests. Yet the 12 and under age group is shown to be arrested most often after larceny-theft for vandalism. These differences may reflect the differential opportunities between younger and older juveniles.

Gender and Adolescent Property Offenders

Property crimes, like violent crimes, are largely committed by male juveniles. Arrest data for 1986 tell us that 3.9 males under the age of 18 were arrested for property crimes for every female juvenile.[5] However, this differential is somewhat smaller than for violent crimes, indicating that male and female delinquents are nearer in their involvement in crimes against property (see Chapter 6 for more on female delinquency).

Race, Ethnicity and Adolescent Property Crime

White youths account for more than 70 percent of the property crime arrests of persons under age 18. This percentage rises to over 84 percent for motor vehicle theft. However, relative to population size, minority youths are overrepresented in property crime arrest figures. As shown in Table 3-3, blacks under the age of 18 accounted for 25.5 percent of the Index property

Table 3-3. Property Crime Arrests of Blacks and Hispanics Under Age 18, 1986

Offense Charged	Black	Percent of all Property Crime Arrests	Hispanic	Percent of all Property Crime Arrests
Burglary	30,341	22.6	16,074	13.9
Larceny-theft	97,356	25.8	35,908	10.8
Motor vehicle theft	16,195	32.5	6,324	14.3
Arson	894	14.3	463	8.1
Index Property Crime	144,786	25.5	58,769	11.8
Forgery & counterfeiting	1,135	15.7	388	5.9
Fraud	8,563	48.3	3,632	21.2
Embezzlement	176	25.3	64	10.2
Stolen property; buying, receiving, possessing	10,112	35.3	3,750	14.4
Vandalism	14,379	15.1	8,013	9.1

Source: U.S. Federal Bureau of Investigation, *Crime in the United States: Uniform Crime Reports 1986* (Washington, D.C.: Government Printing Office, 1987), pp. 183, 186.

crimes in 1986. This compares to their approximately 13 percent share of the juveniles in this country. The disproportion is even more alarming for motor vehicle theft (32.5 percent), fraud (48.3 percent) and stolen property offenses (35.3 percent).

Similarly, Hispanic youths make up about 6 percent of the under 18 population nationwide, yet constitute nearly twice this percentage of the juveniles arrested for felony property crimes. Several property crimes for which Hispanic juveniles are arrested reflect an even greater differential such as motor vehicle theft (14.3 percent), burglary (13.9 percent), and the non–Index property offenses of fraud (21.2 percent) and stolen property; buying, receiving, possessing (14.4 percent).

Table 3–4. Juvenile Arrest Trends for Property Crimes[a], 1986

Offense Charged	1977	1986	Percent Change	1982	1986	Percent Change	1985	1986	Percent Change
				Number of Persons Arrested Under 18 Years of Age					
Burglary	198,132	123,037	−37.9	154,216	119,360	−22.6	135,600	128,901	−4.9
Larceny-theft	369,801	347,046	−6.2	324,375	328,848	+1.4	357,431	363,667	+1.7
Motor vehicle theft	60,514	45,907	−24.1	34,381	45,097	+31.2	40,768	48,636	+19.3
Arson	7,137	5,619	−21.3	5,587	5,518	−1.2	6,420	6,045	−5.8
Index Property Crime	635,584	521,609	−17.9	518,559	498,823	−3.8	540,219	547,249	+1.3
Forgery & counterfeiting	7,510	6,587	−12.3	7,019	6,389	−9.0	7,298	6,956	−4.7
Fraud	21,362	17,360	−18.7	17,814	17,047	−4.3	17,416	17,545	+0.7
Embezzlement	682	657	−3.7	533	629	+18.0	638	679	+6.4
Stolen property; buying, receiving, possessing	29,076	26,651	−8.3	24,915	25,331	+1.7	25,755	27,430	+6.5
Vandalism	99,842	86,674	−13.2	76,514	82,038	+7.2	92,300	91,355	−1.0

[a]Based on different population estimates and agencies for each period.
Source: U.S. Federal Bureau of Investigation, Crime in the United States: Uniform Crime Reports 1986 (Washington, D.C.: Government Printing Office, 1987), pp. 168, 170, 172.

Trends in Adolescent Property Crime

Long term arrest trends indicate that juvenile property crime is on the decline (Table 3–4). For the ten year period of 1977 to 1986, Index property crime arrests of persons under 18 dropped almost 18 percent. The greatest decrease was for burglary at 37.9 percent, followed by motor vehicle theft at 24.1 percent. The decline in juvenile property crime is also reflected amongst non–Index property offenses, with fraud and vandalism showing the greatest downswings over the ten year period. In all, juvenile arrests for every property crime dropped between 1977 and 1986.

The five year trends from 1982 to 1986 also show a decline in juvenile arrests for felony property crimes; the 3.8 percent decrease, however, is considerably less than that recorded over the ten year stretch. Moreover, an almost complete reversal can be seen for motor vehicle theft arrests, which rose more than 31 percent over the five years. Significant increases in juvenile arrests also occurred for embezzlement and vandalism.

Two-year arrest trends may be the most unreliable since fluctuations from one year to the next may be a fluke. However, the 1985 to 1986 arrest data show an increase in most juvenile property crime arrests. The greatest upswing was in motor vehicle arrests which rose 19.3 percent.

The results of these trends, when analyzed together, suggest that while overall juvenile crimes against property appear to be declining, for certain offenses such as motor vehicle theft, juvenile participation in recent years seems to be on the rise.

Larceny-theft

As we have noted, larceny-theft is the most common means by which juveniles engage in criminal violations of the law. The UCR defines larceny-theft as "the unlawful taking, carrying, leading, or riding away of property from the possession or constructive possession of another."[6] Falling into this category of criminality are crimes such as shoplifting, bicycle theft, pocket-picking, purse snatching, and theft of motor vehicle parts and accessories. Larceny-theft offenses accounted for one-fifth of all juvenile arrests and more than half of their arrests for crimes against property in 1986. Juveniles were responsible for 23 percent of larceny-theft clearances nationally and one-third of the aggregate arrests for larceny-theft.

Even with this being said, the research on adolescent larceny-theft is scanty. One way to place their role in this offense in perspective is to examine the nature of larceny-theft. In 1986, $2.9 billion was estimated to have been lost nationally due to larceny-theft. Reported larcenies and their average value in losses were broken down as follows:[7]

	Average Value of Losses
Motor vehicle contents and accessories — 37 percent	$710
Shoplifting — 15 percent	$ 86
Contents from buildings — 15 percent	$646
Bicycles — 8 percent	$167
Purse-snatching — 1 percent	$208
Pocket-picking — 1 percent	$248
Coin machines — 1 percent	$129
Other types of larceny-theft — 22 percent	—
Total average value of property	$400
Total loss due to larceny	$2.9 billion

From this data we can apply juvenile arrest figures. For example, as persons under the age of 18 are involved in just under 40 percent of the arrests for motor vehicle theft, it is likely that they are responsible as well for a similar percentage of the reported theft of motor vehicle contents and accessories.

One study that does shed some light on larceny-theft among adolescents was undertaken by Cheryl Carpenter and colleagues. As part of their examination of drugs and juvenile crime, the researchers looked at the relationship between adolescent theft, gender, and drug use. Their findings can be seen in Table 3-5. As is predictable, male youths committed

Table 3-5. Larceny-theft and Drug Use Among Youths, by Sex and Types

	Type of Larceny							
	Shoplifting		*Petty Theft*		*Burglary*		*Grand Larceny*	
	%	*Number*	*%*	*Number*	*%*	*Number*	*%*	*Number*
Sex								
Male	60	40	69	40	100	29	92	22
Female	40	20	31	19	0	0	8	2
TOTAL	100	60	100	59	100	29	100	24
Type of Drug User								
Heavy user	78	47	83	44	83	24	96	23
Light user	15	9	15	9	14	4	4	1
Non-user	7	4	2	6	3	1	0	0
TOTAL	100	60	100	59	100	29	100	24

Source: Cheryl Carpenter, Barry Glassner, Bruce D. Johnson, and Julia Loughlin, **Kids, Drugs, and Crime** (Lexington, Mass.: Lexington Books, 1988), p. 84.

the vast majority of the reported burglaries and grand larcenies. The gender gap is closer for reported shoplifting and petty theft. The breakdown most open to debate is reported shoplifting, where males accounted for 60 percent of the total. This is contrary to other data which show female youths to constitute the greatest population of shoplifters. The small size of Carpenter's sample and methodology used would seem to account for this discrepancy.

Heavy drug users were found to be the most likely to report involvement in each type of larceny, followed by light users and non-drug users.

Burglary

Burglary is defined as "the unlawful entry of a structure to commit a felony or theft."[8] Forceful entry is not required in UCR terms to classify an offense as a burglary. More than 35 percent of the persons arrested for burglary in the United States in 1986 were under 18 years of age. The highest degree of juvenile participation in burglary was recorded in the nation's smallest cities (under 10,000 in population), where persons under age 18 constituted 28 percent of the clearances.

Burglary victims lost an estimated $3.1 billion in 1986. Two of every three burglaries in 1986 involved residences and 70 percent were classified as forcible entry. Juvenile burglars tend to commit more burglaries during the daytime than adult burglars. Many juvenile burglaries, in fact, take place after school lets out, or between 3 p.m. and 6 p.m.[9] Research also suggests that a large proportion of adolescent burglaries occur within close proximity of their own residence;[10] and that young burglars are more likely than older offenders to use accomplices.[11]

Motor Vehicle Theft

Motor vehicle theft, "the theft or attempted theft of a motor vehicle," is like larceny, largely a youthful offense, even though this constitutes only a small percentage of all juvenile arrests.[12] It is estimated that motor vehicle theft in 1986 cost victims nationwide $6 billion. Persons under 18 years of age were responsible for 20 percent of the clearances for motor vehicle theft across the country in 1986. Although juveniles are most apt to sell or use accessories stolen from a motor vehicle, actual motor vehicle theft is usually perpetrated because of boredom and easy access, and for the purpose of joyriding. This is typically evidenced by the words of a 15-year-old male involved in motorcycle theft:

Nighttime and we didn't want to go home, so we said let's stay out all night and we were trying to think of something to do, and we had known where this motorcycle was and we were gonna take it and we were gonna go to Virginia and ride around and come back the next day. So we took the motorcycle—first we took the bus to where the motorcycle was. . . . We rode around town—we went to the reservoir, and it got a flat—we had a flat tire, so we hid the motorcycle and this lady seen us hiding it and then she called the cops the next day and they picked us up.[13]

Arson

Arson is probably the most frightening property crime because of its destructive capacity. Defined as "any willful or malicious burning or attempt to burn, with or without intent to defraud, a dwelling house, public building, motor vehicle, etc.," arson is estimated to account for 30 percent of the total fire losses in the United States.[14] The estimated value of damage in 1986 as a result of reported arsons was $1.2 billion. Structures account for more than half the arsons; while motor vehicles are the target of arsonists in over 90 percent of the mobile property arsons.[15]

Juveniles are responsible for more than 40 percent of the arrests for arson offenses. The impact of youthful involvement in arson can also be seen in law enforcement clearances. During 1986, the percentage of arson clearances involving only persons under the age of 18 was 35 percent, higher than any other Crime Index offense.[16]

The majority of juvenile perpetrated arsons occur to fulfill a desire for excitement, to "get back at" or challenge authority figures, gain status, or alleviate boredom.[17]

4. The Status Offender

UNQUESTIONABLY THE AREA of juvenile behavior that has drawn the most criticism with respect to juvenile statutes and involvement with the juvenile justice system is that regarding status offenses. These are "offenses" or actions applicable only to juveniles and which are not in violation of criminal laws. Categorizing what constitutes a status offense may be the most difficult challenge, since much of what falls under this term is largely subjective, discriminatory, or of a double-standard. In general, status offenses can be broken down into at least three broad areas:

- *Familial offenses:* running away, ungovernability, disobedience, etc.
- *Ordinance violations:* truancy, curfew and loitering statutes, liquor and tobacco laws, etc.
- *Immoral offenses:* waywardness, incorrigibility, sexual promiscuity, etc.

Given this range, it is reasonable to assume that every juvenile in this country could at some point during their childhood be considered a status offender and, hence, subject to officially being labeled as such and action by the juvenile court.

In this chapter we will examine the implications and dynamics pertaining to the status offender.

Status Offender Statutes

Since the late 1960s, status offender statutes have come under fire by opponents who oppose the juvenile court's jurisdiction over and processing of youths who commit acts that are noncriminal; as well as those who question the notion of the juvenile court as a "child-saving" social agency. In 1967, the President's Commission on Law Enforcement and Administration of Justice recommended that eliminating status offenses from the juvenile court's jurisdiction should be given serious consideration.[1] Others have seconded this motion, including the American Bar Association and the National Council on Crime and Delinquency.[2] The most powerful voice to date against the status quo came from the federal government itself through the Juvenile Justice and Delinquency Prevention Act of 1974 which, amended in 1977, required that federal funds to states be subject to their discontinuing detention of status offenders in closed facilities that include delinquent offenders.[3]

These pressures notwithstanding, presently all 50 states and the District of Columbia continue to include status offenders within the jurisdiction of the juvenile court. Twenty-eight states and the District of Columbia do, however, make a distinction between delinquent juvenile acts (offenses that would also be criminal violations for adults) and status offenses. In seven states, there is still no legal differentiation between status offenders and criminal offenders; while in eight states, some acts that are considered illegal for those under the age of mandatory are defined as status offenses, and others are classified as delinquent acts. In the remaining seven states, status offenders are now only referred to the juvenile court as dependent or neglected children.[4] Preadjudicatory detention of status offenders is now prohibited in most states, as well as postadjudicatory commitment of status offenders to training schools.[5]

The Official Incidence of Status Offenses

How often do juveniles enter the criminal or juvenile justice system for status offenses? And what proportion of all official delinquency falls into this category? The answers are unclear. Table 4–1 presents 1986 arrest figures for "status offenses." The only *pure* status offenses in the UCR program, that is, offenses for which only nonadults are subject to arrest, are runaways and curfew and loitering law violations. In 1986, 211,213 juveniles were arrested for these offenses, representing 12.1 percent of the 1,747,675 total juvenile arrests.

Other offenses that are commonly considered status offenses when applied to juveniles, even though they are also violations of criminal laws or otherwise applicable to adults, include liquor law violations, disorderly conduct, sex offenses, vagrancy, and suspicion. A total of 283,557 persons under the age of 18 were arrested in 1986 for said offenses, accounting for 16.1 percent of the aggregate arrests of juveniles. When looking at all the offenses that could fit under the broad classification of status offenses, a sum of 494,770 juveniles were arrested for these law violations, comprising nearly one-third of all arrests of persons younger than 18.

Because of the subjectivity of what constitutes a status offense, many youths who violate status offender laws may be arrested and charged only as a delinquent offender (an example may be a truant who is arrested for drug abuse). Conversely, some delinquent offenders may be listed in the

Table 4–1. Total Arrests for Status Offenses, 1986

Offense Charged	Number of Arrests	Percent Distribution
Total UCR Offenses[a]	1,747,675	100.0
Runaways	138,586	7.9
Curfew & loitering law violations	72,627	4.2
TOTAL	211,213	12.1
Liquor laws	132,335	7.6
Drunkenness	26,589	1.5
Driving under the influence	22,749	1.3
TOTAL	181,673	10.4
Sex offenses	13,753	0.8
Disorderly conduct	82,986	4.7
Suspicion	2,595	0.1
Vagrancy	2,550	0.1
TOTAL	101,884	5.7
Total Status Offense Arrests	494,770	28.3

[a]*For persons under age of 18.*
Source: U.S. Federal Bureau of Investigation, **Crime in the United States: Uniform Crime Reports 1986** *(Washington, D.C.: Government Printing Office, 1987), p. 174.*

statistics as status offenders (such as runaways who engage in prostitution). Others may be subject to both types of delinquent offense charges. It can vary considerably from one jurisdiction or agency to another.

Being arrested at all for a status or delinquent offense that would draw little to no attention if the party was of adult age indicates the dilemma of police discretion and discrimination the juvenile faces. For example, 13,753 persons under age 18 were arrested in 1986 for sex offenses. Although the UCR does not break down the specific types of sex offenses, we can assume that most involved normal heterosexual relations between consenting adolescents who had the misfortune of being detected for an offense that is not illegal when concerning consenting adults.

Comparison statistical data on status offenders can be seen in status offense cases disposed by juvenile courts during 1983 (Table 4–2). Of an estimated 1,247,000 delinquency and status offense cases, 216,900 or 17.4 percent were referred for status offenses. Another 74,600 cases were referred for what could be considered borderline delinquency offenses (sex offenses, drunkenness, and disorderly conduct). These offenses are generally more associated with the status of being under age than delinquent in conduct. Hence, roughly one-fourth of all the cases handled by juvenile courts may be directly related to the status of being a juvenile.

Table 4-2. Reasons for Referral of Status and Status-Related Offense Cases to Juvenile Courts, 1983

Reason for Referral	Number Referred	Percent Distribution
TOTAL ALL OFFENSES	1,247,000	100.0
Running away	59,900	4.8
Truancy	35,400	2.8
Curfew violations	9,900	0.8
Ungovernability	61,800	5.0
Liquor law violations	49,900	4.0
TOTAL STATUS OFFENSES	216,900	17.4
Sex offenses	14,800	1.2
Drunkenness	21,700	1.7
Disorderly conduct	38,100	3.1
TOTAL OFFENSES	291,500	23.4

Source: Howard N. Snyder and Terrence A. Finnegan, **Delinquency in the United States** *1983 (Pittsburgh: National Center for Juvenile Justice, 1987), p. 6.*

Status Offense Arrestees by Age

The age distribution of persons arrested for status offenses in 1986 is reflected in Table 4-3. For the primary status offenses of runaways and curfew and loitering law violations in UCR data, the peak age of arrestees is 15 and 16 respectively, with the 15 to 16 age group accounting for the

Table 4-3. Age Distribution of Status Offenses Arrestees, 1986 (10,743 agencies; 1986 estimated population 198,488,000)

Offense Charged	Ages Under 15	Ages Under 18	Under 10	10-12	13-14	15	16	17
Sex offenses (Except forcible rape and prostitution)	6,110	13,753	558	1,551	4,001	2,611	2,514	2,518
Driving under the influence	456	22,749	147	33	276	945	5,957	15,391
Liquor laws	10,163	132,335	430	615	9,118	19,264	40,669	62,239
Drunkenness	3,283	26,589	470	247	2,566	4,245	7,293	11,768
Disorderly conduct	22,517	82,986	1,746	5,384	15,387	14,723	20,413	25,333
Vagrancy	539	2,550	32	79	428	520	664	827

	Ages	Ages			Age			
Offense Charged	Under 15	Under 18	Under 10	10-12	13-14	15	16	17
Suspicion	846	2,595	98	172	576	617	600	532
Curfew & loitering law violations	19,260	72,627	654	3,199	15,407	16,781	20,333	16,253
Runaways	55,984	138,586	2,210	9,486	44,288	38,558	31,279	12,765

Source: U.S. Federal Bureau of Investigation, **Crime in the United States 1986**
(Washington, D.C.: Government Printing Office, 1987), p. 174.

majority of juvenile arrests. Juveniles arrested for sex offenses peak at age
15, with the bulk of arrestees concentrated in the 13 to 17 age range. This
parallels with the period of adolescence when juveniles are most precocious
and experimental sexually.

Juvenile arrestees for alcohol-related offenses, disorderly conduct, and
vangrancy tend to be slightly older, with arrests peaking at 17 years of age
and declining the lower the age. Overall, most arrests of juveniles for status
offenses occur during the age 15 to 17 adolescent years. In 1986, 3.15 persons
15 to 17 years old were arrested for status offenses for every juvenile age 14
and under. Similar age distribution patterns are present in juvenile court
cases.[6]

Gender of Status Offenders

Some studies have shown female adolescents to be more likely to be
charged with status offenses, detained, and held for a longer amount of
time than their male counterparts.[7] This is not substantiated by arrest and
juvenile court case data. The only status offense for which girls were
arrested more often than boys in 1986 was runaways. There were 79,985
female arrests for running away compared to 58,601 male arrests for a
female to male ratio of 1.36.[8] However, male youths were arrested substantially more often for every other type of status offense, as we see in Table
4-4.

Cases handled by juvenile courts reflect a similar disparity in particular
types of male and female status offense cases, although the proportion of
overall status offense cases is almost equally divided by sex as shown in 1983
case estimates below:

Offense Charged	Male	Female
Runaway	36%	64%
Truancy	57%	43%

Offense Charged	Male	Female
Curfew	72%	28%
Liquor	73%	27%
Ungovernability	51%	49%
Status Offenses	54%	46%

Table 4–4. Juvenile Arrests for Status Offenses by Sex[a], 1986

	Number of Persons Arrested	
Offense Charged	Male	Female
Runaways	58,601	79,985
Curfew & loitering law violations	54,087	18,540
Liquor laws	98,295	34,040
Drunkenness	22,539	4,050
Driving under the influence	19,731	3,018
Disorderly conduct	67,526	15,460
Vagrancy	2,097	453
Suspicion	2,044	551
Sex offenses	12,760	993

[a]*Based on 10,743 agencies; 1986 population estimated to be 198,488,000.*
*Source: U.S. Federal Bureau of Investigation, **Crime in the United States: Uniform Crime Reports 1986** (Washington, D.C.: Government Printing Office, 1987), pp. 176, 178.*

Fifty-four percent of all status offense cases involved males. Nearly three-quarters of the curfew and liquor law violations favored males, while they were responsible for 57 percent of the truancy cases. Females accounted for 64 percent of the runaway cases, the only status offense in which they were referred to the juvenile court more than males. The closest category of status offense cases of boys and girls was for ungovernability, where the percentages were roughly equal for both sexes.[9]

Although females are proportionately more likely to be securely detained for runaway cases, juvenile court data indicate that a higher percentage of males are detained for running away; while the detention rate for other status offense cases is about the same for males and females.[10]

Race and Ethnicity of Status Offenders

White juvenile adolescents are by far the most likely racial or ethnic group to be arrested or brought before the juvenile court for status offenses. For example, 84.3 percent of the persons arrested for running away in 1986 were white. Arrest data indicate a disproportionate involvement of blacks and

Hispanics in some status offenses such as curfew violations; however, this is likely more of a reflection of differential arrest practices, particularly in lower class or urban areas where minority youths are most often targeted for such arrests.

Trends in Adolescent Status Offenses

There has been a decline in status offenses since the mid-1970s. According to arrest statistics (Table 4-5), in 1986 as compared to 1977, juveniles were arrested less for most status offenses and offenses that are often related to

Table 4-5. Arrest Trends for Status Offenses[a]

				Number of Persons Arrested					
Offense Charged	1977	1986	Percent Change	1982	1986	Percent Change	1985	1986	Percent Change
Runaways	156,776	127,572	−18.6	96,636	120,477	+24.7	129,048	131,993	+2.3
Curfew & loitering law violations	75,672	66,757	−11.8	69,664	63,423	−9.0	63,869	69,721	+9.2
Sex offenses	9,435	12,512	+32.6	9,501	12,230	+28.7	13,600	13,240	−2.6
Liquor laws	101,355	117,748	+16.2	100,642	109,775	+9.1	106,201	125,269	+18.0
Drunkenness	42,439	24,348	−42.6	30,406	24,257	−20.2	22,316	25,361	+13.6
Driving under the influence	20,699	20,147	−2.7	22,328	18,952	−15.1	18,537	21,681	+17.0
Disorderly conduct	90,621	77,446	−14.5	71,254	72,054	+1.1	73,661	78,915	+7.1
Vagrancy	5,028	2,313	−54.0	3,201	2,164	−32.4	2,614	2,439	−6.7
Suspicion	5,305	2,519	−52.5	2,304	2,197	−4.6	2,385	2,204	−7.6

[a]*Trend periods based on different numbers of agencies and population estimates. Some of the offenses are considered criminal violations of the law, depending upon the circumstances of the offense and jurisdiction in which it occurs.*
Source: U.S. Federal Bureau of Investigation, Crime in the United States: Uniform Crime Reports 1986 (Washington, D.C.: Government Printing Office, 1987), pp. 168, 170, 172.

the status of being under age when applied to youths. Runaways and curfew and loitering law violation arrestees dropped 18.6 percent and 11.8 percent respectively over the ten-year period. Other such offenses as vagrancy and suspicion showed decreases of more than 50 percent. Only two status related offenses — sex offenses (+32.6 percent) and liquor laws (+16.2 percent) rose from 1977 to 1986.

Five-year arrest trends also support a decrease in arrests for most status offenses. However, persons arrested as runaways climbed nearly 25 percent between 1982 and 1986. The only other notable increases were for sex offenses, at 28.7 percent and liquor laws with a 9.1 percent jump.

The two-year trends in arrests indicate an increase in most status offense categories, with the highest jumps being recorded for liquor law and other alcohol-related violations. Short-term trends cannot be considered very reliable, since fluctuations are more likely from year to year.

Juvenile court case loads support the reduction in juvenile status offenses, or at least those handled by the courts. Between 1975 and 1983 there was a 39 percent decrease in status offense cases processed by the juvenile courts.[11] In part, this reflects a general deemphasis of status offense cases disposed in the juvenile court system and more responsibility being imposed upon child welfare agencies.

Secure detention of status offenders has also declined in recent years, due primarily to the Juvenile Justice and Delinquency Prevention Act of 1974. For instance, in 1975 juveniles charged with status offenses were considerably more likely to be securely detained than youths referred in any other offense category. However, by 1983 status offenders were the least likely juveniles to be detained.[12]

Runaways

The runaway youth perhaps best epitomizes the status offender since runaways, particularly chronic ones, are the most likely status offender group to have crossed over into every other status offense at some point. Additionally, background determinants of runaways often reflect those of other status offenders. Understanding the dynamics of the runaway can tell us a lot about the adolescent status offender as a whole.

How many runaways are there? By most accounts the numbers are frighteningly high, with estimates ranging from several hundred thousand to more than two million youths who run away from home annually.[13] In comparison, 138,586 persons under the age of 18 were arrested as runaways in 1986. A national survey reported that more than half a million families were victimized by children running away within a year, and that runaway rates were similar for white and black families as well as families with blue collar or white collar household heads. Rates of running away were shown to be higher in single parent families than those where both parents were present. Juveniles were more likely to run away from homes in large cities and small towns than in suburban or rural communities.[14]

The majority of runaways in the United States are white (the estimate is at least 70 percent), from middle and upper class homes, and with a median age of 15. Although females constitute the largest proportion of runaway youths, when age and sex are considered, males age 12 and under tend to run away at a greater rate than females in the same age group.[15]

The reasons why children abandon their homes are many. The most pressing and predictable reason seems to be physical or sexual abuse at the hands of their parents. However, other causes have been shown to be just as significant, including other family dysfunction (such as marital and disciplinary problems), school difficulties, sexual relations/romance outside the home, mental illness, boredom, and the thrill of a new experience (such as drugs or moving to a new, exciting city).

C.J. English identified four types of runaways based upon the commitment to remain away from home and the circumstances that led to running away:

- *Floaters* — juveniles who leave home for a short period of time, usually until things "cool off."
- *Runaways* — children who often stay away from home for a long period (weeks or even months), usually due to a destructive family situation or a serious and unsharable problem.
- *Splitters* — youths who are pleasure seekers. They also seek to acquire status among their peers.
- *Hard-Rock Freaks* — runaways who leave home for good, having opted for life on the streets, generally because of extreme family problems.[16]

Throwaways

Throwaway children are a separate branch of runaway youths, yet an even more frightening prospect for these are children who are literally thrown or "kicked" out of the house by their parents, or forced to flee due to intolerable conditions. These youths are generally not reported missing by their parents, making the problem of identifying such children that much more difficult than other runaways. About one in three children on the streets are believed to be throwaways. The National Network of Runaway and Youth Services recently estimated that 40 percent of the country's homeless youths are throwaways.[17]

Like the typical runaway, throwaway children tend to come mostly from suburban or urban America and are the victims of parental-child conflicts relating to such areas as incorrigibility and inability to relate to parental authority.

Rat Packers

A more recent trend in the growing number of troubled youths who have found their way out onto the streets are "rat packers." This offshoot of the runaway reflects the rebellious adolescents who resent parental or other authority such as the school. When parents seek to institute control, many of these youths leave home for days, weeks or months, often grouping together with other teens in what police describe as "rat packing."

Rat packers are largely suburban youths. It is estimated that more than 30,000 troubled middle, upper-middle, and upper class adolescents become rat packers annually.[18] Expressed one observer, these teenagers "glory in anarchy and destruction," often stealing what they want (or need), drink and use drugs, and participate in petty crimes or "childish pranks," such as vandalism.

The Runaway Road to Disaster

Children who run away from home often face a fate far worse than that they escaped from. This is effectively delineated in the introduction of journalist Robin Lloyd's provocative book on American male juvenile prostitution:

> The children who run look for companionship, friendship, and approval from those they meet. Many such youths are easy marks for gangs, drug pushers and pimps. Runaways often sell drugs or their bodies, and steal to support themselves.[19]

What may be the biggest threat to the runaway is the deadly AIDS virus. Given that many runaways are forced into prostitution and drug use, both of which are strongly linked to AIDS, suggests that our focus more than ever must be on stopping youths from trying to survive on their own.

Progress has been made in this regard since the late 1970s as more and more runaway shelters have sprung up around the country, many as a result of federal funding through the Runaway and Homeless Youth Act of 1978 (see Chapter 18). However, the fact that many runaway cases are still handled by the juvenile court illustrates how such youths continue to be viewed as "offenders" rather than victims.

The Grim World of the Runaway

Across the country, tens of thousands of youths run away from home and take up residence on the streets, at bus stations, airports, abandoned buildings, and anywhere else necessary for survival. Many of these runaways seek refuge from physically, sexually, or emotionally abusive homes. What they most often find in their no-win dilemma is prostitution, drug abuse, petty or serious criminality, disease, sickness and death. "As a group, runaway children have a high mortality rate," notes June Bucy of the National Network of Runaway and Youth Services. "They suffer from malnutrition, venereal disease, a high incidence of suicide, and they are frequently sexually exploited."[20]

Writer Dotson Rader recently traveled around the country and interviewed a number of runaway children. He recounts several typical stories in this Close-up:

> I went to Los Angeles and talked to runaways cruising Hollywood Boulevard and Santa Monica. I interviewed a girl who said she had fled Milwaukee when she was 12 because her father and uncle raped her. Now, at 14, she lived in an abandoned bathhouse on Venice Beach with several other kids and pushes drugs. She was four months pregnant and didn't know by whom.
>
> Under Santa Monica pier, I found a 16-year-old boy asleep. Later, he told me he had run away from Spokane because his grandparents, with whom he had lived, couldn't care for him any more. In Los Angeles, he said, he was picked up by a man and woman who ran a sadomasochistic sex club. Now he lives on the beach and is terrified of being inside buildings.
>
> In New Orleans, I interviewed runaways on Bourbon Street and on Canal. They lived one day at a time.
>
> I met Nicky at Miss Brown's, an all-night coffee shop on San Francisco's Polk street. . . . His voice was somewhat high and unsteady. He was 16. He told me he was originally from Portland. . . . His parents were divorced, and his step-mother had thrown him out when he was 14.
>
> "I didn't know what to do," he said. "I was just a kid. Finally, another kid told me about Camp − − that's an area in Portland where all the boys and girls sell themselves. So I did, and I lived in a dirty hotel. Then I got beat up by pimps a couple of times, and I came here to San Francisco and got involved down here. I've been here a year or two, I guess."[21]

The Unmeasurable Adolescent Sex Offender

The one status offense that may be the most elusive to track down and equally difficult to contain is the sexual behavior and promiscuity of adolescents. The incidence and range of juvenile sex offenses (excluding rape and prostitution) is largely unknown since, like adult sexual habits, most consensual juvenile heterosexual or homosexual relations, including those that involve adults, are usually private and undetected. Even the number of children arrested or incarcerated for sex offenses is unclear, since many juvenile courts mask the offense under such categories as indecent behavior or loitering in order to protect the juvenile.

The following recent figures give some rise to the dimensions of teenage sexual activity, and perhaps more importantly the increasing commonness and condoning of adolescent sex:

• In the United States, 11.5 million adolescents have engaged in sexual intercourse; 6.5 million males and 5 million females.
• Seven of every 10 females have been sexually active by age 20.

- Eight of every 10 males have had sexual relations by age 20.
- Four of every 10 women become pregnant before reaching the age of 20.
- More than 1 of every 10 adolescent females get pregnant each year.
- The 10 to 24 age group accounted for more than 60 percent of the gonorrhea cases and 40 percent of the cases of syphilis in 1985.[22]

For our purposes, the argument is not over the moral, psychological and developmental implications of illicit sexual behavior among youths, but rather the double standard that encourages juvenile sexual practices. Clearly youths are strongly influenced by the standards and normative values of sexually permissive adulthood in addition to their own burgeoning sexual drive. That sexual promiscuity and adventure among unmarried or cheating adults as well as children is woven into our culture via television soap operas, theatrical movies, literature, and adult magazines—all of which are easily accessible to and sometimes even targeted for children—makes it almost inevitable that such practices will be learned and emulated by the underage group. As a result, it is less practical to look at juvenile violations of the sex codes as an offense of adolescence than as a response to the society in which we live.

5. Juvenile Prostitution and Pornography

PERHAPS NO AREA pertaining to juvenile delinquency has drawn both contempt and sorrow as much as adolescent prostitution. On the one hand, the child prostitute is seen as merely a juvenile (and therefore delinquent) version of the adult in this sex-for-sale industry. Yet underage prostitutes are also generally viewed as victims of exploitation, troubled and abusive backgrounds, and a society that does not care. Related yet separate from juvenile prostitution is child pornography. Although juvenile participation in the pornography industry is largely looked upon as victimization rather than delinquency, per se, there is evidence that many of these children are drawn into pornography through prostitution, promiscuity, and other forms of delinquency. Juvenile involvement in the sex market has taken on greater implications in recent years with AIDS, drugs, family disintegration, and crime all posing major related problems.

Adolescent Prostitution

Juvenile prostitution is generally defined as the use of or participation of under age persons (usually age 17 and under) in sexual acts with adults or other minors where no force is present. This differs from statutory rape and incest in that it involves payment, usually in monetary terms, but also through drugs, clothing, gifts, food or other items. Adolescent prostitutes can be readily found practicing their trade in major urban areas, middle class suburbs, and the smallest of towns. That there is an active market for underage prostitutes illustrates both the presence of young prostitutes and the near futility in stopping this form of child sexploitation.

How many juveniles are actively working as prostitutes? While there are no precise figures, estimates vary from tens of thousands to well over one million adolescent prostitutes. Recent data gathered from police departments nationwide showed that there are somewhere between 100,000 and

200,000 juvenile prostitutes.[1] Other sources suggest the figures are at least double that amount and include only prostitutes under 16, with the number doubling again when the 16- and 17-year-old prostitutes are considered.[2]

There is evidence that adolescent prostitution is on the rise. A recent 50 state survey found that juvenile prostitution had increased in 37 percent of the affected cities.[3] This rise was largely attributed to greater numbers of juveniles leaving troubled homes. The study also found that most adolescent prostitutes tend to be runaways, drug and/or alcohol abusers, ages 13 to 17; with the majority practicing their trade in central business districts, arcade game rooms, and bus and train depots.

The relationship between adolescent prostitution and the runaway has been strongly supported in the literature.[4] Most of these children have run away from abuse, neglect, broken families, or loneliness. Contrary to popular belief, juvenile prostitutes are not merely a product of the lower class and underprivileged, but come from across the socioeconomic strata. A study of adolescent prostitutes in Minnesota found that nearly one-quarter of those at a shelter had parents with some college education and many had fathers who were in skilled or professional occupations.[5]

What most youths are indoctrinated to in life on the streets is hunger, fear, loneliness, the elements, pimps, prostitution, drugs, pornography, violence, and other realities they rarely were prepared for and realistically can rarely fully overcome.

Female Adolescent Prostitutes

When we think of juvenile prostitutes, the one image that readily comes to mind is the female adolescent hustling on the streets of New York's Times Square, or Los Angeles' Hollywood Boulevard. Females appear to comprise the majority of adolescent prostitutes; some estimates suggest that females account for upwards of two-thirds of the juveniles selling themselves on the streets.[6] Female juveniles are also more likely than males to be arrested for prostitution and commercialized vice. In 1986, there were 1,442 such arrests of females under the age of 18 compared to 750 male juvenile arrests. Adolescent females further tend to be arrested more as runaways than do male adolescents, one of a number of charges police employ when arresting juveniles who were soliciting for prostitution.[7] There is some evidence that differential treatment may account for these discrepancies in arrest.[8]

Age Distribution

Female juvenile prostitutes can range in age from 10 to 17. Most findings point toward the 15 to 17 age group as constituting the bulk of adolescent female prostitutes.[9] Jennifer James, who has done extensive research on female prostitutes, placed the mean age for female juvenile prostitutes at 16.9 years.[10] This is supported by 1986 arrest data which shows females at age 17 as being arrested for prostitution nearly twice as often as those at age 16, with arrests declining the lower the age thereafter.[11]

However, much of the research has found that the majority of adolescent prostitutes are actually younger than 16 when they first participate in prostitution, with the average age for that first experience being 14.[12]

Race and Ethnicity

Adolescent female prostitutes are distributed across all racial and ethnic groups; however, most evidence suggests that white females make up the vast majority of girl prostitutes. Studies in San Francisco[13] and Minneapolis[14] revealed that 80 percent of the samples were white, while 62 percent of James' sample were white adolescents.[15]

Blacks account for the second greatest percentage of adolescent female prostitutes, with estimates ranging from just over one-tenth to around one-half of those sampled.[16] The larger the sample, the lower the percentage of black prostitutes there is likely to be. Other racial and ethnic group female juveniles also are involved in prostitution, though the numbers are believed to be much lower than white and black participants. Different studies have found Hispanics and Native American girls to comprise of between 2 percent and 11 percent of the sample.[17] Asian juvenile females have the lowest racial incidence of adolescent prostitution.

Socioeconomic Characteristics

Female adolescent prostitutes are represented in every socioeconomic group. While some studies consisting of small samples have shown a higher incidence of prostitutes with lower and working class backgrounds,[18] other research featuring larger sample groups indicates a more prominent representation of the middle and upper classes. In her study of prostitutes, Mimi Silbert reported that 70 percent of the female adolescents sampled were from families of average or higher incomes.[19] James found a similar high rate of average and higher income backgrounds among her sample. She also noted a "phenomenal" increase in the number of "affluent and overindulged" juvenile prostitutes.[20]

Family Dynamics

Research indicates that most adolescent female prostitutes are victims of broken homes. In Maura Crowley's study, 85 percent of the respondents reported the absence of at least one parent during their childhood[21]; 70 percent of James' sample[22] and the Huckleberry House[23] study were characterized by the absence of one or both parents. The consensus among researchers is that at least two-thirds of all juvenile prostitutes come from disrupted families.

A solid relationship has been shown as well between girl prostitutes and parental relationship beset by conflict and stress. The Huckleberry House project found that few female prostitutes demonstrate positive and caring relationships toward their parents.[24] Seventy-five percent of Diana Gray's sample described their relationships with parents as "poor" and "very bad."[25] Other studies such as Crowley's notes this discord by the gender of the parents; 42 percent of the mothers and 25 percent of the fathers were the source of the prostitutes' poor parental relationships.[26]

One area of family dynamics pertaining to female juvenile prostitution that has been given inadequate attention is the factor of a mother who is a prostitute. Some studies have suggested a link between adolescent female prostitutes and promiscuity or prostitution of their mothers.[27] However, further exploration of this relationship is needed.

Sexual and Physical Abuse

The most common background variable associated with girl prostitutes is sexual abuse. The literature is replete with works that correlate female prostitution with intrafamilial and nonfamilial sexual mistreatment including incest, molestation, rape and sexual exploitation.[28] The Huckleberry House research approximates that 90 percent of the female prostitutes have been sexually abused.[29]

Physical abuse is also strongly documented as a childhood feature of female prostitutes. More than two-thirds of the prostitutes reported physical abuse in Crowley's sample and the Huckleberry House study.[30] In most research, at least half of the juvenile prostitutes, and usually more, are estimated to have experienced some form of childhood physical abuse.

The Role of Pimps

It is generally accepted that most juvenile female prostitutes are physically, psychologically, and emotionally coerced by a pimp into becoming a prostitute. Both James[31] and Dorothy Bracey[32] speak of the pimp's charm, flattery, and emotional manipulation as prominent in a girl's decision to enter the prostitution business. However, empirical studies have not supported the notion that adolescent females are physically forced into prostitution by pimps. One study found that only 5 percent of the subjects entered into prostitution because of physical threats of coercion by a pimp.[33] The apparent rarity of this practice is indicated by Bracey, who notes: "Although we have heard stories of kidnappings and of totally innocent girls being raped and then 'turned out,' none of the girls interviewed claimed to know anyone who had been started in prostitution in these ways."[34]

Nevertheless, the evidence indicates that once a young girl is in a pimp's stable, she is generally subject to his rules, regulations, and manipulation which includes falling in love, working for him, believing him, giving him much of her earnings, and violence.[35]

Typology of Female Adolescent Prostitutes and Prostitution

The vast majority of underage female prostitutes are street walkers.[36] Girls also engage in prostitution through phone solicitation, in nightclubs, hotels, saunas and massage parlors. Nor are the services they perform limited to sexual intercourse. Notes Kelly Weisberg in her detailed study of adolescent prostitution, other services solicited are oral sex, anal sex, homosexual activities, multiple partner sex, sadomasochistic activities, urination or defecation, and obscenity related sexual performances.[37]

Motivational Factors in Female Prostitution

Researchers have studied female juvenile prostitution in terms of psychoanalytic, situational, and economic motivations. Psychoanalytical studies have pointed toward such motivating factors as emotional deprivation, schizophrenia, and depression[38]; while situational studies have focused on the role of incest, rape, early sexual experiences, child abuse and neglect and other such situational motivations for children entering prostitution.

However, the most grounded motivational source seems to be that pertaining to economics. A number of studies have found juvenile prostitution to be motivated primarily by economic necessity. James forwards this view: "The apparent reason for prostitution among adolescents is for economic survival and to meet other needs."[39] Most juvenile prostitutes interviewed have acknowledged that money and material items are the most important motivations for entry into prostitution and continuing it.[40] Logic suggests this to be true as well, since most long-term runaways ultimately find prostitution to be one of the few ways for unskilled, undereducated, underaged persons to make money for food and shelter.

Delinquent Female Adolescent Prostitutes

Although we have noted many of the victimizational correlates of female adolescent prostitution, not all girls who engage in this profession do so because of shattered or abusive backgrounds or economic impoverishment. Many young females are motivated by fun, excitement, new experiences, promiscuity, peer group pressures, and simply extra money to satisfy their particular needs such as more clothes. Bracey concluded from her research that many female adolescents choose to enter prostitution because they know other young females who are in the profession.[41] One article observed that "a lot of kids take to prostitution as an 'on and off job'—when you need a few bucks."[42] Through counseling female adolescent prostitutes, a San Francisco social worker commented: "Sex is no longer for love and procreation, but solely for enjoyment. But this leads to fleeting sexual contacts which turn out to be meaningless. What gives them meaning is the profit."[43]

This theme of young females who almost frivolously engage in prostitution as a way to acquire what they want is further elaborated on in the following depiction made by a person who worked with female adolescent prostitutes:

> There are more younger hookers, thirteen and fourteen-year-olds. They just don't care. It's a way they can have all the clothes they want, all the blue jeans and shoes they want. . . . Girls sell their bodies to get money. If it was legal and had a tax on it, they would find something else.[44]

Delinquent female adolescent prostitution among affluent girls is motivated by means other than those most associated with young prostitutes from other classes, according to James. She describes this difference:

> It appears that for [affluent adolescent female prostitutes] it is basically entertaining to dress up with your friends and go down on the street and con, cajole, and be the aggressor. The extravagant sensations from the illegality, projected immorality, and danger of prostitution is a relief from the neutrality of suburbia.[45]

Drug and Alcohol Usage

The correlation between adolescent prostitution and the use of drugs or alcohol is strong. Virtually all juvenile prostitutes have at least tried one substance or another, and estimates are that between one-fifth and one-half of all underage prostitutes use drugs regularly.[46] Marijuana is the drug of choice most often among adolescent prostitutes,[47] although psychedelic and narcotic drug use as well as alcohol abuse have also been frequently associated with juvenile prostitutes.[48] Many young prostitutes report that drug or alcohol usage helps them to relax and makes their profession more bearable.

Violence Perpetrated Upon Customers

Violent crime perpetrated by young prostitutes against their customers is a common occurrence. One study reported that half the adolescent prostitutes admitted robbing customers regularly.[49] Other violent acts such as "cutting" a customer are also utilized by juvenile prostitutes either in the course of robbery or in self-defense.

Female Adolescent Prostitutes as Victims

Adolescent females who enter the world of prostitution often as victims frequently are victimized as well throughout their life as prostitutes, including violence by their pimps, customers, and others such as muggers and drug addicts.[50] Rape is a common occurrence among many prostitutes, primarily because of their exposure and high crime locality in which they operate.[51] Young female prostitutes are also subject to high incidences of pregnancy, abortion, venereal diseases, and differential involvement with the criminal justice system.[52]

Male Adolescent Prostitutes

Although the portrayal of the teenage prostitute in literature, theatrical releases and television has been largely that of young women, more attention has been given in recent years to the male juvenile prostitute with the threat of the deadly AIDS virus. Just how big is the problem of teenage male prostitution? The best indication was offered by Robin Lloyd in his study of boy prostitution, *For Money or Love.* He estimated that there were 300,000 adolescent males under the age of 16 active as prostitutes in the United States.[53] As the book was written in 1976, we can be sure that the estimate would be much higher today. Some sources in fact suggest that at least a half million boys are plying this trade.

A number of interesting terms are used to describe the male juvenile prostitute and his customer. The most common are "chickens" (boy prostitutes) and "chicken-hawks" (men who cruise the streets in search of young males). Much male adolescent prostitution occurs in large cities with substantial gay populations; however it also is a phenomenon in suburbia and rural communities. These male youths can generally be found hanging around adult bookstores, public parks, or standing in alleys and doorways of businesses.

Categorizing the Adolescent Male Prostitute

Unlike adolescent female prostitutes, juvenile male prostitutes are comprised of several types and subtypes. Weisberg identifies two distinct adolescent male prostitution subcultures: the peer-delinquent subculture and the gay subculture. She describes the makeup of these subcultures as follows:

> For youth in the first subculture, prostitution is an integral aspect of delinquent street life. These adolescents engage indiscriminately in prostitution, drug dealing, panhandling, and petty criminal activity. They sell their sexual favors habitually as a way of making money, viewing prostitution as just one aspect of "hustling"—as the term is used to mean procuring more than one gives.
>
> Youth in the gay subculture engage in prostitution for different reasons. Prostitution is one outlet for their sexuality. They find in the gay male subculture a means of identification, and prostitution satisfies their needs for social interaction with gay persons and for sexual partners. Simultaneously, it provides a way of making money, since the purchase and sale of sexual activity is a product of the sexual mores of that community.[54]

Within these subcultures, several interchangeable categories of juvenile male prostitutes have emerged:

- *Situational Prostitutes:* Adolescent males who participate in prostitution only under certain circumstances and who regard prostitution as an occasional pastime.
- *Habitual Prostitutes:* Male youths engaged in inner-city street life of which prostitution is an integral part of a life that also involves such criminality as robbery, petty theft, and drug dealing.
- *Vocational Prostitutes:* Juvenile males who see prostitution as either a career or a stepping stone to one, and who look upon themselves as professionals.
- *Avocational Prostitutes:* Vocational male adolescent prostitutes who fancy their prostitution as part-time employment.[55]

Characterizing the Juvenile Male Prostitute

Teenage male prostitutes have many common personal and background features with their female counterparts, as well as specific differences. The first national study of the adolescent male prostitute was conducted recently by the Urban and Rural Systems Associates of San Francisco.[56] Their major findings on the typical male juvenile prostitute are as follows:

- Adolescent male prostitutes sell their bodies to survive economically, explore their sexuality, or make contact with gay men.
- The average age of the juvenile male prostitute is 16.
- Two-thirds of the male adolescent prostitutes are white; one-fourth black.

• Most boy prostitutes come from broken homes; have been physically, sexually, or emotionally abused; and have experienced school failure.
• The majority of male juvenile prostitutes are runaways.
• Delinquent and criminal behavior characterize the teenage male prostitute.
• Pimps are virtually nonexistent in the juvenile male prostitution profession.
• Money is the motivating force for most boy prostitutes.
• Gay-identified prostitutes find the lifestyle initially exciting.

   Although most studies find young male prostitutes to be predominantly runaways, Jon Herzstam, a health worker in San Francisco, recently called this into question. He estimated that 50 percent of the boy prostitutes are "thrown out of their houses because of sexual identity issues."[57]

   Most male juvenile prostitutes are street prostitutes. Weisberg's study found that 94 percent of the sample conducted their trade on the streets.[58] Drug and alcohol use is also common among boy prostitutes. The Huckleberry House project reported that 83 percent of the male youths tried marijuana, and 77 percent continued to smoke it.[59] Another study found that 29 percent of the juvenile male prostitutes regularly used hard drugs, while 42 percent were heavy drinkers or alcoholics.[60] In Weisberg's sample, the reason most often applied for using drugs while engaging in prostitution was the enjoyment of "being high."[61]

   Like female adolescent prostitutes, teenage male prostitutes face the constant threat and reality of violence, including rape and murder; as well as drug addiction, illness, and sexually transmitted diseases.

Law Enforcement and Adolescent Male Prostitution

Despite the fact that studies show male juvenile prostitutes to be involved in other serious crimes more often than female juvenile prostitutes, most indications are that boy prostitutes are less likely to be arrested or otherwise involved with the juvenile or criminal justice systems for prostitution. In 1986, for example, the female-to-male ratio of arrest for prostitution or commercialized vice was 1.92. D. Sweeney estimated that about 70 percent of the adolescent male prostitutes never come into contact with the systems of justice because they have never been caught.[62] This compares to data on girl prostitutes that suggest approximately 75 percent have had involvement with the police, courts, or detention at some point during their prostitution life.[63] When young male prostitutes are arrested, it is often for shoplifting or for noncriminal activities such as runaways and loitering and curfew violations.

   The main reason attributed to the low involvement of adolescent male prostitutes with law enforcement is the difficulty in identifying them, compared to female prostitutes whose professional activity is more spread out and often clearly evident. Laws also tend to vary regarding the limits of what undercover police officers can do or say when targeting boy and girl prostitutes.

Weisberg's research did indicate a high incidence of juvenile male prostitutes involved with the legal system. Roughly two-thirds of the adolescents sampled had been arrested at least once, with prostitution-related offenses accounting for 33 percent of the arrests.[64]

Adolescent Prostitution and Aids

The most serious implication of juvenile prostitution at present is the possibility of contracting AIDS. Since the two most common ways of catching AIDS, or Acquired Immune Deficiency Syndrome, are through sexual contact and the sharing of needles in drug use, this illustrates the seriousness of the situation for adolescents in the business. Very little information is currently available on juvenile prostitutes who have AIDS. However, there are several indications that the numbers are significant. Recently, 27 percent of the juveniles tested at New York City's largest shelter for runaways, Convenant House, were HIV-positive (Human Immunodeficiency Virus), or afflicted with AIDS. It was estimated that 15 percent of the 11,000 adolescents who passed through the shelter yearly would test positive for AIDS, while more than 50 percent of those who are prostitutes would.[65] A Center for Disease Control Report found that the rate of AIDS among prostitutes is well above that of the general population[66]; a study at the University of Miami found that 41 percent of the street prostitutes tested were infected with AIDS.[67]

Thus it is clear that young people who turn to prostitution not only are at risk to violence and exploitation, but now an early and painful death.

Street Kids and the Aids Factor

If the threat of AIDS to the adolescent community is grave, the children who are on the streets as prostitutes and runaways face an even greater risk of never making it to the next century. Patricia Hersch, who has studied homeless youth and worked with New York City's Convenant house, recently wrote an article on the realities of street life, street kids and AIDS. What follows are excerpts of her research:

> Each section of the city holds new horrors. There are children everywhere. Block after block, I see female prostitutes, some as young as 12 years old, dressed in G-strings, stiletto heels and not much else. They're bizarre caricatures of little girls playing dress-up as they work to turn 8 to 10 tricks

a night. Boys too young to shave are dressed in the most exaggerated stereotypes of gayness. No one has helped them to understand what it means to be homosexual, nor offered support and positive models for the realities of their sexual preferences.

Like other adolescents, street kids spend a lot of time in sexual exploration with multiple sex partners, only they are more active. They trade sex for money, lodging, drugs and nurture. "They go home and sleep with their [old] friends, they sleep with their parents, they sleep with each other—there is hardly anybody they don't sleep with. And, of course, they sleep with their johns, who sleep with their wives and who may also be sleeping with their kids and their secretaries."[68]

Many people believe these adolescents will become part of the third wave of the AIDS epidemic. Karen Hein, a physician, . . . testified . . . before the Select Committee on Children, Youth and Families that in the AIDS epidemic, "geography can be destiny." The risk-related behavior of runaway and homeless adolescents puts them directly in the path of the disease. . . . Runaway and homeless kids gravitate to the very locations around the country where their risk is greatest. Not only are these kids at higher risk with every sexual contact . . . but they also have higher levels of drug use and sexually transmitted diseases . . . [increasing] the risk for developing AIDS.[69]

Juvenile Pornography

Juveniles are also strongly represented in the pornography industry. In many instances, children are involved in both pornography and prostitution.[70] Juvenile pornography, often referred to as "chicken porn" and "kiddie porn" is generally defined as photographs, films, magazines, books, and motion pictures which depict juveniles (sometimes as young as age 2) engaged in sexually explicit acts with other children, adults, or animals. Some materials present juveniles being abused or tortured. Child pornography is big business, with some estimates of the money generated annually as much as $6 billion.

Approximately 7 percent of the pornography in America involves juveniles.[71] One recent study found that at least 264 different magazines are produced and sold in the United States each month that graphically illustrate sexual activity between children and man or beast.[72] A magazine of obscene pictures of children can be produced for as little as 50 cents and sold for as high as $12.50. In Los Angeles, law enforcement recently estimated that more than 30,000 juveniles were sexually exploited in the city that year[73]; in Houston, a recent raid of a warehouse netted 15,000 color slides of boys engaged in homosexual acts, more than 1,000 magazines and paperbacks, and 1,000 reels of film of child pornography.[74]

Mirroring the background characteristics of juvenile prostitutes, most child participants in pornography come from broken, discordant homes and range from runaways to children induced to participate by pimps, family members, friends, or pornographers. Yet many juveniles who enter the business come from stable backgrounds but become involved as a means to make quick money or for the thrills or excitement attached to the experiences. Children in pornography are at risk to be sold into white slavery, sexually or physically abused or contract sexually-transmitted diseases such as AIDS.

Because of the secretive nature of much of the child pornography business and the inconsistent and sometimes nonenforceable laws surrounding pornography in general, it has been relatively easy for child pornographers to establish their lucrative business and keep it under tabs and in operation for years.

The Battle Against Juvenile Sexual Exploitation

A number of measures have been employed in recent years through legislation, law enforcement, and community groups, aimed at curbing juvenile involvement in prostitution and pornography. These include increasing penalties for sexually exploiting children, establishing more specialized law enforcement units to deal with investigations into the sexual exploitation of juveniles, and greater public awareness. Chapter 18 examines some of these advancements more closely.

6. The Delinquency of Females

IN RECENT YEARS there has been much debate over the prevalence of female criminality, its nature, its proximity to male criminality, and explanations that purport to account for the incidence and patterns of female known and unknown crime. While much of the discussion has focused on females in general or women, the female juvenile has also received a fair share of attention with respect to the same issues. In this chapter, we will elaborate on the delinquency of the juvenile female.

Official Indicators

Arrest statistics are the most reliable official means for assessing the participation of female juveniles in criminal and delinquent behavior. In 1986, 390,871 females under the age of 18 were arrested. Table 6-1 reflects the breakdown by offense of these arrests. We can see that more than one-

Table 6-1. Total Arrests of Females Under 18 Years of Age, 1986 (10,743 agencies; 1986 estimated population 198,488,000)

Offense Charged	Number of Persons Arrested	Percent of Aggregate Female Juvenile Arrests
TOTAL[a]	390,871	100.0
Murder and nonnegligent manslaughter	93	.02
Forcible rape	89	.02
Robbery	1,938	0.5
Aggravated assault	5,794	1.5
Burglary	10,171	2.6
Larceny-theft	100,722	25.8
Motor vehicle theft	5,479	1.4
Arson	625	0.2
Violent crime[b]	7,914	2.0

Offense Charged	Number of Persons Arrested	Percent of Aggregate Female Juvenile Arrests
Property crime[c]	116,997	29.9
Crime Index total[a]	124,911	31.9
Other assaults	19,534	5.0
Forgery and counterfeiting	2,359	0.6
Fraud	4,370	1.1
Embezzlement	282	0.1
Stolen property; buying, receiving, possessing	2,649	0.7
Vandalism	8,653	2.2
Weapons; carrying, possessing, etc.	1,614	0.4
Prostitution and commercialized vice	1,442	0.4
Sex offenses (except forcible rape and prostitution	993	0.2
Drug abuse violations	9,861	2.5
Gambling	40	.01
Offenses against family and children	952	0.2
Driving under the influence	3,018	0.8
Liquor laws	34,040	8.7
Drunkenness	4,050	1.0
Disorderly conduct	15,460	3.9
Vagrancy	453	0.1
All other offenses (except traffic)	57,114	14.6
Suspicion	551	0.1
Curfew and loitering law violations	18,540	4.7
Runaways	79,985	20.5
Non-Index total[a]	265,960	68.1

[a]*Because of rounding, the percentages may not add to total.*
[b]*Violent crimes are offenses of murder, forcible rape, robbery, and aggravated assault.*
[c]*Property crimes are offenses of burglary, larceny-theft, motor vehicle theft, and arson.*
Source: U.S. Federal Bureau of Investigation, **Crime in the United States: Uniform Crime Reports 1986** *(Washington, D.C.: Government Printing Office, 1987), p. 178.*

quarter of the arrests of girls was for larceny-theft, which accounted for the highest number of female juvenile arrests. Property crimes, led by larceny-theft, constituted the bulk of the Crime Index arrests. Only 2 percent of these arrests were for violent crimes.

The most significant observation may be that more than two-thirds of the arrests of females under 18 in 1986 were for Part II or less serious offenses.

Running away accounted for the highest percentage of Part II arrests and one-fifth of all female juvenile arrests. All other offenses (except traffic) were responsible for the nearly 15 percent of the aggregate arrests. When you combine these two offenses with others such as curfew and loitering law violations, disorderly conduct, and liquor law violations, it becomes clear that over half of the female juvenile arrests are for status or minor offenses. Even for offenses commonly associated with young females, such as prostitution, sex offenses, and drug abuse violations, the arrest percentages relative to their aggregate arrests are very small.

Age Distribution of Female Juvenile Arrestees

The distribution of juvenile female arrests by age gives us further insight into the typology of the delinquent girl. As we see in Table 6–2, the peak age group of female juvenile arrestees in 1986 was 15 to 17, with arrests reaching their highest point at age 16. The ratio of arrests for the 15 to 17 to under 15 age groups was 1.96, or nearly twice as many girls over 14 were arrested for those 14 and under.

Table 6–2. Juvenile Female Arrests, Distribution by Age, 1986 (10,743 agencies; 1986 estimated population 198,488,000)

	Age					
Offense Charged	Under 10	10–12	13–14	15	16	17
TOTAL	7,385	25,510	99,082	86,156	91,275	81,463
Percent distribution[1]	0.4	1.4	5.5	4.8	5.1	4.5
Murder & nonnegligent manslaughter	1	2	6	17	49	18
Forcible rape	4	14	31	18	11	11
Robbery	10	87	468	444	454	475
Aggravated assault	92	356	1,453	1,144	1,415	1,334
Burglary	429	1,071	2,844	2,043	2,069	1,715
Larceny-theft	2,637	10,650	26,616	19,737	21,010	20,072
Motor vehicle theft	20	177	1,523	1,483	1,332	944
Arson	75	84	206	115	76	69
Violent crime[2]	107	459	1,958	1,623	1,929	1,838
Percent distribution[1]	0.2	0.9	3.9	3.2	3.8	3.6
Property crime[3]	3,161	11,982	31,189	23,378	24,487	22,800
Percent distribution[1]	0.8	2.9	7.7	5.8	6.0	5.6
Crime Index total[4]	3,268	12,441	33,147	25,001	26,416	24,638

	Age					
Offense Charged	*Under 10*	*10–12*	*13–14*	*15*	*16*	*17*
Percent distribution[1]	0.7	2.7	7.3	5.5	5.8	5.4
Other assaults	435	1,713	5,531	3,992	4,060	3,803
Forgery & counterfeiting	16	54	302	383	625	979
Fraud	53	337	1,322	1,397	448	813
Embezzlement	1	–	14	17	86	164
Stolen property; buying, receiving, possessing	25	107	564	522	714	717
Vandalism	514	1,121	2,388	1,635	1,546	1,449
Weapons; carrying, possessing, etc.	16	68	401	313	388	428
Prostitution & commercialized vice	9	7	121	186	397	722
Sex offenses (except forcible rape & prostitution)	62	146	287	177	181	140
Drug abuse violations	26	226	1,698	1,913	2,700	3,298
Gambling	–	1	8	6	14	11
Offenses against family & children	274	61	199	171	146	101
Driving under the influence	25	3	63	158	905	1,864
Liquor laws	78	248	3,679	6,635	10,642	12,758
Drunkenness	41	63	773	888	1,051	1,234
Disorderly conduct	286	1,037	3,782	3,088	3,485	3,782
Vagrancy	6	13	81	112	126	115
All other offenses (except traffic)	1,497	2,914	12,634	11,387	14,394	14,288
Suspicion	23	24	140	156	123	85
Curfew & loitering law violations	105	704	4,622	4,709	4,999	3,401
Runaways	625	4,222	27,326	23,310	17,829	6,673

[1]*Because of rounding, the percentages may not add to total.*
[2]*Violent crimes are offenses of murder, forcible rape, robbery, and aggravated assault.*
[3]*Property crimes are offenses of burglary, larceny-theft, motor vehicle theft, and arson.*
[4]*Includes arson.*
Source: U.S. Federal Bureau of Investigation, Crime in the United States: Uniform Crime Reports 1986 (Washington, D.C.: Government Printing Office, 1987), p. 178.

The actual patterns of juvenile female arrests by age are fairly constant across age strata. In each age group, for example, larceny-theft constituted the greatest number of arrests, while gambling accounted for the lowest. Some differences, however, can be seen in individual offenses. Arrestees charged with running away peak at age 15 and decline drastically by age 17; whereas arrests for drug abuse and liquor law violations were highest at age 17 and decreased the lower the age group.

Juvenile-Adult Differences in Female Arrests

Juvenile females account for only about one-fifth of all female arrests. According to 1986 arrest figures, females under 18 constituted 21.6 percent of the female arrests, compared to 78.4 percent for persons 18 and over.[1] The differential is slightly greater for violent crimes and slightly less for property crimes. The only non–Index offenses in which juvenile girls are arrested more than their adult counterparts are runaways and curfew and loitering law violations — offenses which apply predominantly to persons under age 18. Hence, we can say that female crime is largely a product of adult women.

Male-Female Differences in Juvenile Arrests

Despite some arguments that young females are coming closer to young males in the incidence and types of crimes committed, aggregate arrest statistics indicate a wide differential between boys and girls in their delinquent activities. In 1986, males under the age of 18 were arrested 3.5 times for every female age 17 and under. The male-female ratio for Crime Index arrests was 4.1. The differential was nearly twice as great for violent crime arrests at 8.0; while male juveniles were 3.9 times as likely to be arrested for property crimes as females under the age of 18. The only offenses in which female juveniles were arrested more often than males were prostitution and commercialized vice and runaways, with ratios of 1.9 and 1.4 respectively.[2]

Female Juvenile Court Cases

Another official indicator of the incidence and nature of juvenile female delinquency is the females referred to juvenile courts. In 1983, females were responsible for approximately one-fourth of the 1,247,000 delinquency and status offense cases disposed by the nation's juvenile courts. Females were involved in only 19 percent of the delinquency cases (these include offenses against the person, property crimes, and drug offenses); and 46 percent of the status offense cases.[3]

Although males also outnumber females in status offense cases, females are most strongly represented as status offenders in juvenile court referrals. Females are charged most frequently with running away (the only offense category in which the majority of cases usually involve females) and ungovernability.

When age is considered, juvenile court data indicate that female case rates for delinquency tend to peak in the 15 through 17 age group with little variance between the ages. For status offense cases, the rates of female referrals generally peak at age 15 and decline considerably by age 17. The exception to this is commonly for liquor offense violations where the rate of juvenile female cases peaks at age 17.[4]

Race, Ethnic Origin, and Female Delinquency

The UCR does not subdivide race and ethnic origin by gender. However, arrest data that reflects the race and ethnic origin of persons under age 18 generally is representative of female juvenile arrestees as well. That is, white young females make up the vast majority of girls arrested; but black and Hispanic adolescent females tend to be overrepresented in arrest figures. Native American and Asian female juveniles have low arrest figures.[5]

Some self-report studies have examined various aspects of female delinquency by race. Two such studies have shown nonwhite adolescent females to have higher rates of involvement in serious crimes such as fistfighting and use of weaponry than their white female counterparts.[6] Steve Cernkovich and Peggy Giordano concluded that white juvenile females were more resembling of white juvenile males in their involvement in delinquent acts than nonwhite female juveniles; while nonwhite adolescent girls were more similar to nonwhite adolescent boys in their delinquencies than they were similar to white adolescent girls.[7] They also found that for nonwhite females, blocked opportunity was not a factor in subsequent delinquent behavior; however, the perception of blocked opportunity was a strong predictor of delinquent conduct by white females.[8]

Self-Report Surveys

Many believe self-report surveys, which rely on offender respondents, to be the most accurate gauge of delinquent behavior. As was shown in Chapter 1, self-report research indicates that the disparity between the male-female incidence of delinquency is smaller than reported through official data. Whereas most official reports of gender ratios tend to be over 3 to 1 in male-female juvenile delinquency differentials, self-report findings have consistently shown the ratio to be less than 3.0. Early studies by Nancy Wise[9] and F. Ivan Nye and James Short[10] yielded juvenile sex ratios of 2.3 and 2.4 to 1, respectively. Similarly, recent self-report surveys by Cernkovich and Giordano[11] and Peter Kratcoski and John Kratcoski[12] found the male-female juvenile ratio of admitted delinquency to be 2.1 and 2 to 1.

Some self-report studies have found the ratio to vary when considering such factors as offense, race and class.[13] In most research, however, the male-female ratio is closer for petty and status offenses than violent crime.[14] Where official and self-report data agree is that female juveniles participate in less delinquency and less serious crime than male juveniles.

Trends in the Incidence and Nature of Female Delinquency

The interest generated over female crime and delinquency since the 1970s has centered on three questions: (1) Has overall female delinquency increased significantly from past years? (2) Are delinquent girls closer today to delinquent boys in the incidence of "nontraditional" female crimes? and (3) Is the delinquency and behavior of females more varied today than it was in the past? Let us address each of these issues separately.

Trends in Aggregate Female Delinquency

Official statistics indicate that the total incidence of juvenile female criminality ballooned between 1960 and 1986. As shown in Table 6–3, arrests of females under 18 years of age went from 70,925 in 1960 to 341,080 in 1986, an increase of 380.9 percent. This percentage is somewhat

Table 6–3. Total Arrest Trends[a] for Females Under the Age of 18

	1960	1986	Percent Change
Total Arrests	70,925	341,080	+ 380.9
	1977	1986	
Total Arrests	394,403	359,190	– 8.9
	1982	1986	
Total Arrests	322,087	341,080	+ 5.9
	1985	1986	
Total Arrests	362,606	373,840	+ 3.1

[a]The trend periods are based on different agency and population figures.
Source: U.S. Federal Bureau of Investigation, *Crime in the United States: Uniform Crime Reports (Washington, D.C.: Government Printing Office, 1961–1987).*

misleading since the 1960 figures were so low relative to juvenile male arrests, meaning that inflated arrest trends would occur as the incidence of female arrests rose. The actual quantitative disparity between male and female juvenile arrests has changed little over the years.

The more recent ten year period, 1977 to 1986, shows that aggregate arrests of female juveniles declined nearly 9 percent. However, the shorter five (1982–1986) and two (1985–1986) year trends indicate that arrest of girls is on the rise. These conflicting data may be the result, in part, of differences in the number of law enforcement agencies reporting during these periods. Short-term trends are a less accurate measure of actual patterns of crime, since year-to-year fluctuations can more readily occur.

Self-report surveys also reveal that female delinquency has increased since the 1960s. Patricia Miller's study showed that although the rate of male delinquency remained relatively constant during the 1960s and early 1970s, female involvement in delinquency rose considerably.[15] Martin Gold and David Reimer's research found that female delinquency increased 22 percent from 1967 to 1972, however, they attributed that mainly to an increase in the use of drugs and alcohol.[16] The Institute for Juvenile Research study further supports an increase in the delinquency of females.[17]

Other self-report studies, however, have shown female delinquency to be similar in relative terms to that in the past or actually on the decrease. Using self-report surveys conducted between 1955 and 1977, Darrell Steffensmeir and Renee Steffensmeir compared the differences in male and female delinquency over the course of time. They found that the disparity in male-female self-reported delinquency was fairly stable during much of this period, although they noted slight increases in female property damage and petty theft.[18] Suzanne Ageton's analysis of the extent of female delinquency from 1976 to 1980, in which she used a national probability sample of adolescents, revealed that the incidence of female delinquency generally drops or maintains stability as females pass through adolescence, while the proportion of girl delinquents decreases significantly during this period. Ageton also found that fewer females in the primary delinquency years, 15 to 17, are being attracted to delinquent conduct than in the past.[19]

Overall, both official and self-report data has shown that girls are more active in delinquency in the late 1980s than in the prior two decades. Nevertheless, they still lag far behind their male counterparts in absolute delinquency figures.[20]

Trends in Adolescent Female Violent Crime

A major area of concern in recent years has been the notion that young females have somehow become more violent and aggressive, or nearer to young males in delinquent activities. This proposition has surfaced due in large part to UCR data and interpretations of its meaning. Freda Adler's work, *Sisters in Crime,* may have drawn the most noticeability in this regard. Relying heavily on UCR arrest statistics, Adler has advanced that a new female criminal has emerged, one that is moving toward parity with males in the commission of violent and aggressive criminality. States Adler: "Although males continue to commit the greater number of offenses, it is the [females] who are committing those same crimes at yearly rates of increase now running as high as six and seven times faster than males."[21] She credits the women's liberation movement and the entry of females into nontraditional occupations as the driving forces behind this increase in female violent criminality. Regarding adolescent female criminality, Adler contends that delinquency among girls is on the rise because they are abandoning traditional female juvenile offenses such as running away, promiscuity, and incorrigibility, and participating more in acts of violence and aggressive behavior.[22]

There has been very little support for Adler's assertions. A number of critics have called into question the argument that the rate of female violent crime is nearing that of male violent crime.[23] Some, in fact, have suggested that male violent crime has risen at a rate greater than violent crime among females;[24] while others have even argued against the notion of a "liberated" female criminal.[25]

Below is a comparison of females and males arrested for violent crimes in 1960 and 1986.

	Females			Males		
	1960	1986	Percent Change	1960	1986	Percent Change
Number of Arrestees	10,139	49,090	+ 384.2	84,912	399,432	+ 370.4

We see that female arrests climbed 384.2 percent over the 26-year period, while male arrests rose 370.4 percent for a differential of 13.8 percent. Even though this shows a slight narrowing of the gap between male and female violent crime arrestees, the female gain is only in relative terms. Males continue to show a considerable advantage in quantitative arrests for crimes of violence.[26]

Similarly, arrests of females under age 18 for violent crime has risen 507.5 percent between 1960 and 1986, a figure greater than their male counterparts, but of little consequence in the overall differential between boys and girls arrested for violent crimes.[27] Furthermore, more recent 5- and 10-year trends show that juvenile female arrests for most violent crimes are on the decline (see Table 6-4). From 1977 to 1986, arrests of females under the age of 18 decreased more than 20 percent for three of the four major violent crimes; only aggravated assault arrests showed an increase. A comparable drop in juvenile female arrests can be seen as well in the 1982 to 1986 figures. Overall, violent crime declined nearly 2 percent.

Self-report studies also dismiss the assertion of a more violent delinquent girl. Cernkovich and Giordono found that the least frequently committed types of delinquent acts by females and males are the more serious violent and property crimes, but that boys participate in these more often than girls.[28] Flowers' research also concluded that female juveniles are yet to be equally represented in the more serious violations of the law.[29]

Table 6–4. Trends in the Arrests of Female Juveniles for Violent Crime[a]

Offense Charged	Ten Year Trends			Five Year Trends		
	1977	1986	Percent Change	1982	1986	Percent Change
Murder & nonnegligent manslaughter	126	87	− 31.0	106	88	− 17.0
Forcible rape	92	73	− 20.7	59	53	− 10.2
Robbery	2,373	1,850	− 22.0	2,152	1,835	− 14.7
Aggravated assault	4,596	5,299	+ 15.3	4,954	5,159	+ 4.1
Total violent crimes	7,187	7,309	+ 1.7	7,271	7,135	− 1.9

[a]*Each trend is based on different agency and population figures.*
Source: U.S. Federal Bureau of Investigation, Crime in the United States: Uniform Crime Reports 1986 (Washington, D.C.: Government Printing Office, 1987), pp. 169, 171.

Trends in Adolescent Female Property Crime

Much has also been made in terms of an "explosion" in nontraditional female crime and a narrowing of the bridge between males and females about an increase in female property crime. Most prominent in this perspective is the work of Rita Simon. From her analysis of arrest statistics during the span of 1953 to 1972, Simon advanced that were the present trends in female property crime to continue, approximately an equal number of males and females will be arrested by the 1990s for larceny-theft, fraud and embezzlement; and by the 2010s a similar proportion will be arrested for forgery and counterfeiting.[30] Many disagree with Simon's conclusions, pointing toward her methodology and interpretation of her data among other reasons.[31]

Arrest data does in fact support a significant increase in female property crime, particularly larceny-theft, and relative female gains on male property crime offenders. Between 1960 and 1986, female arrests for property crimes rose an incredible 915.5 percent compared to 269.2 increase in male arrests. However, as we see in the property crime arrest figures presented, the absolute margin between male and female property crime arrestees is still considerable.

	Females			Males		
	1960	1986	Percent Change	1960	1986	Percent Change
Number of Arrestees	38,526	391,247	+ 915.5	336,311	1,241,562	+ 269.2

The wide differential in the percentage increases is more a reflection of the low arrest total for females in 1960 than an "absolute explosion" in the incidence of female property crime relative to male property crime. Moreover, the greatest increases have been for offenses considered traditionally female in nature, such as petty theft and vandalism.[32]

Property crime among juvenile females has followed much the same pattern of increase as females in general. Arrests of females under the age of 18 for crimes against property rose some 488.1 percent from 1960 to 1986, with the most significant jump in larceny-theft which increased by 509.9 percent.[33] The most recent 10- and 5-year property crime arrest trends of females and males under the age of 18 can be seen in Table 6-5. Decreases in major property crime arrests for the period of 1977 to 1986 were recorded for both male and female juveniles. Although the differences in aggregate percentages indicate a slight narrowing of the arrests for serious property offenses, in qualitative terms male youths were nearly four times as often arrested for Index property crimes as females in 1986.

Females showed small relative gains in Part II property crimes during the ten year span. The most significant gain was for embezzlement. Yet this is clearly not representative of a shift in the nature of female crime as Simon suggested, since embezzlement accounted for only 1/10 of 1 percent of the total arrests of juvenile females in 1986.

Table 6-5. Juvenile Arrest Trends for Property Crimes[a] (1977-1986)

	Female			Male		
	Total			Total		
Offense Charged	1977	1986	Percent Change	1977	1986	Percent Change
Burglary	12,102	9,334	− 22.9	186,030	113,703	− 38.9
Larceny-theft	106,558	92,618	− 13.1	263,243	254,428	− 3.3
Motor vehicle theft	5,546	5,015	− 9.6	54,968	40,892	− 25.6
Arson	659	551	− 16.4	6,478	5,068	− 21.8
Property Crime Total	124,865	107,518	− 13.9	510,719	414,091	− 18.9
Forgery & counterfeiting	2,052	2,147	+ 4.6	5,458	4,440	− 18.7
Fraud	4,397	4,253	− 3.3	16,965	13,107	− 22.7
Embezzlement	148	271	+ 83.1	534	386	− 27.7
Stolen property; buying, receiving, possessing	2,530	2,487	− 1.7	26,546	24,164	− 9.0
Vandalism	7,537	7,849	+ 4.1	92,305	78,825	− 14.6

Table 6–5. Juvenile Arrest Trends for Property Crimes[a] (1982–1986)

	Female			Male		
	Total			Total		
Offense Charged	1982	1986	Percent Change	1982	1986	Percent Change
Burglary	10,449	9,209	− 11.9	143,767	110,151	− 23.4
Larceny-theft	86,785	87,620	+ 1.0	237,590	241,228	+ 1.5
Motor vehicle theft	3,834	4,888	+ 27.5	30,547	40,209	+ 31.6
Arson	691	544	− 21.3	4,896	4,974	+ 1.6
Property Crime Total	101,759	102,261	+ 0.5	416,800	396,562	− 4.9
Forgery & counterfeiting	2,264	2,090	− 7.7	4,755	4,299	− 9.6
Fraud	3,804	4,156	+ 9.3	14,010	12,891	− 8.0
Embezzlement	141	244	+ 73.0	392	385	− 1.8
Stolen property; buying, receiving, possessing	2,278	2,271	− 0.3	22,637	23,060	+ 1.9
Vandalism	6,331	7,531	+ 19.0	70,183	74,507	+ 6.2

[a]*Five and ten year trends are based on different agency and population figures.*
Source: U.S. Federal Bureau of Investigation, **Crime in the United States: Uniform Crime Reports 1986** *(Washington, D.C.: Government Printing Office, 1987), pp. 169, 171.*

The five-year arrest trends of 1982 to 1986 indicate that the percentage increase of male juveniles arrested for larceny-theft, the offense that accounts for the greatest proportion of juvenile crime for both sexes, was slightly higher than that of female youths. This suggests female adolescents may not even be gaining on their male counterparts in this category of offense. Furthermore, no appreciable rise in larceny-theft arrests occurred for either group. While young females also show some gains in relative terms in other property crime arrests such as motor vehicle theft and vandalism, they continue to account for only a very small percentage of female juvenile arrests.

The overall evidence indicates that Simon's conclusions do not hold up under scrutiny, particularly for juvenile females.

Trends in the Variance of Female Adolescent Delinquency

Has female delinquency become more varied and similar in variety to male delinquency than in years past, as some argue? Both official and self-report data seem to confirm this. In virtually every UCR offenses, girls are being arrested more today than two decades ago as more opportunities and convergence of sex roles are occurring. Self-report studies support this contention. Michael Hindelang found the actual kinds of delinquency being perpetrated by male and female youths to be much the same.[34] Kratcoski and Kratcoski found the same to be true for status offenses, but less so for more serious crimes.[35] Gary Jensen and Raymond Eve's analysis of research revealed a wide degree of variation in the delinquency of both sexes.[36]

Despite the similarities in delinquent behavior among youth, males continue to commit far more acts of delinquency. This was pointed out in the Jensen and Eve study,[37] Ageton and Delbert Elliot's findings,[38] and by J. Williams and Martin Gold, who found that female juveniles perpetrated less frequent and major acts of crime and delinquency than did their male counterparts.[39]

Although girls may be more varied in their delinquent activities on the whole, the vast majority of their antisocial behavior is still concentrated in traditional female delinquency such as shoplifting, running away, substance abuse, and minor assaults.[40]

The Adolescent Female Shoplifter

The most typical and frequent form of delinquency perpetrated by the adolescent female is shoplifting. In one study it was found that over 60 percent of all shoplifters apprehended were females under age 17.[41] A 16-year-old girl who began shoplifting at age 10 and has been a habitual shoplifter ever since spoke about it in a question and answer session with a researcher:

> GIRL: After I stole those records, I didn't do it for a long time. Then my friends started doing it, so I started doing it. Only little things mostly . . . just like necklaces.
> INTERVIEWER: Do you think that's a pretty common thing?
> GIRL: To steal?
> INTERVIEWER: Shoplifting.
> GIRL: Uh-huh. 'Cause it is. Everybody does it.[42]

This example seems to typify the young female shoplifter and her rationale for shoplifting. There are a number of reasons why shoplifting appeals to girls more than any other delinquent violation of the law. The most prominent is the opportunity presented—the more access female adolescents have to stores and their goods, the greater the likelihood they will shoplift.[43] A second reason is appearance, which has been shown to be of great importance to most girls.[44] Other explanations relate to the influence of peer group pressure, impulsive behavior, and the challenge or excitement of doing something illegal and getting away with it.

Anne Campbell, who studied adolescent female shoplifting, summed up the circumstances that compel many female adolescents to shoplift:

> With so many demands on incomes that are often quite low, it is hardly surprising that girls are heavily involved in shoplifting. The pressures — material, psychological, social, romantic — assault from every side. The shops invite them to touch, smell, feel, and wear everything that they need for instant success in all these spheres. When the temptations are all weighed up and the chances of detection calculated, it is remarkable that so few girls do it.[45]

Explanations for the Delinquency of Female Adolescents

Most of the theories of delinquency as addressed in chapters 9–12 are applicable to both males and females. However, there have also been some explanations of delinquent and criminal behavior that have focused specifically on the female offender which deserve to be mentioned.

Biological Perspectives

Biological explanations of female delinquency date back to Cesare Lombroso's work as presented in his 1903 book, *The Female Offender.*[46] Based on examinations of female prisoners, Lombroso related female criminality to atavism, or the recurrence of primitive genetic traits. His major propositions regarding "born" female criminals are that they are (1) biologically more primitive and less evolved than their male counterparts, (2) less intelligent with fewer variations in their mental capabilities, (3) more immoral and menacing than male criminals, and (4) jealous, vengeful, and less compassionate and sensitive to pain. Lombroso's theories have long since been dismissed as sexist and methodologically unsound.

Despite limited support for biological views of crime and delinquency, biological research on female delinquency has continued to surface in recent years. T. Gibbens noted a high rate of sex chromosomal anomalies in female delinquents.[47] J. Cowie and associates identified genetic factors as the primary cause of delinquency, specifically relating overweight girls to sexual promiscuity, and menstruation to the distress females feel in recognizing that they can never be males, thereby making them more susceptible to delinquent conduct.[48]

Other researchers have also focused on the menstrual cycle and its phases in explaining female criminality. Studies have linked both menstruation and premenstrual syndrome (PMS) to female deviant behavior, pointing to such associated conditions as increased aggression, tension and irritability.[49] Research in this area is still sketchy and as a result has yet to gain wide acceptance or credibility.

Psychological Perspectives

A number of psychological and sociopsychological theorists have examined the deviance of females. In his 1923 book, *The Unadjusted Girl,* William Thomas explores female delinquency in terms of innate instincts and as influenced by the social environment.[50] He advanced that female juveniles (particularly prostitutes) are ruled by four basic desires: for security, recognition, response, and new experience. He attributed the delinquency of females to immorality rather than criminality. Thomas' critics have emphasized his liberal paternalism and unproven assumptions as major weaknesses in his work.

A psychoanalytic perspective of female delinquency has been advanced largely through the writings of Sigmund Freud. He viewed females as biologically inferior to males. According to Freud, females become traumatized, jealous, and immoral because they are without a penis. It is this anatomical deficiency and "penis envy" that makes girls morally inferior, less able to control their impulses, and thus delinquent.[51] Freud's penis envy approach has been rejected by most. Karen Horney posited that both boys and girls were mutually envious, and that the male femininity complex was the more severe.[52] Modern psychiatry has largely abandoned Freud's proposals.

Gisela Konopka's detailed study of delinquent females produced four key elements that contribute to adolescent female antisocial behavior: (1) the uniquely dramatic biological onset of puberty, (2) a complex process of identifying with their mothers, (3) the changing cultural position of females, and (4) a "faceless" adult authority, resulting in loneliness and low self-esteem.[53]

Psychological maladjustment and dysfunction of female delinquents has been supported as well through other research.[54]

Sociological Perspectives

Early sociological approaches to the delinquency of females can be seen through the work of Sheldon and Eleanor Glueck and Otto Pollak. The Gluecks' 1934 writing, *Five Hundred Delinquent Women,* linked female delinquency to physical, psychological and socioeconomic factors. They concluded that a high percentage of delinquent girls were mentally defective, came from large and poor families, and had been arrested primarily for illicit sexual acts.[55] Critics have attacked the Gluecks' conclusions for their biases and sexist methodology, such as the routine examination of the sexual histories of their sample.

In his 1950 work, *The Criminality of Women,* Otto Pollak argued that female crime is more prevalent than recognized, but it is largely hidden or unreported due to the traditional social roles of females and chivalry. He suggested that women are more deceitful than men in their criminality and teach this deceit to girls. He also ascribes the delinquency of girls to (1) early physical development and sexual maturity, allowing females more opportunities to commit delinquent acts; and (2) their home life (broken home, criminal parents), causing them to turn to other maladjusted female juveniles as family substitutes, eventually leading to a career of petty criminality.[56] Pollak's propositions have been attacked mostly for their biases and the lack of substantiation for his arguments.

Opportunity Theory

An opportunity theory has been used to explain why many youths become involved in delinquency. According to this view, juveniles are most apt to turn to delinquent behavior when legitimate means for achieving success goals are closed, but illegitimate or delinquent avenues are open. Although this school of thought has generally been applied to male delinquency, some studies have investigated limited opportunity and female delinquency. Susan Datesman and colleagues' research on girl delinquents and differential opportunity found that the perception of blocked opportunity was more closely related to female delinquency than the delinquency of males.[57] Cernkovich and Giordano's study of self-report research derived from 1355 female and male high school students revealed that, overall, blocked opportunity was a greater predictor of delinquency for both sexes than any other variable.[58]

The Women's Liberation Movement

Some theorists have blamed the women's liberation movement for the rise in female crime and delinquency, pointing toward the increased participation of females in the labor force concomitant with an increase in the opportunities to commit crimes, and the changing identity and self-concept of females. Freda Adler was one of the first to associate the increase in the criminality of females with the "consciousness-raising" of the women's movement.[59] Rita Simon also contributed strongly in this inference in her exploration of the political and social implications of the movement in relation to the labor force and female criminality.[60]

Much criticism has been directed at the notion that the liberation movement significantly figures into female delinquency and crime. Carol Smart argues, based on examining official arrest statistics in the United States and England, that dramatic increases in female criminality is not a new phenomenon.[61] Laura Crites contends that female offenders are often poor, single, under- or unemployed, lowly educated, and racial and ethnic minorities who have not taken part in the women's movement and greater economic opportunities.[62] Joseph Weis' article on liberation and female crime and delinquency advanced that official and self-report data on female delinquent behavior reveals that the new female criminal is more a matter of social invention rather than an empirical reality.[63]

In all, little support is given for a major influence of the women's liberation movement on juvenile female delinquency.

Differential Treatment of Adolescent Females in the System of Justice

A considerable body of research exists that supports the existence of discrimination against juvenile females in the juvenile justice system. Some studies present evidence of chivalrous and paternalistic attitudes towards females by the system of justice.[64] However, it is this protective philosophy that often works against juvenile females. Studies show that girls are more likely than boys to be arrested for minor offenses and certain status offenses such as running away and sexual activities; held in detention, where they are more likely than males to have to undergo genital examinations for sexual diseases (and pregnancy); and given harsher dispositions.[65] Furthermore, female adolescents placed in long-term institutions tend to be sent there more often for status offenses than for delinquent offenses.[66] Even where it involves nondelinquent detention, such as for neglect, physical or sexual abuse, girls are more likely to be referred to the juvenile court than boys.[67]

Although there is a greater trend today toward diverting female status offenders from the jurisdiction of the juvenile court and there is less detention of girls for status offenses, overall there continues to be a double standard in the juvenile justice system with respect to differential treatment of young female offenders.

7. Substance Use and Abuse Among Adolescents

THERE IS VIRTUALLY a unanimous consensus among researchers, juvenile justice officials, teachers, parents, and even adolescents themselves that alcohol or drug use by persons under age 18 is a fairly common occurrence throughout the American adolescent culture. Most juveniles are guilty of at least trying an alcoholic beverage or drug, usually beginning at a young age. According to the National Council on Alcoholism and the National Institute on Drug Abuse, the average age of first alcohol use is 12, while the average age of initial drug use is 13.[1] The relationship between adolescent involvement with drugs or alcohol and delinquent behavior presents itself in several ways. First is the fact that the purchase, possession of, and use of illegal (or illegally used prescription) drugs and alcohol by juveniles is prohibited by law. Second is the role of adolescent alcohol or drug use as a correlate of serious and economic crimes (violent crimes, property crimes, or drug dealing). Third is the significance of substance use or abuse as a factor in other types of delinquency such as prostitution and family offenses. Last is the effect of juvenile drug or alcohol use on school performance. The fact that each of these areas are often interrelated underscores the serious implication of drug and alcohol use by adolescents.

Adolescent Involvement with Alcohol and Drugs

It is perhaps best to first analyze juvenile involvement with alcohol and drugs in terms of arrest data. The UCR reported that in 1986 there were 250,024 persons under age 18 arrested for alcohol- or drug-related offenses (see Table 7-1). This comprised 14.3 percent of all juvenile arrests. Liquor law violations represented by far the offense for which juveniles were most often arrested, nearly doubling the number of drug abuse arrests.

Offenses that are commonly associated with juvenile violations of alcohol or drug laws are disorderly conduct, vagrancy, and curfew and loitering law violations. These accounted for 8.9 percent of the aggregate arrests of persons under 18 in 1986. In all, the offenses listed in Table 7–1 indicate that 408,187 arrests of juveniles were made for offenses directly or often indirectly related to involvement with alcohol or drugs — constituting nearly one-quarter of all juvenile arrests.

Table 7–1. Alcohol and Drug-Related Arrests[a] of Juveniles, 1986

Offense Charged	Number of Arrests	Percentage of Total Juvenile Arrests[b]
Liquor laws	132,335	7.6
Driving under the influence	22,749	1.3
Drunkenness	26,589	1.5
Drug abuse violations	68,351	3.9
Total	250,024	14.3
Disorderly conduct	82,986	4.7
Vagrancy	2,550	0.1
Curfew & loitering law violations	72,627	4.1
All Listed Offenses	408,187	23.3

[a]Based on 10,743 agencies; estimated population 198,488,000.
[b]Percentages may not add up because of rounding.
Source: U.S. Federal Bureau of Investigation, *Crime in the United States: Uniform Crime Reports 1986 (Washington, D.C.: Government Printing Office, 1987)*, p. 174.

Distribution of Juvenile Arrests by Age

Juvenile arrests for all alcohol and drug related crimes peak in the 16 to 17 age group, as shown in Table 7–2, with most arrests occurring at age 17 and decreasing the lower the age category. The exception to this in 1986 was arrests for drunkenness and driving under the influence, which were significantly higher among the under 10 age group than the 10 to 12 age category. This interesting inconsistency with the other declining patterns of juvenile arrests may be a reflection of the greater number of years in the under 10 category compared to the 10 to 12 group, the greater accessibility of alcohol than drugs for younger juveniles, and more involvement with drugs than alcohol for juveniles over age 10.

Overall, adolescent use of drugs and alcohol is largely a preoccupation of older youths. In 1986, 9.7 adolescents ages 15 to 17 were arrested for drug or alcohol-related violations for every juvenile under age 15.

Table 7-2. Substance Use Violations of Juveniles, Distributed by Age, 1986

Offense Charged	Under 15	Under 18	Under 10	10-12	13-14	15	16	17
				Age				
Drug abuse violations	9,374	68,351	187	959	8,228	12,181	20,008	26,788
Driving under the influence	456	22,749	147	33	276	945	5,957	15,391
Liquor laws	10,163	132,335	430	615	9,118	19,264	40,669	62,239
Drunkenness	3,283	26,589	470	247	2,566	4,245	7,293	11,768

Source: *U.S. Federal Bureau of Investigation, Crime in the United States 1986 (Washington, D.C.: Government Printing Office, 1987), p. 174.*

Gender and Adolescent Arrests for Alcohol and Drug Offenses

Similar to gender differentials of most other juvenile violations of the law, males are much more likely to be arrested for drug or alcohol related offenses than females. As we see in Table 7-3, there were 199,055 such arrests of males under 18 years of age in 1986 compared to 50,969 female juvenile arrests, for a male-female ratio of 3.9. The differential between males and females was greatest for driving under the influence, where males were arrested at a ratio of 6.5 to every 1 female, and drug abuse violations

Table 7-3. Total Adolescent Arrests[a] for Drug and Alcohol-Related Offenses, by Sex, 1986

Offense Charged	Number of Persons Arrested Male	Female	Male-Female Ratio of Arrests
Total	199,055	50,969	3.9
Drug abuse violations	58,490	9,861	5.9
Liquor laws	98,295	34,040	2.9
Driving under the influence	19,731	3,018	6.5
Drunkenness	22,539	4,050	5.5

[a]*Based on 10,743 agencies; estimated population of 198,488,000.*
Source: *U.S. Federal Bureau of Investigation, Crime in the United States: Uniform Crime Reports 1986 (Washington, D.C.: Government Printing Office, 1987), pp. 176, 178.*

with a 5.9 male-female ratio. Self-report findings suggest the disparity between adolescent male and female substance abusers/users is much closer.

When relating age distribution and gender, arrest data indicate that male and female juvenile arrests for drug and alcohol offenses peak at age 17 and generally decreases as the age group lowers. More arrests of males under age 10 were recorded in 1986 for driving under the influence and drunkenness than in the 10 to 12 age group; females younger than 10 were arrested more often than those ages 10 to 12 for driving under the influence.[2]

Race, Ethnicity, and Adolescent Arrests for Alcohol and Drug Abuse Violations

The race and ethnic breakdown of juveniles arrested for alcohol and drug related offenses in 1986 can be viewed in Table 7-4. White adolescents make up the vast majority of juvenile arrestees in each category, accounting for more than 91 percent of the alcohol-related arrests and over 72 percent of

Table 7-4. Percentage of Adolescent Arrests[a] for Alcohol- and Drug-Related Crimes, by Race and Ethnic Origin, 1986

Offense Charged	Race					Ethnic Origin		
	Total	White	Black	Native American[b]	Asian[c]	Total	Hispanic	Non-Hispanic
Liquor laws	132,059	95.5	2.9	1.2	0.5	123,949	5.8	94.2
Drunkenness	26,517	91.7	6.5	1.5	0.2	24,488	25.4	74.6
Driving under the influence	22,580	95.9	2.6	1.1	0.4	20,959	12.2	87.8
Drug abuse violations	67,455	72.1	26.6	0.4	0.9	61,375	18.9	81.1

[a]Race and ethnic origin figures are based on different agency and estimated population numbers.
[b]Includes American Indians and Alaskan Natives.
[c]Includes Asians and Pacific Islanders.
Source: U.S. Federal Bureau of Investigation, Crime in the United States: Uniform Crime Reports 1986 (Washington, D.C.: Government Printing Office, 1987), pp. 183, 185.

the arrests for drug abuse violations. Black youths were responsible for the second most arrests by race in each category; however, only for drug abuse violations were their arrests disproportionate to their general population figures. In this instance, their 26.6 percent of the drug abuse violations more than doubled the approximately 13 percent blacks under 18 in this country.

Although their percentage of arrests is quite low, Native American youths were arrested out of proportion to their numbers in the population at large for each of the alcohol-related offenses. Asians have a low rate of arrest for drug and alcohol violations.

Hispanic adolescents are highly overrepresented in 3 of the 4 offense categories in Table 7-4. Whereas they constitute some 6 percent of the youths under 18 in the nation, they accounted for more than 25 percent of the 1986 juvenile arrests for drunkenness, nearly 19 percent of the arrests for violations of drug abuse laws, and over 12 percent of the driving under the influence arrestees.

The disproportionate arrest of minorities for drug and alcohol violations is evidence of a serious problem of substance abuse by minority youths, but also may reflect discriminatory patterns of arrests.[3]

Juvenile Court Statistics

Supplemental official data on adolescent involvement in alcohol and drug law violations can be seen in juvenile court statistics. The most recently available national estimates of delinquency and status offense cases disposed by juvenile courts is 1983 data. This indicates that of 1,247,000 cases handled by the courts, just over 10 percent involved a drug or liquor law violation, broken down as follows:

Drug law violations	4.5 percent
Liquor law violations	4.0 percent
Drunkenness	1.7 percent

Only liquor law violations are classified as a status offense. Males were responsible for 82 percent of the cases involving drug law violations, and 73 percent of the liquor law violations. For drug and liquor law violations, the male and female case rates accelerated at around age 12 and peaked at age 17. Males were slightly more likely to be detained than females when charged with a drug or liquor law violation.[4]

Trends in Adolescent Arrests for Alcohol and Drug Offenses

Trends in the arrest of adolescents for alcohol and drug related offenses seems to be following a path of society at large; that is, a shift away from the heavy usage of drugs that characterized the 1960s and 1970s and more involvement with alcohol use and abuse. As indicated in Table 7-5, from 1977 to 1986, aggregate arrests of persons under 18 for drug and alcohol offenses went from 276,438 to 224,642 for a drop of nearly 19 percent. Juvenile arrests decreased most for drug abuse violations at 44.3 percent. Male arrests dropped 42.8 percent and female arrests for drug abuse violations fell 51.6 percent. Adolescent arrests for drunkenness also showed a

Table 7-5. Adolescent Arrest Trends[a] for Alcohol and Drug Offenses, 1986

	Number of Persons Arrested Under 18 Years of Age								
	Total			*Male*			*Female*		
Offense Charged	*1977*	*1986*	*Percent Change*	*1977*	*1986*	*Percent Change*	*1977*	*1986*	*Percent Change*
Liquor law violations	101,355	117,748	+ 16.2	79,334	87,426	+ 10.2	22,021	30,322	+ 37.7
Drunkenness	42,439	24,348	− 42.6	36,533	20,641	− 43.5	5,906	3,707	− 37.2
Driving under the influence	20,699	20,147	− 2.7	18,762	17,457	− 7.0	1,937	2,690	+ 38.9
Drug abuse violations	111,945	62,399	− 44.3	93,447	53,455	− 42.8	18,498	8,944	− 51.6
Total	276,438	224,642	− 18.7	228,076	178,979	− 21.5	48,362	45,663	− 5.6

[a]*Based upon 8,494 agencies; 1986 estimated population 180,790,000.*
Source: U.S. Federal Bureau of Investigation, Crime in the United States: Uniform Crime Reports 1986 (Washington, D.C.: Government Printing Office, 1987), pp. 168–169.

significantly noticable decline of 42.6 percent, however, liquor law violations rose more than 16 percent over the period.

Male arrests generally reflect those of all persons under 18. Twenty-one percent fewer male juveniles were arrested for alcohol- and drug-related crimes in 1986 than 1977. Arrests of females under age 18, on the other hand, decreased by only 5.6 percent over the 10-year period. Females showed a much greater increase (37.7 percent) in arrests for liquor law violations than aggregate or male juvenile totals; as well as a huge jump in arrests for driving under the influence compared to the decline in this category for male arrestees. Although this suggests females are narrowing the gap in alcohol-related arrests, male juveniles are still about three times as likely as female juveniles to be arrested for liquor law violations and 6.5 times more likely to be arrested for driving under the influence.

Despite the apparent drop in drug involvement by young persons, their arrest figures for drug violations are still well above those recorded in 1960 when a total of only 1,461 males and females under the age of 18 were arrested for violations of drug abuse laws.[5]

Adolescent Use of Alcohol

Alcohol is currently the drug of choice among adolescents. Several self-report studies illustrate the pervasiveness of alcohol use among the United

States teenage population. The National Institute on Drug Abuse, through nationwide surveys of high school seniors conducted between 1975 and 1980, revealed that 93.2 percent of the students admitted to using alcoholic beverages during their lifetime. Nearly 88 percent reported usage within the last 12 months, including 72 percent within the past 30 days.[6] Lloyd Johnson and associates' national survey of high school seniors from 1975 to 1982 attained similar results. More than 90 percent of the students acknowledged trying alcohol, while nearly 70 percent had used alcohol during the last month.[7]

A study by the Research Triangle Institute concluded that the majority of American adolescents drink alcoholic beverages, with one-third of the high school students in this country problem drinkers.[8] The National Institute on Alcohol Abuse and Alcoholism estimates that 3 million adolescents between age 14 and 17 experience problems in their lives that are associated with alcohol abuse; approximately 25 percent of the 10th through 12th graders have at least one drink a week; around 15 percent of this group are heavy drinkers; and 6 percent of all 12th graders are daily drinkers.[9]

Gender and Adolescent Use of Alcoholic Beverages

Self-report research suggests that male and female youths are much closer in their incidence of alcohol usage than indicated through arrest data. One recent survey found that 79 percent of the boys and 70 percent of the girls were drinkers; 23 percent of the males and 15 percent of the females were classified as problem drinkers.[10] A federal government report on alcohol and health found that by the time they reach their senior year in high school, 89.9 percent of the males and 83.2 percent of the females will have at least tried an alcoholic beverage once.[11] In Peter Kratcoski and John Kratcoski's study of changing patterns of delinquent activity, the authors actually found that a greater percentage of females (90 percent) had purchased or drunk beer, liquor, or wine that the males sampled (88 percent).[12]

The convergence of sex roles may be more true for adolescent use of alcohol and drugs than any other juvenile violation of the law.

The Legal Ramifications of Adolescent Use of Alcohol

Alcohol-related behavior by adolescents differs legally from that involving drug use in that the former represents both a status offense and often delinquent behavior, whereas drug abuse is entirely a violation of delinquent or criminal laws. The purchase and consumption of alcoholic beverages by persons under the age of majority represents a status offense, or a practice that is legally acceptable for most adults.[13] However, such related offenses as drunkenness and driving under the influence are violations of criminal laws applicable to people of all ages. This inconsistent double standard complicates the process of determining if a youth involved with alcohol should be classified as a status or delinquent offender, the disposition of their case by the juvenile justice system and police, and even the statistical interpretation of juvenile alcohol users.

Compounding this confusion is the fact that in some states persons age 18, or adults in every other sense, are legally unable to purchase or drink alcohol. They thus could be viewed, if arrested, as status or criminal offenders, dependent upon the jurisdiction and state, and dealt with accordingly, including arrest and detention.

In spite of the legal restraints against juvenile and young adult drinking, the evidence suggests that young persons neither obey the laws very often with respect to alcohol purchase and consumption nor find it very difficult to obtain alcoholic beverages. One study found that 7 out of 10 high school students indicated that they could virtually always purchase or get hold of alcohol products with little to no problem.[14]

Adolescent Alcohol Abuse and Traffic Fatalities

Where adolescent use of alcohol seems to draw the most attention is with respect to drunk driving and automobile accidents. The statistics are indeed frightening. In a recent year, teenagers accounted for fewer than 10 percent of the nation's 148,000,000 licensed drivers, yet were responsible for around 15 percent of the year's 65,000 traffic fatalities.[15] One of every five automobile fatalities in the U.S. involve drivers younger than age 20, and in 60 percent of such accidents the drivers were found to have been drinking.[16] Many studies have documented the strong correlation between adolescent drinking, driving, and motor vehicle caused deaths.[17]

It is this dangerous and significant relationship that has led many states to raise the drinking and driving ages as well as imposing curfews on underage drivers.[18] This notwithstanding, adolescent drinking mixed with driving continues to end up with tragic results.

Adolescent Use of Drugs

Adolescent involvement with drugs outside of alcohol may be of even greater consequence. The United States has the highest rate of adolescent drug use in the industrialized world.[19] Studies show that drug use among juveniles is 10 times more prevalent than parents are aware of.[20] The National Institute on Drug Abuse has produced the following data on teenage drug abuse as derived through nationwide self-report measures:

- Marijuana is the most popular drug among juveniles, followed by cocaine.
- One out of every three 12- to 17-year olds has tried marijuana, while one in every six currently uses it.
- Almost one in every five high school seniors has tried cocaine or crack cocaine.
- The use of marijuana and cocaine by adolescents is on the rise.
- Adolescent use of stimulants such as amphetamines or "speed" and Ritalin is rapidly increasing.
- Adolescent involvement with sedatives, including tranquilizers and barbiturates, and hallucinogens such as LSD and PCP is on the decline.
- Experimentation with other hallucinogens has shown an increase among juveniles.
- Narcotics, such as heroin, morphine, and opium, are the least popular type drugs with adolescents.[21]

Other studies are just as revealing about the character and nature of adolescent drug use. The Institute for Social Research recently found in its national probability sample of high school seniors that the use of marijuana and cocaine had increased strikingly; while adolescent use of stimulants and inhalants had risen at a lower rate.[22] In the Department of Health, Education and Welfare's *Marijuana and Health* reports, steady increases in the use of marijuana among adolescents are noted.[23] The emergence of crack cocaine usage by juveniles may represent their most consequential involvement with drugs (see following section on crack).

The frequency and type of drugs used by adolescents appears to vary according to such factors as age, gender, social class, geography, peer pressure, and the current fad.

Crack: The Latest Deadly Menace to Strike Adolescents

Crack, a highly addictive, inexpensive form of cocaine, may be the most harmful drug ever to hit the streets. Known also as "rock," crack is smoked rather than snorted. It absorbs quickly through the lungs and provides an intense rush to the brain in just seconds in a highly concentrated form of cocaine. A former addict depicts what it feels like to use crack: "It goes straight to the head. It's immediate speed. It feels like the top of your head is going to blow off."[24] Unlike regular cocaine addiction that takes three to four years to develop, crack abusers usually become addicted within six to ten weeks.

The National Cocaine Hotline estimates that over a million Americans in 25 states across the country have tried cocaine, noting that children as young as 12 have called the coke hotline out of desperation.[25] The rapidly increasing use of crack has led some professionals to fear an epidemic of cocaine addiction in the United States rivaling or surpassing that of the wave of heroin addiction in the 1960s.

Crack is believed to be responsible for a growing proportion of the drug-related and violent crime across the country, particularly that involving criminal gangs. A recent survey indicates that much of the cocaine-related crime takes place in predominantly minority and inner city areas.[26] The same sociodemographic characteristics apply as well to the typical crack cocaine user, although crack addicts can be found across the socioeconomic and racial strata.

It is unknown how many adolescents are involved with crack either as dealers or users; however, there is good reason to believe that juveniles are highly represented in both instances. In Los Angeles, for example, teenage street dealers have taken up much of the selling trade with the crackdowns on crack-based houses in the city.[27] Around 20 percent of the 12th graders have at least tried cocaine or crack.[28]

A typical example of an adolescent crack user was recently reported in a *Time* magazine article:

> "Eva" is a 16-year-old patient at New York City's Phoenix House drug rehabilitation center who got hooked on crack two years ago. The product of a troubled middle-class family, she was already a heavy drinker and pot smoker when she was introduced to coke by her older brother, a young dope pusher. "When you take the first toke on a crack pipe, you get on top of the world," she says.
>
> She first started stealing from family and friends to support her habit. She soon turned to prostitution and went through two abortions before she was 16. "I didn't give a damn about protecting myself," she said. "I just wanted to get high. Fear of pregnancy didn't even cross my mind when I hit the sack with someone for drugs."[29]

And obviously neither did AIDS.

Gender and Adolescent Drug Use

Drug use by adolescents has been shown through some self-report studies to be more prevalent among females than males. Kratcoski and Kratcoski's research showed that 40 percent of the females had used or sold drugs, compared to 35 percent of the males.[30] Similarly, in Nechama Tec's study, it was found that 40 percent of the female teenagers and 39 percent of the male teens used marijuana. However, a higher percentage of the males (13 percent) were regular users than the females (11 percent).[31] The significance of such studies relative to gender is to illustrate how male and female adolescents are much closer in their involvement in the teenage drug culture than official figures would have us believe. This seems particularly true for marijuana use.

Adolescent Use of Drugs and Alcohol in Combination

Evidence exists to support a dual use of alcohol and drugs by many adolescents.[32] That this occurs is not surprising considering the common availability of both type substances at teenage parties, on the streets, and even within the home, and the attraction of drugs and alcohol for the highs, feelings and status they present to young people. Yet the dangers of mixing alcohol and drugs are far greater than the average juvenile is aware of. The chemical ingredients of alcohol and one or more drug substances combined could cause a violent reaction, overdose, or death. One researcher explains the danger of adolescents' using alcohol concurrently with other substances: "Teenagers typically take the sedative and tranquilizing drugs in combination with alcohol or other drugs. When depressants are taken with alcohol, the intensity of intoxication increases, and the combination is potentially lethal."[33]

Adolescent Drug Use and Drug Dealing

The literature indicates that adolescents who deal in drugs are often drug users.[34] It is estimated that some 10 percent of all juveniles participate in illicit drug transactions in a given year, some of which are regular drug dealers.[35] Numerous studies have shown a direct correlation between drug selling and use of drugs. Bruce Johnson and colleagues found that youth drug dealing is highly concentrated. Their national sample of adolescents revealed that while fewer than 3 percent were cocaine users, nearly 60 percent of these youths who used cocaine sold illegal drugs, one-fourth of which were drugs other than marijuana.[36] Cheryl Carpenter and associates revealing study of youth, drugs and crime found that the majority of adolescents who sold a drug used the same drug, and many were regular users of marijuana and alcohol.[37]

Marijuana is the most commonly used and sold drug by adolescents. However, other drugs such as crack are also easily accessible and affordable to youths throughout this country, and thus likely figure significantly in adolescent drug dealing as well. Most adolescents who sell and distribute drugs do so in order to obtain drugs for their own use and to make money.[38]

Although adolescent drug dealers are predominantly male, young females are becoming increasingly involved in the selling of drugs, primarily as a means to make money or to support a habit. A 16-year-old female drug addict describes her experience as a seller of drugs to fellow adolescents:

> It is really easy to make money off of drugs. It has got to be the easiest job anyone could do. All you have to do is sit on your butt and wait for people to call. My boyfriend was dealing in drugs, and he was making nearly $200

a day. The money is nice, but when you get caught, it is another story. But I have never been caught. I've broken into homes, too, but I have never been caught doing that either.[39]

Adolescent Alcohol or Drug Use and Other Crimes

Alcohol and drug use by adolescents are believed to significant correlates of other types of juvenile crime. A recent survey of juvenile and family court judges estimated that between 60 and 90 percent of all crime perpetrated by youth is connected to use or abuse of substances.[40]

Violent Crime

A number of studies have documented a relationship between adolescent alcohol and drug usage and crimes of violence such as aggravated assault, sexual assault, homicide, and gang violence.[41] Serious youthful offenders have been shown to be habitual marijuana and alcohol users, as well as to exhibit less frequent involvement with such drugs as cocaine, pills, speed, and hallucinogens.[42] Violent crime by adolescents who use alcohol or drugs seems to be more related to a history of violent behavior rather than the influence of substances.[43] Moreover, such violence is often motivated by precipitating factors other than the drug or alcohol use itself, including drug distribution run-ins, gang warfare, racial hostilities, and revenge.[44]

Property Crime

The strongest link between adolescent use of drugs and alcohol and juvenile criminality is that involving economic or property crimes. Studies have shown that this relationship is governed primarily by two things (1) the need or desire for alcohol or drugs, and (2) the money or other property which can be used to purchase drugs or alcohol, or support a habit.[45] Carpenter and associates described theft among adolescent substance users as "partly a product of a consumeristic mentality."[46] They used this term to refer to the desire of their sample group to obtain what they wanted or needed as the major impetus of their theft activities which involved direct acquisition of valued goods, property stolen for resale, and theft as a direct source of money.

The researchers found that rather than committing property crimes in order to buy drugs or alcohol, most delinquents cited their objectives as more importantly to have fun, acquire valued goods, or obtain money for various reasons. While some theft involved drugs or property to purchase drugs or alcohol, adolescents were greater motivated by the acquirement of consumer goods such as clothing and stereo components, which they considered they needed in order to be popular among their peers.

Sex Offenses

Alcohol and drug use and abuse are frequently associated with adolescent sex offenses, most notably prostitution, commercialized vice, and pornography. D. Kelly Weisberg[47] and Ronald Flowers[48] cite research to support this relationship. Much of the substance abuse by adolescents who are sexually exploited occur in order to "deaden memories and desensitize present experiences."[49] Many young prostitutes and other sex offenders, such as rapists, already had experience or problems with drugs or alcohol prior to their sex crimes.[50]

Lesser evidence exists on the relationship between premarital juvenile sexual activity and drug or alcohol use. Yet logic suggests that the association is strong given the high rate of both adolescent sexual relations and the use of alcohol or drug substances.

Family Offenses

Numerous studies have established a correlation between adolescent substance abuse and various family offenses such as parent abuse, child abuse, and intergenerational violence. Some research has attributed violent behavior by adolescents towards members of their family to drug or alcohol influence.[51]; whereas other studies have linked child abuse and neglect or other family dysfunction with the onset of juvenile use of alcohol and drugs.[52] Further findings report a cycle of family substance abuse.[53] Overall, it appears that a significant proportion of the adolescent involvement with drugs and alcohol has its roots in a troubled or dysfunctional home life.

Beyond the Legal Implications of Adolescent Substance Abuse

Aside from the legal ramifications, teenage alcohol and drug use takes its toll in addiction and other physical and emotional health problems such as mental illness or impairment, heart and liver ailments, and death by association. In the case of drugs, AIDS is a potential affliction when it involves intravenous use. Further implications of adolescent use of alcohol and drugs can be seen in the high costs of dependency treatment and drug abuse education, the residual effect on family and friends, and school performance.

The relation between adolescent drug and alcohol use and problems in school has been documented in a number of studies. In a survey of Ohio teachers, drug use was perceived as an in-school problem by 40 percent of the high school teachers, 21 percent of those in junior high school, and 9 percent of the elementary school teachers. Alcohol use was also cited by 8 percent of the high school teachers as a problem with students.[54] Kenneth Polk and Steven Burkett's study of adolescent drinking revealed that intoxication had a negative effect on students' grade point average, time spent doing homework, and self-image. They also found that adolescent drinkers are more likely than nondrinkers to reject authority figures; and teen beer drinkers were more prone to receive low grades and participate in delinquent activities than nondrinkers, irrespective of social class.[55]

Why Adolescents Use Alcohol and Drugs

Adolescent involvement with drugs and alcohol can generally be traced to one or more of the following reasons:

- Peer group pressure.
- The perception of being grown up when using alcohol or drugs.
- The easy accessibility of drugs and alcohol.
- The attractiveness of substance use as portrayed through television, motion pictures, and literature.
- A breakdown in family discipline and stability.
- A family cycle of alcohol or drug use.
- Boredom.

Peer group influence is probably the strongest factor in alcohol and drug use among teenagers. Few youths are able to escape the pressures of belonging or fitting in with those of their inner circle or with whom they aspire to be grouped or associated with.

Other explanations linked to adolescent use of drugs or alcohol include addiction, use in order to reduce inhibitions, and substance intoxication as a means to commit other illegal acts.[56]

The Battle to Contain Adolescent Use of Alcohol and Drugs

In recent years, efforts have been stepped up to try to control the incidence of alcohol and drug use among adolescents. Some states have raised the legal age for drinking and driving; others have established curfews for underage drivers. More than 200 drunk driving statutes have been adopted across the country since 1980.[57] An even greater push has been made to stop drug use by teenagers. The slogan, "just say no to drugs" has become a popular theme in recent years in the wake of several headlined drug-induced deaths of young people. Many states have contributed to the fight against drugs by toughening drug laws and considering antiparaphernalia legislation criminalizing the manufacture, distribution, and sale of drug-related paraphernalia.[58] These efforts notwithstanding, the evidence indicates that we are still a long way from solving the problem of adolescent alcohol and drug use.

8. Adolescent Gang Delinquency

ONE OF THE MOST SERIOUS delinquent problems to confront law enforcement, particularly in inner city areas, is adolescent gang delinquency. Youth gangs have been in existence in the United States since the early 19th century. Although they have often been associated with violence and terrorizing local neighborhoods, today's delinquent gangs seem to have become even more deadly, sophisticated, distorted in values, and uncontrollable. Almost daily, it seems, we are confronted with news stories about youth gang violence, death, drug deals, and law enforcement attempts to deal with this branch of teenage delinquency. There are some who believe that gang delinquency lies at the root of most adolescent antisocial behavior.

Defining the Adolescent Delinquent Gang

What constitutes a youth gang? Because juveniles often group together either in disorganized or organized association for a variety of purposes, we will limit our attention to what could be considered a delinquent youth gang. Even here, there is little consensus among researchers in composing a uniform definition to apply to all juvenile gangs. Among the first to define the adolescent gang was sociologist Frederick Thrasher in the 1920s who defined it as

> an interstitial group originally formed spontaneously and then integrated through conflict. It is characterized by ... meeting face to face, milling, movement through space as a unit, conflict, and planning. The result of this collective behavior is the development of tradition, unreflective internal structure, espirit de corps, solidarity, morale, group awareness, and attachment to local territory.[1]

Walter Miller defined the youth gang as part of his national survey in the 1970s of various persons and organizations connected with or knowledgeable or urban gangs. According to Miller, a delinquent juvenile gang is

98

a group of recurrently associating individuals with identifiable leadership and internal organization, identifying with or claiming control over territory in the community, and engaging either individually or collectively in violent or other forms of illegal behavior.[2]

A 1988 definition of the typical adolescent delinquent gang might be

a loosely organized or disorganized group of juveniles distinguished by colors, race and ethnicity, neighborhood, and principles; and whose delinquent and criminal activities relate to status, respect, revenge, celebrity, satisfaction, and profit, and include murder, gang wars, and drug dealing.

Structural Features of the Juvenile Gang

There is considerable variation in the structural makeup of juvenile gangs. Some are composed of taut, strongly integrated, and formalized structures and bylaws; while others are made up of very loose, purposeless organization. Lewis Yablonsky described adolescent gangs as having "diffuse role definition, limited cohesion, impermanence, minimal consensus on norms, shifting membership, disturbed leadership, and limited definitions of membership expectations."[3] This is in stark contrast to John Quicker's observation that juvenile gangs have strong ties and gang structure, as well as fierce loyalty.[4]

In general, most teenage gangs are composed of a hierarchy involving a core or elite leadership, a group of regular or full-time members, and additional "hangers-on" or peripheral members. Yablonsky estimated that 10 to 15 percent of the typical gang consists of a "hard-core" or elite group that leads the gang and manages its day to day activities, with the other members serving as their followers.[5] One source describes the typical requirements for leadership in a gang:

Retention of the top leadership position in the gang may be dependent upon meeting the physical challenges presented by other candidates, demonstrating "heart" by fearlessly leading the gang into battle, or showing the ability to "look out for" the other gang members through cunning and manipulation. The other leadership positions are frequently conferred as a result of extraordinary performance in the gang's behalf.[6]

Entrance into a gang often involves initiation rites and demonstrations of personal valor, such as proving one's sexual prowess or tolerance for pain. Gang solidarity and structure is strongly connected to the names of gangs, gang emblems, gangs' meeting places, use and collection of weapons, and distinctive modes of dress.

The Extent and Character of Delinquent Gangs

The most important empirical research on juvenile gang delinquency was largely conducted during the 1950s and 1960s. Today more attention seems to be directed toward examining and explaining adolescent antisocial behavior in general. There have been some studies on gang delinquency in recent years, most notably the work of Walter Miller. His investigation of juvenile urban gangs in the 1970s revealed that some 2,200 gangs existed nationally, consisting of approximately 96,000 members spread over 300 communities. He concluded that gang members were responsible for roughly one-third of all crimes of violence, terrorizing entire communities, and maintaining a state of siege in many inner city schools.[7]

Miller specified six major cities as having serious gang problems: New York, Los Angeles, Chicago, Detroit, Philadelphia, and San Francisco. Gang violence was broken down into four categories:

* "Normal" gang violence — violence directed against other gang members.
* Violence against nongang members with similar social characteristics to members of gangs.
* Gang criminality directed toward the general public.
* Attacks upon young children, females, elderly, or noncommunity members.[8]

Table 8-1 reflects the distribution of victimization by gang violence in four of the problem cities. Gang members were the victims of more than 60

Table 8-1. Victims of Gang Violence in Four Cities, 1973-1975

Type of Victim	City				
	NYC N = 80	Chicago N = 58	Los Angeles N = 108	Philadelphia N = 55	Four Cities N = 301
Gang Member	51.2	56.9	66.7	65.5	60.5
Via rumble, warfare	36.2	22.4	35.2	28.2	31.9
Via band, individual assault	15.0	34.5	31.5	36.2	28.6
Nongang Member	48.8	43.1	33.3	34.6	39.5
Peers	11.5	8.6	11.1	18.2	11.9
Children, adults	37.5	34.5	22.2	16.4	27.6
	100.0	100.0	100.0	100.0	100.0

Source: Walter Miller, Violence by Youth Gangs and Youth Groups As A Crime Problem in Major American Cities (Washington, D.C.: U.S. Department of Justice, December, 1975), p. 39.

percent of the gang directed violence; however, nearly 4 out of 10 victims of gang violence were nongang members, illustrating the serious effect of gang delinquency on the general public.

Age Distribution of Gang Members

Most members of gangs have been shown to fall within the age 10 to 21 range. Miller found that 82 percent of the gang members arrested in the four largest "gang problem" cities were between ages 14 to 19. Just over 4 percent were under age 14.[9] These figures correspond with those reported in earlier studies.

Gender and Adolescent Gang Involvement

Juvenile gang members are predominantly male by most accounts. In Miller's research, 90 percent or more of the gang members were male. Nevertheless, female members of male gangs or female gangs have been documented through several studies. Peggy Giordano's study of institutionalized female delinquents found that over half of the 108 girls sampled reported having been a part of a gang complete with a name.[10] In a study of Philadelphia females involved with gangs, Waln Brown indicated that female gang members are generally participants in sexually integrated youth gangs as opposed to autonomous female gangs, and perform such tasks as spying on other gangs.[11] Miller supports the belief that independent female juvenile gangs are limited and that female gang members are much less violent than their male counterparts.[12]

However, some research suggests that many female gang members are involved in serious and violent forms of delinquency as well as independent gangs. Freda Adler has advanced that girls are becoming "more highly integrated in male gang activity and were moving closer to parallel but independent, violence-oriented, exclusively female gangs."[13] In *Girls in the Gang,* Anne Campbell also notes the violence capacity of female gang members, which she says, "tends to erupt faster [than male gang violence] and end more quickly. The weapons used are most likely to be fingernails, teeth, and knives rather than crowbars and guns."[14]

Race and Ethnic Composition of Juvenile Gangs

Blacks are believed to be involved in adolescent delinquent gangs more than any other racial or ethnic group. Part of this assumption is associated with the greater attention given to the delinquent activities of inner city youth groups and differential enforcement of laws, since studies have shown that black youths are more likely to be labeled as gang members, arrested, and incarcerated than youths of other ethnic or racial persuasions.[15]

Nevertheless, black adolescent gang members have been shown to be disproportionately involved in violent gang activity. The same can be said for Hispanic youth. This can be seen in Table 8-2, which reflects the racial and ethnic breakdown of youth gang members in six major cities with a serious gang problem. Blacks accounted for nearly half of the total, while

Table 8-2. Major Racial and Ethnic Categories of Gang Members in Six Cities

Race/Ethnicity	Number	Percent
Black	29,000	47.6
Hispanic	22,000	36.1
Non-Hispanic White	5,400	8.8
Asian	4,600	7.5

Source: Walter B. Miller, Violence by Youth Gangs and Youth Groups As A Crime Problem in Major American Cities (Washington, D.C.: U.S. Government Printing Office, 1975), p. 26.

Hispanic youths made up over 36 percent of the gang members. Combined, black and Hispanic adolescents represented over 83 percent of the members of gangs. Since this study, which took place in the mid-1970s, Asian gang members have become increasingly more prominent in number and violent activities.[16]

Class Variations in Delinquent Gang Activity

Much of the serious and violent youth gang activity has been shown to occur in lower class and slum areas of large cities.[17] Although there is no doubt a class bias at work in the study and conclusions of gang activity, this cannot account for the strong correlation between lower class gangs and violence. This seems especially true in urban areas such as New York and Los Angeles. In Los Angeles County alone, the gang-related homicides for the period between 1980 and 1985 were 351, 267, 205, 214, 355, and 269 respectively. In 1987, 387 such homicides were recorded in the county, a record 207 of which occurred in the city of Los Angeles.[18]

Notes the head of Los Angeles' city attorney's gang unit: "These gangs are extremely violent today. They're killers. We literally have dead bodies all over the place."[19] Another observer of L.A.'s serious gang problem put it in perspective: "We're not talking about kids with zip guns. We're talking about kids with Uzis."[20]

The problem of gang delinquency is not limited to major metropolitan areas, but can also be found in suburbia and small towns. Howard

Myerhoff and Barbara Myerhoff's study of middle class gangs documented not only their existence, but the similarities to urban gangs in their objectives such as status, protection, belonging, and monetary gain.[21] Dale Hardman's exploration of small town juvenile gangs revealed much of the same in their goals, while also noting that their activities ranged from petty crimes to violent crimes such as rape and murder.[22] Hardman found, interestingly enough, that small town gangs differed from inner city youth gangs in that females were included as full fledged members as opposed to simply auxiliary members of the gang. Nor are white youths exempt from gang status. Miller cited seven white delinquent gangs in a large metropolitan area. The most criminally active gang, the Senior Bandits, was composed primarily of Irish Catholic youths between the ages of 16 and 18. Members of this gang were frequently convicted and institutionalized.[23]

Los Angeles — The Melting Pot of Gangs and Gang Violence

If there is one city in the United States that best defines the ethnic and racial diversity of youth gangs and their penchant for violence, it is Los Angeles. Referred to by police as the gang capital of the nation, L.A. is believed to have about 600 different gangs totaling some 70,000 members, or seven times as many as are estimated to be among Chicago's 100 gangs, which is said to represent the second greatest concentration of gangs and members in the country.[24] Los Angeles boasts gangs of virtually every ethnic group including black, white, Mexican, Filipino, Vietnamese, Samoan, and Salvadoran. Their criminal activities are broad and include drug trafficking, extortion, intimidation, prostitution, and murder.

The black gangs of Los Angeles have established the reputation of being the most violent, dangerous, and powerful. Rival factions of black gangs such as the Crips and the Bloods have branched out into other cities such as Sacramento, Denver, Portland, Tulsa, Seattle, and Phoenix where they peddle drugs and often resort to violence. So much attention has been focused on the problem of black gang warfare and indiscriminate gang violence in L.A. in recent years that a theatrical movie dealt with the subject.

There are approximately 25,000 members of Los Angeles' black gangs, most of which are armed with automatic weapons. Local police officials contend that black gangs have become the central distributors of crack cocaine throughout the West. They are also believed by some experts to be the best organized youth gangs, "fighting for control of the drug traffic with a disdain for human life — their own and others."[25]

An official of the Youth Gang Services, an agency that mediates gang disputes, speaks of the frustrating and frightening spectre of L.A.'s black juvenile gangs:

The black gangs have progressively gotten more violent and affluent. Also the relative value of life has decreased. They don't give a damn about their own lives or anybody else's. We've got people willing to risk their own lives and prison for a few short months on the high life. The alternatives to them are not that great.[26]

Despite Los Angeles' continual war on gangs, including raids on drug houses, beefed up police forces, "gang summits," and even secret witness rewards, there were still a record number 207 gang killings in the city in 1987. As of late 1988, gang related deaths were still occurring at an alarming rate, as were other forms of gang violence and drug trafficking. Notes the Youth Gang Services official bleakly: "You're talking about a whole subclass of folks who have pretty much given up on themselves, their future, their community.[27]

Organized Delinquent Gangs

There is indication that the nature of gang delinquent activities has undergone significant changes from past periods. Whereas once upon a time the primary objective of the youth gang was protection and control of their "turf," as of the late 1980s adolescent gang delinquencies had broadened into drug dealing, theft, prostitution, extortion, and other crimes. Many believe that today's youth gangs have become "organized criminals" in many respects. In *Minorities and Criminality,* Ronald Flowers presents evidence of organized criminal activity among various minority gangs.[28] Black, Hispanic, and Asian youth gangs have interspersed traditional gang activities with nontraditional involvement in criminality previously associated primarily with racketeers.

In Los Angeles, Robert Ruchhoft, a veteran member of the city's police department specializing in gang activity, recently commented on the changes in black and Asian gang delinquency. He observed that black youth gangs have stepped up from traditional turf wars and knife fights to drug distribution and murder or, as he described it, their delinquency is "disorganized crime on the threshold of organized crime."[29] Although Asian youth crime has traditionally been low, Asian gangs are beginning to make their presence felt as a force in organized criminal activities such as extortion and robbery. Says Ruchhoft, Asian gangs are "the closest thing we've got to real organized crime in Los Angeles."[30]

In addition to an expansion to such criminal pursuits as drug dealing, prostitution, and robbery, adolescent gangs of the 1980s have also taken to other forms of loosely organized "street hustling" including larceny-theft, burglary, and con games.

A common feature of today's more dangerous and sophisticated adolescent gang is the stockpiling and almost casual use of weaponry ranging from handguns to automatic weapons. In some states, law enforcement has been forced to upgrade their own weaponry just to keep pace with the advanced arms of gang members.

Causes of Adolescent Gang Delinquency

As noted earlier, the most substantive studies of delinquent gangs occurred in the 1950s and 1960s and today continue to offer us the most influential theoretical perspectives on gang formation and delinquent behavior. In this section we will review the propositions of four of the major contributors to this field of study.

Reaction-Formation Theory

It was in the 1955 book, *Delinquent Boys: The Culture of the Gang,* that Albert Cohen first proposed his reaction-formation theory of gang delinquency.[31] According to this theory, lower class juveniles turn to gang delinquency as a necessary group response or reaction to the failure to acquire status as determined by middle class norms and values. Cohen maintained that middle class goals and values (such as success through hard work, ambition, and using one's skills to progress) are desired by lower class youth, but they are generally at a disadvantage in institutional settings such as the school, where they are measured by middle class standards; and otherwise find themselves deprived of approved opportunities to attain culturally prescribed goals.

Due to these blocked opportunities and conflicts with middle class social institutions, Cohen theorized that lower class youth undergo a deviant behavioral response to their limitations which he refers to as "status frustration" or a "reaction-formation against a middle class organized status dilemma in which the lower class boy suffers status frustrations in competition with middle status boys."[32] This causes many of these adolescents to band together in juvenile gangs or a delinquent subculture, where they participate in behavior that is nonutilitarian, malicious, negativistic, and hedonistic.

Cohen contended that the values of this delinquent subculture are the opposite of middle class values. Because of an emotional attachment to middle class goals that are unachievable, these youths must reject such goals and develop their own standards by which success can come and with it status, self-esteem, and solidarity.

Thus, Cohen's theory attributes the formation of juvenile delinquent gangs with lower class living and the rejection of middle class values, and blames this delinquent subculture on the structural failures of the system (i.e., the family, institutional settings).

Although Cohen is credited with being one of the first to associate the school system with delinquency, there are a number of holes in this theory. The most significant is that his premise has not been validated empirically. Also, there is little evidence to support the contention that lower class youths repudiate middle class values. Another problem area relates to the broad generalization with which he uses such terms as malicious and nonutilitarian to describe gang members. Finally, Cohen places too much value on the rejection of middle-class standards in explaining juvenile gang delinquency, while giving little attention to the relative influence of such variables as family, race, and demographic characteristics in delinquency causation.

In response to the criticism of his work, Cohen, in collaboration with James Short, Jr., later expanded upon his original theory by suggesting that there is more than one kind of lower-class gang subculture. They advanced that a *parent subculture* was the primary type with other gang orientations specialized offshoots from it, including a middle class subculture and a drug addict subculture.[33]

Opportunity Theory

Richard Cloward and Lloyd Ohlin made a substantial contribution to the study and understanding of delinquent subcultures with their 1960 work, *Delinquency and Opportunity: A Theory of Delinquent Gangs.*[34] Inspired by Merton's theory of anomie, Sutherland's differential association theory, and Cohen's view of middle class values being desired by all classes of people, Cloward and Ohlin proposed an opportunity theory, also referred to as differential opportunity theory. This theory argues that one's access to both legitimate and illegitimate means is largely influenced by the social structure. That is, while differential opportunity exists in reaching culturally prescribed goals through legitimate means so too does differential opportunity operate in the use of illegitimate means for attaining socially approved goals.

Opportunity theory explains juvenile gang delinquency in terms of a discrepancy between the aspirations that lower class youths aspire for and what they have access to, assuming that "discrepancies between aspirations and legitimate chances of achievement increase as one descends in the class structure."[35] Because lower class juveniles are unable to lower their aspirations as derived from middle class standards, their lack of access to legitimate means to reach culturally defined goals results in deep frustrations and deviation to illegitimate means to achieve these cultural goals.

According to Cloward and Ohlin, two types of opportunities are distributed unequally: access to "learning structures," or the "appropriate environments for the acquisition of the values and skills associated with the performance of a particular role," and access to "performance structures," or the opportunity to organize with others who share a related problem of adjustment and the opportunity to receive peer approval for one's behavior.[36] Opportunity theory posits that it is the social structure of a community that determines the access youths have to learning and performance structures. Hence, the type of juvenile gang and delinquent subculture in a given area is determined to a great extent by the community social structure or environment.

Cloward and Ohlin have identified three primary types of lower class adolescent gangs, or subcultural reactions to blocked legitimate or illegitimate avenues for success — each or all a product of the available means: criminal gangs, conflict gangs, and retreatist gangs.

The Criminal Gang. Adolescent criminal gangs take on criminal values and skills as learned from adult and organized crime figures. These gangs are driven primarily by the acquirement through illegitimate means (such as larceny-theft and extortion) of material gain, power, and prestige.

The Conflict Gang. Youth conflict gangs develop under conditions in which both legitimate and illegitimate opportunities for success are closed or hampered. Membership in conflict gangs allows juveniles to achieve prestige, status, or a reputation for toughness among their peer groups, often by way of forceful means or the threat of force. The conflict gang's principle delinquencies involve fighting, violence, and inter-gang conflict.

The Retreatist Gang. Retreatist juvenile gangs emerge when youths are denied or reject success through legitimate and illegitimate means. Retreatist teenagers often submerge into a world of substance abuse and take on secondary criminal pursuits to support their habit, such as prostitution and drug dealing. They gain personal status from their inner circle by aiming to be the "coolest" person around.

Cloward and Ohlin's opportunity theory may succeed in its recognition of various delinquent gang subcultures according to differential opportunity structures. The major weakness of the theory is its concentration on lower class gang delinquency, while not adequately accounting for individual delinquency or the gang delinquencies of other social classes. Further, the researchers fail to explain why some communities have different types of delinquent gangs at once. Some critics also question whether or not lower class juveniles aspire to the values of the middle class.[37] These criticisms aside, Cloward and Ohlin's theory of differential opportunity is credited with having a profound impact on delinquency theory.

Lower Class Culture Theory

Walter Miller offered a theory of delinquency that suggested the existence of a lower class culture and gang delinquency as a reflection of that culture. Unlike Cohen and Cloward and Ohlin's premise that lower class gang delinquency is centered around the rejection of middle class values, Miller argued that lower class gang delinquency is the result of positive attempts by youths to attain goals as determined by the values or focal concerns of the lower class culture.[38]

Miller identifies six such lower class focal concerns, or areas that represent the main concerns of lower class youths: trouble, toughness, smartness, excitement, fate, and autonomy. These are described as follows:

- *Trouble* refers to circumstances that result in undesired involvement with law enforcement. Miller regards staying out of trouble and getting into trouble as a daily concern of lower class youth.
- *Toughness* is associated with masculinity, physical superiority, daring, and bravery.
- *Smartness* is the capacity to outsmart, outwit, or "con" others while avoiding being duped or deceived.
- *Excitement* relates to the desire for thrills, risks, and to avoid boredom.
- *Fate* concerns interests or beliefs associated with luck, fortunes, and jinxes. Miller holds that members of the lower class often perceive themselves as having little or no control over their lives due to fate.
- *Autonomy* is closely related to fate and is in reference to a desire to be in control of one's own life or destiny.

According to lower class culture theory, the delinquent gang acts as a social setting in which juveniles can achieve prestige through actions in relation to lower class focal concerns.

Miller's theory of lower class culture seems to have some merit in linking differential lower class values (specifically those of lower class gangs) to gang delinquency. However, a number of critics reject the notion that lower class adolescents do not adhere to the norms and values of society at large.[39] Lower class culture theory does not explain how these focal concerns originated, and also fails to differentiate between lower class law violators and lower class law abiding citizens.

The more recent contributions by Miller in the study of juvenile gangs have been more productive in terms of their usefulness in probing the problem and demographic variables of gang behavior.

The Violent Gang

A final contributor to gang delinquency that deserves mention is Lewis Yablonsky. In his book, *The Violent Gang,* he classifies youth gangs into three types: social gangs, delinquent gangs, and violent gangs. *Social gangs* are made up of juveniles who aspire to achieve their individual social goals as part of a group. *Delinquent gangs* are concerned primarily with material gain through delinquent activity. *Violent gangs* seek emotional gratification by way of violent behavior.[40]

Yablonsky proposed that these violent or conflict-oriented gangs are a product of certain conditions present in the urban slums, which contributes to a sociopathic personality in adolescent delinquents. These sociopathic persons largely make up the core leadership of violent youth gangs. According to Yablonsky, the primary function of the violent gang is to offer a means by which youths can act out aggressions or hostilities in a way more acceptable than that present in the general community.

Because of the difficulty in classifying specific gangs and gang members as fitting solely into one classification or another, Yablonsky's typology cannot be viewed as representative of all, if any, violent gangs. More likely, violent gangs are composed of violent, social, and delinquent youths, and interchangeable typologies depending upon the individual and the metamorphosis of the gang. Yablonsky's view of the violent gang can also be criticized for its unsubstantiated reliance on slum conditions in creating adolescent sociopathic personalities. Nevertheless, on the whole Yablonsky succeeds in offering a classification scheme for the violent youth gang as differentiated from other adolescent gangs.

Trends in Youth Group Crime and Delinquency

The 1980s have spawned a number of frightening and often violent manifestations of adolescent gangs and gang crime and delinquency. These include "wilding," a street term for violent pack mischief by mostly urban, impoverished teens; skinheads, neo–Nazi youth groups distinguished by shaven heads and racial attacks; and satanic cults, featuring bizarre rituals and sacrifices. Similar to traditional gang formation, these variations of delinquent youth groups can be attributed to adolescent frustrations, peer group pressure, alienation, remorselessness; as well as drugs, lack of positive role models, hatred, and racism.

Controlling Adolescent Gang Delinquency

Efforts to control gang delinquency and violence include "gang-intelligence" units within police departments, street worker programs aimed at redirecting gang objectives into more constructive activities, and "gang summits" involving community members and gang leaders in an attempt to establish a truce in gang warfare. These efforts have had only limited success.

9. Biological Approaches to Delinquency

BIOLOGICAL OR BIOGENIC theories offer one of the earliest criminological attempts to explain delinquent and criminal behavior. These theories are based on the premise that criminal deviance is preestablished primarily by genetic anomalies. That is, theorists of the biological school of criminology propose that certain biological factors such as heredity and physiology predisposes some to criminal behavior. Most biological theories of crime have been rejected by modern criminologists and sociologists who prefer environmentality based explanations of criminality. However, the biological influence on the study of crime and delinquency should be recognized as well as the more recent biological research that has, at least to some extent, brought this school of thought back into prominence.

Early Biogenic Theories

Atavistic Theories

Cesare Lombroso, an Italian physician, is generally recognized as pioneering the research into the relationship between criminality and biological characteristics. Referred to as the "father of criminology," Lombroso's major thesis as originally formulated in his 1876 book *L'Uomo Delinquente,* was that some people are biologically predisposed or born to be criminals.[1] He believed criminals to be a product of atavism, or biological throwbacks to primitive genetic forms, and termed this species of man *homo delinquens.*

Lombroso, who was highly influenced by the work of Charles Darwin, derived his propositions through his scientific examinations of Italian prisoners and Italian army personnel. He postulated that criminals and noncriminals could be differentiated by physical stigmata. Physical anomalies such as fat lips, enormous jaws, flattened nose, and particular skull shapes; as well as such preferences for tattoos and orgies were indicative of a predisposition to criminal or deviant behavior. This criminal stigmata consisted of various combinations and distinguished one type of criminal from another.

Although Lombroso later modified some of his hypotheses, his basic philosophy remained. In 1913, Charles Goring refuted Lombroso's atavistic approach in his book, *The English Convict*.[2] Comparing the physical measurements of 3,000 English prisoners to the same number of nonprisoners, Goring could find no differences of consequence.

Lombroso's work has further been discredited because of, among other things, the small size of his prison samples, lack of general population control groups, and his inability to account for biological determinants that might be the result of such factors as malnutrition rather than heredity. Nevertheless, Lombroso's contribution to the biological-positivistic school of criminology remains considerable.

Body Type Theories

The relationship between body type and criminal behavior took on renewed interest with the 1939 publication of Ernest Hooton's *Crime and the Man*.[3] An advocate of Lombroso, Hooton compared thousands of measurements of the physical characteristics of prisoners and nonprisoners. He concluded that most criminals were physically as well as mentally inferior to noncriminals. Hooton believed that criminals could be identified by such physical traits as mixed eye color, reddish hair, and long necks; and even typecast criminals according to their particular physical characteristics. For instance, he believed tall, heavy men were more likely to be murderers.

It was the work of William Sheldon in the 1940s that first sought to systematically show a relationship between body types and juvenile delinquency.[4] Based upon extensive collection and comparison of physical measurements, Sheldon described three basic body types or somatotypes which he related with certain personality or temperamental traits. The endomorphic is depicted as fat, soft and round; extroverted, and desires comfort. The ectomorphic is thin, fragile, weak; introverted, shy and sensitive. The third type, mesomorphic, is characterized as muscular and hard; aggressive, assertive, and active—and the most likely to engage in delinquent behavior. Sheldon contended that there were specific somatotype and personality differences between delinquents and nondelinquents.

Sheldon and Eleanor Glueck also examined body types in their study of delinquents. Using Sheldon's principles, the Gluecks found that mesomorphs were disproportionately represented among the institutionalized delinquents they studied. Mesomorphic types characterized 60.1

percent of the delinquents compared to only 30.7 percent of the non-delinquents.[5] More recently, J. Cortes and F. Gatti's study of adolescents supported the Gluecks' finding of proportionately more mesomorphic youths among the delinquent group.[6]

Body-type theories are no longer, if they ever were, considered credible in explaining criminal and delinquent behavior. The foremost of such theories is the lack of a conclusive physiological association between body type and antisocial behavior or delinquency. The methodology used in most of these studies (i.e., prisoners as representative of *all* criminals) has also been called into question. Additional fault with the body type perspective is that most of the delinquent body characteristics can also be found in nondelinquents.

Heredity-Genetic Theories

The role of heredity in delinquent behavior has long been given attention in the biological school of criminal behavior. The notion that abnormal behavior such as delinquency, mental illness, and alcoholism, is somehow the result of genetic transmission of mental or physical traits or abnormalities from one generation to the next has had its share of supporters. Once Lombroso's atavistic propositions were largely rejected, many biological theorists turned to inherited mental deficiencies as a possible explanation for criminality and delinquency. Some of the more interesting research in this regard were studies by Richard Dugdale[7] and Henry Goddard[8] which attempted to document the long histories of social aberrations such as prostitution, idiocy, feeblemindedness, fornication, and delinquency within certain families.

Although such research has long since been ridiculed as defective and methodologically unsound, there continues to be some appeal in the characterization of the "black sheep," "bad apple," "bad blood" to describe those who are predisposed to badness or antisocial behavior because of similar behavioral traits by parents or other blood relatives. Even the entertainment industry is capitalizing on this fascination as evidenced by a recent television movie about a child murderess, appropriately titled, *The Bad Seed*.

Modern Biological Research

Twin Studies

Interest in the genetic influence of criminal and delinquent behavior led to the inevitable study of twins. Such research has compared the criminal patterns and incidence of crime among twins developed from a single egg — monozygotic (MZ) twins — or identical twins, to that of twins who came from separately fertilized eggs — dizygotic (DZ) twins — known as fraternal twins. The implication is that if criminal tendencies are in fact inherited traits, then identical twins will be more alike in their criminal behavior than fraternal twins.

A prominent concept in twin studies is *concordance,* a genetic term that refers to the degree in which twins or related subject pairings both show a specific condition or behavior. A number of early studies, such as that conducted by Johannes Lange of Bavarian prisoners, have found that identical twins had a higher concordance rate of criminal behavior than fraternal twins.[9]

Subsequent, more advanced research, has also shown a considerably higher rate of criminal concordance among identical twins, though not as great as that reported in earlier studies. For instance, Karl Christiansen's study of 444 pairs of twins who were born in Denmark between 1870 and 1910 and who reached the age of 15, found that the concordance rate for MZ or identical twins was more than three times the rate of DZ or fraternal twins.[10] This compares to a rate of concordance in the Lange study of identical twins that was more than six times the percentage of twins who were fraternal.

In a review of twin studies, Hans Eysench concluded that the consistent differential in concordance between identical and fraternal twins indicates that heredity is "beyond any doubt . . . an extremely important part in the genesis of criminal behaviour."[11]

Despite such findings, not all researchers are in agreement. A study by Odd Dalgaard and Einar Kringlen showed no significant difference in concordance rates between identical and fraternal twins.[12] Other studies have supported this finding.

Most theorists that advocate a genetics-delinquency link also recognize the importance of environment in behavior, thereby mitigating somewhat the role of heredity. Furthermore, even with the differences shown between identical and fraternal twins with respect to criminality, it has yet to be established whether they are inherited or environmental in nature, or to what degree either variable may come into play.

Adoption and Fosterling Studies

The relative weight of genetic and environmental influence on delinquent behavior has also been explored through adoption and fosterling studies. Such research seeks to examine the relationship between the criminality of adopted or foster children and that of their biological and adoptive or foster parents. The assumption is that if these children exhibit behavior more like that of their biological parents, then this offers stronger support that behavior is genetically transmitted. On the other hand, should adopted or foster children more closely resemble the behavioral characteristics of their adoptive or foster parents, then a more solid case can be made for the environment as the greater influence in deviant behavior.

Typically, adoptions and foster home provisions occur shortly after birth; hence such children have only brief contact with, and little knowledge of, their biological parents. However, because adoption and fostering agencies seek to place children with families similar to that of their natural parentage in terms of race, physical appearance, and socioeconomic status, the ability to accurately differentiate biological and environmental influence on such children would seem to be questionable. Nevertheless, research in this area has offered support for heredity as a significant causal agent in delinquent and criminal behavior.

One of the first adoption studies was undertaken in Denmark by F. Schulsinger.[13] Comparing the incidence of "psychopathy" in the biological families of adoptees, Schulsinger found that 3.9 percent of the biological relatives of psychopathic adoptees were in his classification psychopathic, compared to only 1.4 percent of the control groups' biological families. However, definitional and methodology problems hamper these findings.

A more advanced study of genetics and environment with respect to criminality was conducted by Bernard Hutchings and Sarnoff Mednick.[14] They examined 1,145 male adoptees and the same number of nonadoptees, controlling variables such as age, sex, and occupation of fathers. It was concluded that nearly twice as many adoptees had criminal records as nonadoptees and that there was a strong relationship between the criminality of the adoptees and that of their fathers. The biological fathers of the adoptees were more than three times as likely to be criminal participants than either the adoptive fathers or the fathers of the nonadopted control sample. The criminality of the adoptees was twice as high (22 percent) when the biological father had a criminal record and the adopted father (11.5 percent) did not than vice versa. When both the biological and adoptive parents had criminal records, the likelihood that the adoptee would follow suit was much greater. Although Hutchings and Mednick advanced that genetic factors were strongly influential in the propensity toward criminality, they also noted that environmental variables played an important role.

In one of the most comprehensive studies of adoptees, Mednick, W. Gabrielli, and Hutchings compared the conviction records of 14,427 adoptees to the conviction records of their biological and adoptive parents. They concluded that genetic transmission of deviant tendencies increased the probability of children becoming delinquent or criminal.[15]

It appears that genetics may in fact be influential in the behavior patterns of some people. Even then, though, it is doubtful that such influence would manifest itself without the trigger of environmental variables.

The XYY Chromosome Factor

Another genetic theory of delinquency and criminality that has gotten its share of attention and controversy is that surrounding an XYY chromosomal pattern in males. It was in the early 1960s that researchers discovered that a genetic abnormality exists in some males. The normal human chromosome count is 46; with the male configuration being XY and the female pairing XX. The observation that some males possess an extra Y sex chromosome or a complement of XYY, led researchers to findings that associated this unusual chromosomal configuration with aggressive and violent behavior. Most of the studies have been of tall, institutionalized prisoners and mentally retarded persons with the XYY complement. These XYY males have been shown to be in disproportion to the general population.[16]

A cohort study of tall men in Denmark by Herman Witkin and colleagues found that XYY males (12 out of 4,139) participated in more criminal behavior than the XY males of comparable height, age, and social status. However, the researchers also found no evidence that the XYY group was any more violent prone than the XY group.[17]

Recent research has generally failed to support the association between the XYY chromosomal complement and criminality. Some criminologists have refuted the notion that XYY prisoners are significantly disproportionate to XYY individuals in the population at large; while others have argued that XYY persons have a lower tendency toward aggressive behavior than those with a normal chromosomal arrangement.[18]

Brain Disorder Studies

The biological approach to delinquent behavior has focused in recent years on brain dysfunctions and impairments in learning capabilities. Some evidence indicates that delinquents have a higher rate of epilepsy through which seizures may diminish self-control.[19] Other research has shown abnormal electroencephalogram (EEG) recordings of the brain activity in criminals and delinquents, relating this to violent and aggressive behavior, destructiveness, limited impulse control, and poor social adaptation.[20]

Dysfunctions of the brain have also been linked to such learning disabilities as dyslexia, aphasia and hyperactivity, which some researchers contend predisposes these persons to deviant behavior, rejection and poor educational achievement.[21] Further study has established a relationship between violent criminal behavior and brain tumors.[22]

Although there does appear to be some basis for brain dysfunction theories in delinquent behavior, there is still too little evidence of a direct causal relationship to know what role, if any, brain disorders play in adolescent delinquency.

Biochemical Research

Other modern biological explanations of delinquent behavior have focused on such areas as nutritional deficiencies, hypoglycomia, allergies, and the role of environmental contaminants on the body.[23] Much of this work is still too recent to be able to evaluate adequately.

10. Psychological Propositions of Juvenile Criminality

PSYCHOLOGICAL OR PSYCHOGENIC approaches to delinquent behavior have been around for some time. These theories, in contrast to biological research, are heterogeneous in the perspectives they offer to explain adolescent criminality. Formulated by psychologists, psychiatrists, and other mental health professionals, the psychological school of thought attributes delinquency and criminality to a variety of mental, emotional and personality disorders. Despite a number of faults with psychological propositions of delinquent behavior, this discipline is generally believed to be more credible in some of its assumptions than the biological school.

Psychoanalytic Theories

Sigmund Freud's psychoanalytic proposals paved the way for much of the psychoanalytic research with respect to personality, crime and delinquency. Freud, a Vietnamese physician, advanced that the personality is composed of three integral parts: the id (the source of instinctive energy and biological drives), the ego (the component of the psyche that experiences and reacts to the surrounding world), and the superego (the conscience of the psyche; it intercedes between the drives of the id and moral values).[1] Fundamentally, psychoanalytic theories regard delinquent behavior as the conflict between these basic drives and unresolved instincts.

Although Freud is credited with establishing a correlation between deviant behavior and personality formation, particularly an unconscious sense of guilt the person develops during childhood, it is the work of psychoanalyst August Aichorn that is most responsible for applying the psychoanalytic perspective to delinquency and criminality. Upon studying adolescents, Aichorn posited that they were psychologically predisposed to commit criminal and delinquent acts. He described this as latent delinquency, which he believed to be present in juveniles whose personality compelled them to act instinctively, impulsively and for self-satisfaction without feelings of guilt.[2]

More recently, C. Schoenfeld suggested, with respect to psychoanalytic theory and the superego, that most delinquent acts are not due to criminal tendencies, but rather a weak, incomplete, or defective superego that is unable to control adequately the primitive and strong early childhood urges, resulting in delinquent behavior.[3]

Supporters of the psychoanalytic approach believe that the solution to these behavioral problems is psychoanalysis — an individualistic therapy program which concentrates on delving deep into the individual's past experiences to uncover the unconscious conflicts.

The primary criticism against psychoanalytic theories is that they cannot be tested empirically. Because the personality parts are neither observable nor measurable, the basis of psychoanalytic conclusions is essentially the "analyst's interpretation of a patient's interpretation of what is occurring in the subconscious."[4]

Personality-Disorder Theories

Personality-disorder theorists tend to focus on personality flaws and emotional problems to explain delinquent behavior, while not necessarily relating this to unconscious conflicts.

Emotional Problems

Since the early 1900s psychiatrists, psychologists and other researchers have studied the relationship between emotional difficulties and delinquency, independent of the psychoanalytic perspective. Cyril Burt found that 85 percent of the criminals he studied in the 1930s were emotionally impaired.[5] Similarly, William Healy and Augusta Bronner's comparison of 105 delinquents and their nondelinquent siblings resulted in the researchers concluding that more than 90 percent of the delinquents were presently or previously unhappy, discontented, or "extremely emotionally disturbed because of emotion-provoking situations or experiences."[6] This compared to 13 percent of the control group.

For the most part, the association between emotional variables and delinquency has been rejected by critics, who find fault with the methodology and samples used in such studies and the subjectiveness of the definition of problems as emotionally based. A review of studies of personality variables and delinquency by Gordon Waldo and Simon Dinitz revealed no significant relationship between the two components.[7] Michael Hakeem also examined research findings of emotional disturbances among adolescent delinquents. He concluded that the results were likely more representative of psychiatric biases than the characteristics of the delinquents.[8]

Undoubtedly, emotional difficulties play some role in most deviant behavior. However, the evidence does not support the notion that this role is more prominent in relation to other variables.

Interpersonal Maturity Levels Theory

A social-psychological theory that is concerned with the personality and moral development is the Interpersonal Maturity Levels (I-Levels) System. Developed in California's juvenile correctional system, this theory has advanced that there are a series of stages in the socialization process. In each stage there exists a core structure of the personality around which a person's behavior revolves and which significantly affects their responses. The theory proposes that although there are seven stages of interpersonal maturity we each move through in becoming socialized, not everyone reaches the highest levels of interpersonal maturity or competence. Hence, some remain at a lower stage of development. I-Levels theorists have argued that delinquents generally tend to be at lower levels of maturity than their nondelinquent counterparts.[9]

Much of the criticism of the I-Levels proposition is not with its socialization thesis which is supported through other social-psychological research, but rather the contention that adolescent offenders are less mature than youths who conform to social convention. This proposition has not been validated through comprehensive comparative examinations of the maturity levels of nondelinquents. Also, I-Levels research does not adequately account for the high levels of delinquency uncovered through self-report surveys perpetrated by those who would not otherwise be considered delinquent.

Psychopathy

One variation of personality-theories that has been given much attention as a correlate of delinquency is the psychopathic personality theory. The psychopath or sociopath in its simplest yet broadest terms has been defined as an individual who is mentally unstable, antisocial, amoral, hostile, egocentric, insensitive, callous, and fearless, with limited social ties. That this definition is so ambiguous indicates the difficulty in applying the concept to particular individuals. Yet there are many who contend that such persons are present in great numbers within the juvenile population.

Psychopathic or sociopathic personalities are generally viewed in modern psychiatry as persons who lack normal feelings of obligation to conform to social norms and are without moral constraints. William McCord and Joan McCord, who have done extensive study on the psychopath, advanced that two traits in particular that sets the psychopath apart from other people are guiltlessness and lovelessness. The researchers suggested that the origins of the psychopathic personality are in brain damage, physical trauma, and most typically, extreme childhood emotional deprivation.[10]

The most prominent shortcoming of the psychopathic theory with respect to adolescents is that there has been very little empirical evidence to relate psychopathy to delinquency. Lee Robins' follow-up study of 524 patients at a child guidance clinic 30 years after their treatment at the clinic, sought to establish some link between psychopathic personalities, delinquency and adult criminality. A control group of 100 normal children were also followed.[11] More than 70 percent of the clinic juveniles had been referred by the juvenile court for "antisocial" behavior such as truancy, running away, and theft. Robins found that most of the clinic patients in the antisocial category exhibited adult lives marked by frequent arrests for crimes and drunkenness, divorce, psychiatric problems, unstable work lives, and dependency on social welfare agencies. The implication of the study is that the clinic group generally had severely troubled adult lives compared to the control group. For instance, 44 percent of the antisocial males had been arrested for a serious crime, whereas only 3 percent of the control subjects had a serious criminal record.

Robbins' study really does little to support the psychopathic theory of criminality since his parameters of the psychopath are not clearly established (22 percent of the clinic group and 3 percent of the control group were diagnosed as sociopaths). A second problem with these findings lies in the weak association between childhood "antisocial" behavioral patterns such as truancy, running away, and theft and the adulthood designation of psychopathic personality which applied to only about one-fifth of the clinic patients. Furthermore, most evidence suggests that psychopaths constitute a very small percentage of the delinquent and criminal population. For example, Herbert Quay, who has studied the personality patterns of delinquents in-depth, notes that while adult sociopathic criminals probably make up less than 25 percent of all criminals, adolescent offenders who could be defined as psychopaths are proportionately much smaller.[12]

The Criminal Personality Theory

The more recent notion of a deviant personality existing early in life as an explanation for delinquency and criminality can be attributed to the work of Samuel Yochelson and Stanton Samenow.[13] After years of study on violent criminal patients, the researchers posited that in all of the subjects there existed certain patterns of deviant thinking. According to Yochelson and Samenow, the offenders considered normal interaction with family and others to be dull and sought out excitement, with crime being the ultimate form of excitement. This abnormal pattern of thinking develops in early childhood. The researchers reject explanations of delinquency and criminality outside the individual (such as poverty and environment), although they note that offenders often purport to having been victimized by family or others.

There are supporters for the criminal personality theory who suggest that it accounts for the criminal or delinquent who seemed to have no apparent familial or other background problems yet still resorted to criminality. However, there are a number of rather distinct faults with this theory. For one, Yochelson and Samenow fail to adequately explain why criminal behavior comes into being. Also, their lack of a control group to compare with their clinical findings makes such findings most suspect in relation to the population at large. A final major problem with the criminal personality theory is that the researchers disregard for explanations of criminal behavior outside the individual is in essence a rejection of the wealth of research that supports such social and environmental causes of delinquency and crime.

Intelligence Quotient Theories

A theory of delinquency causation that contains both psychological and biological elements relates to the much debated relationship between intelligence and criminal behavior. A number of early criminologists firmly believed that an intrinsic lower than average intelligent quotient (IQ) among delinquents and criminals was the major cause for their antisocial behavior.[14] Today, most criminologists dismiss this theory as unsound because of consistent cultural biases, methodological problems, and lack of substantive findings.

However, there now appears to be findings that give some credence to the link between delinquency and IQ. The most significant is the review of key IQ research by Travis Hirschi and Michael Hindelang. On the basis of their examination, they argue that there is a strong correlation between delinquency and IQ, independent of social class and race.[15] The researchers suggest that a low IQ affects school performance, in turn producing failure and incompetency. It is these variables which they believe lead to juvenile delinquency. Supporting this contention is a review of the literature by R. Loeber and T. Dishion.[16] It is likely that IQ does to some extent, in combination with other variables such as peer group pressure and environment, constitute a viable element in the establishment of delinquent and criminal behavior.

Mental Illness

There have always been those who ascribed delinquent behavior to mental illness. Opponents of this argument have pointed to the very small percentage of youths who suffer from the delusional systems and hallucinations that characterize mental illness in psychiatric terms. These theorists prefer to favor environmental and situational variables as more critical in delinquency formation.

The overall evidence does not indicate that mental illness can be seriously considered as an important cause of delinquency. A recent study of juveniles referred to a juvenile court found that 75 to 80 percent were classified as "normal delinquents," with only 12 to 17 percent believed to be psychologically or emotionally disturbed.[17] This is consistent with a recent report of the President's Commission on Mental Health that suggested that between 5 and 15 percent of children aged 3 to 15 suffer from some type of persistent, socially interfering mental problems.[18] The same relative percentage could be said to exist in the delinquent population.

11. Sociological Concepts of Adolescent Crime and Delinquency

SOCIOLOGICAL PERSPECTIVES of delinquency generally regard it as a "normal" response to the social structure, environment, social life, and other circumstances related to crime formation. This is in contrast to psychological and biological theories of delinquency that seek to explain delinquent behavior in terms of individual abnormalities or flaws. Sociological or sociogenic criminological and delinquency theories primarily fall under four major perspectives: social control, strain, cultural transmission, and radical/critical. In this chapter will will examine these perspectives and some of the more prominent delinquency theories that they contain.

Social Control Theories

Social control theories take the position that all persons have the potential and opportunity to commit delinquent or criminal acts, but fear and social constraints keeps most of us as law abiding citizens. This perspective explains delinquent behavior in terms of inadequate external social control and internalized social values for some juveniles, which creates a freedom in which delinquency becomes possible. Control theorists are less concerned with the motivations to deviate from the norm than the social institutions that produce conditions favorable to either violating or refraining from breaking the law.

Social Disorganization

The concept of social disorganization was established by the Chicago School—which the University of Chicago's sociology department and its sociologists came to be referred as—in the early 1960s. Social disorganization was used to describe the breakdown in social conventional structures within a community characterized by largely transitory, heterogeneous, and economically underprivileged people; and the incapability of organizations, groups, and individuals as part of that community to effectively solve its problems. Researchers found that this social disorganization or ineffective social controls in certain areas correlated with their having the highest rates of delinquency.

This perspective of social disorganization was given its greatest boost due to Ernest Burgess' zonal model of urban ecology. Along with Robert Park, Burgess studied the ecological patterns of crime and delinquency in Chicago. They found that delinquency rates were highest in the central cities and decreased the further the distance away from the center. This high inner city crime and delinquency rate was attributed to their highest concentration of physical and social conditions commonly associated with delinquency and crime.[1] Clifford Shaw and Henry McKay were the first to apply this zonal model systematically. Their research supported the concept of social disorganization in inner city areas and the inverse relationship between delinquency rates and distance from the center of the city.[2]

Frederic Thrasher's study of 1,313 Chicago gangs effectively depicts the social control/disorganization concept of delinquency. He advanced that in all neighborhoods juveniles establish play groups; but these groups are differentiated in socially disorganized neighborhoods by the inability of social institutions to control the delinquent behavioral patterns of these groups.[3] Without social control, believed Thrasher, juveniles need not be motivated to commit delinquent acts since unconventional conduct represents a more exciting option than conventional behavior. He further posited that structured adolescent gangs only emerged upon a perceived threat from an outside source such as competing juvenile gangs.

Social disorganization as a concept was strongest in its accounting of the high rate of delinquency in certain areas. It was not until the work of the Chicago School was modified through later social control theories that more attention was given to explaining why juveniles in socially disorganized communities commit delinquent and criminal acts.

Social Bonding Theory

In his book *Causes of Delinquency,* Travis Hirschi may have offered the most influential sociologically based social control theory with his social bonding proposition.[4] He described as a social bond the ties juveniles have to the social order. This social bond consists of four components: attachment (ties to others such as family and friends), commitment (the devotion to social conformity), involvement (in legitimate activities), and belief (attitudes toward conformity). The degree and strength of these components or a person's adherence to the values and norms of society vary from person to person. According to Hirschi, the less an individual believes they should conform to social convention, the more likely they are to non-conform or break the law. He posited that delinquents are without the intimate attachments, goals, and moral standards that bind people to the norms and values of society; and therefore, are free to commit acts of crime and delinquency.

Although many see the social bonding theory as being sound and consistent, some criticism has been raised in opposition. Probably the most vocal is Hirschi's belief that attachment to others helps prevent delinquency, even if these others (such as friends) are delinquent themselves. Hirschi later suggested that a weakened social bond and delinquent attachments are directly correlated with delinquent conduct. Another argument of social bonding theory is that it fails to adequately explain the variance in the frequency of delinquent acts.

Containment Theory

Another social control theory was proposed by Walter Reckless. His containment theory postulates that youths are restrained from committing delinquent or criminal acts by a combination of inner containment (a positive self-concept, self-components, well developed superego, high tolerance level, and positive goal orientation), and outer containment (positive social ties, strong parental supervision, institutional support of the juvenile's positive self-concept).[5] These containments, according to Reckless, act as buffers against the influences of delinquent behavior (such as the delinquent subculture, temptations, and other deviant-based environmental factors). He held that although both inner and outer containment components were the most effective counter-delinquency measures, strong inner containment could compensate for defective or weak outer containment and vice versa.

The major criticisms leveled against Reckless' hypothesis concern methodological weaknesses and questions with the validity of his self-concept measures. Overall, there is indication that outer containment factors may be more prominent in delinquency involvement than inner containments.[6]

A Critique of Social Control Theories

Social control theories have been successful in explaining some aspects of delinquency such as how we can comprehend the episodic delinquency of most adolescents and why even the most delinquent youths engage in delinquency only under certain circumstances. However, these theories are problematic in that they do not sufficiently explain the role of internalized norms and values; nor do they fully account for the social-structural causes of delinquency. Nevertheless, empirical studies of control theories support their basic premise.

Strain Theories

Strain theories also evolved from the research of the Chicago School. These theories explain juvenile delinquency as a response of adolescents to their lack of socially approved opportunities. The concept of strain is seen as a shared problem of adjustment that originates from the social position common to a group of people.

Theory of Anomie

The concept of anomie was developed by Emile Durkheim, a preeminent sociologist at the turn of the century. Anomie referred to a condition of relative normlessness within a group or society.[7] Durkheim saw this anomic condition as occurring when the existing social structure was unable to control man's desires. Anomie generally was the result of social disruption, due to natural or human-induced disasters such as economic depression and war.

It was Robert Merton who adapted the concept of anomie to societal conditions and cultural values present in the United States.[8] He sought to relate particular modes of behavior to the social position of the persons participating in such behavior. It was Merton's contention that deviant behavior is the result of the anomic interaction of two elements of society: culturally defined goals and the socially structured means for attaining them. Since some people have unequal access to approved means, they are unable to achieve societal goals unless they deviate from the norm.

Merton outlined five modes of adaptation to the goals and means in our society. The two most applicable to delinquent behavior are innovation and retreatism.

> *Innovation* refers to the acceptance of culturally prescribed goals of success without abiding by the institutional means for their attainment.

> *Retreatism* concerns the rejection of both the culturally prescribed goals and the conventional means.

Innovation, for example, would be relevant to describe the juvenile who shoplifts an expensive pair of Reebok tennis shoes rather than pay for them. This resorting to illegitimate means to achieve a desired goal may occur because legitimate means are blocked (such as no money or the inability to find a job). Retreatism applies to juveniles who, for instance, turn their backs on both conventional goals and the means to achieve them; and instead engage in an escapist pastime such as alcohol.

There have been numerous assaults on Merton's theory of anomie. One is that it does not explain why some innovators choose theft and others robbery or why some retreatists use drugs and others alcohol. A second criticism of the theory is that there is some question as to whether all Americans share common goals and expectations of success. Furthermore, although the theory accounts for the criminality of the disadvantaged, it does not explain the delinquency of upper class individuals, or the patterns of delinquent behavior.

Despite the weaknesses in Merton's theory it was the sophistication of his work that was most influential in subsequent theory into the relationship between criminality and differential economic opportunity.

Subcultural Theories

Delinquent subcultural theories were spawned in the 1950s in the study of juvenile gangs. Influenced by the work of Durkheim and Merton, there have been a number of important contributors to the subculture thesis such as Albert Cohen,[9] Walter Miller,[10] and James Short.[11] However, it was the delinquent subculture theory of Richard Cloward and Lloyd Ohlin that is most credited with the emergency of this explanation of delinquent behavior.[12] They argued that there exists a delinquent opportunity structure as well as a legitimate opportunity structure. The basic thesis of the Cloward and Ohlin theory rests on the structural conditions that lead to lower class gang delinquency. They also seek to explain the development of other delinquent subcultures.

In general, subcultural theory regards a delinquent subculture as a group that fosters beliefs legitimizing delinquent activities. Within this context, the theory proposes that the culture, goals, and strategies of the lower class or of subgroups within these classes are significantly different from those of the middle class. Lower class youths have their own lifestyles, traditions and focal concerns, which attach importance to "toughness," "living by one's wits," and "hustle." Conformity to this lifestyle, therefore, suggests deviation from middle class standards.

Subculture theory has been attacked on a number of fronts. Foremost is the belief by many that most lower class members adopt the middle class norms of material success, educational and occupational achievements. The theory has also been criticized for its inapplicability to the majority of delinquents. Furthermore, it appears likely that most lower class gang members ultimately abandon their delinquent lifestyle and turn to more conventional norms as adults.

Refer to Chapter 8 for a closer examination of gang delinquency and opportunity structures.

School and Delinquency

The role of schooling and education in delinquency has been examined through a number of perspectives. The strain approach, in particular, has incorporated educational performance and the educational system in its study of adolescent goals, motivations, expectations, and delinquent behavior. Some researchers, for example, have suggested that the educational system itself contributes to delinquent behavior in its fostering of conditions (such as language barriers, inadequate education, and differential instruction) that socialize adolescents whose subculture system placed more value on delinquent conduct than normative behavior.[13]

Other theorists have attributed lower class delinquency, particularly for black adolescents, to their perception that educational pursuits are less feasible for them; hence they lack the motivation for higher learning and instead turn to delinquent behavior which "constitutes a tempting alternative to poverty."[14] Critics of this hypothesis argue that most minority or lower class youngsters, even if performing poorly in school, are educationally motivated just as middle class youths are.[15]

Studies have shown a correlation between educational failure and delinquency—both of which are disproportionate among lower class youths.[16]

That school-related factors are influential in delinquency cannot be argued. However, how significant educational variables are in delinquency formation when placed in context with other determinants such as opportunity and learned behavior has yet to be sufficiently established.

Cultural Transmission Theories

Cultural transmission theorists regard delinquency as learned behavior, that is, it is a reflection of the norms, beliefs, values, and behavioral characteristics one learns from those they interact with. Hence, cultural transmission theory proposes that juvenile delinquency is caused primarily by conforming to the behavioral norms of a culture or subculture that are contrary to conventional norms and values with respect to behavior and the law. Delinquent norms are further seen as intergenerational in both the socialization process and the techniques of committing deviant or delinquent acts.

Differential Association Theory

The cultural transmission theory that has received the most attention is Edwin Sutherland's differential association theory. Sutherland first introduced this theory in the 1939 edition of his text *Principles of Criminology*, but modified it in 1947.[17] Basically, differential association theory is concerned with explaining the reasons for the crime or delinquency rate distribution among various groups and why a particular person engages in or refrains from deviant behavior.

As it relates to juvenile delinquency, the theory posits that the probability of delinquent behavior varies directly with the priority, frequency, duration, and intensity of a person's contacts with patterns of delinquent and criminal behavior, and inversely, with their nondeviant contacts. Interaction with antisocial elements tends to take place most often when an individual's perception of their circumstances is supportive of violations of the law. Hence, many types of nonconformity such as delinquency, crime, and mental illness are likely to be concentrated in inner city areas that are characterized by cultural traits that often alienate persons from both one another and middle class norms.

Differential association theory posits that delinquency is learned; and also outlines the general conditions under which there is likely to be more delinquent behavior rather than less to be learned, leading to a greater probability that the adolescent will acquire a set of "definitions" more favorable to delinquent than nondelinquent behavior. Additionally, the theory contends that delinquency is a social rather than antisocial behavioral pattern. Thus, if most of a juvenile's interaction is with people who frequently violate the law and who express beliefs that seek to justify their behavior, then the juvenile has a greater chance of becoming delinquent or criminal than one who interacts with persons who do not violate the laws or disapprove of such violations.

Sutherland's theory of differential association is generally supported by most criminologists for its explanation of delinquent and criminal behavior. However, there are some problems with it. The most conspicuous is that with a lack of clarity in its terminology and definitions, the theory cannot be validated through empirical testing. A second fault lies in the failure to explain the origin of crime and delinquency. Nor is the nature of the "learning" process, which is the basic tenet of the theory, outlined. A final criticism is that differential association theory does not establish the basis for differential susceptibility to deviant patterns for different people.

Social Learning Theory

Due to some of the weaknesses of differential association theory with respect to its learning propositions, some sociologists have sought to modify the theory to mitigate its limitations. The most prominent of this research is Ronald Akers' social learning theory, also referred to as reinforcement theory.[18] Basically, this theory proposes that juveniles learn to commit delinquent or criminal acts through social interaction with those who constitute their primary source of reinforcement. Akers sees these social reinforcements as mostly symbolic and verbal rewards for supporting group norms and expectations. He also notes the lesser role of nonsocial reinforcement, which relates mainly to physiological variables that may be relevant for some offenses such as substance abuse.

Critics of social learning theory have argued that nonsocial reinforces are stronger than social ones in deviant behavior. There is also some question as to whether this theory's proposition can be sufficiently tested any more than differential association theory.

Labeling Theory

Labeling theory has elements of several different criminological perspectives, but can most often be referred to as a cultural-transmission theory. However, rather than concern itself with the person's response to or interaction with deviant behavioral norms, labeling theory focuses principally on the societal response to such persons, their behavior, and the results of this response. Edwin Schur speaks of the mechanism of labeling in his book, *Labeling Deviant Behavior:*

> Human behavior is deviant to the extent that it comes to be viewed as involving a personally discreditable departure from a group's normative expectation, and it elicits interpersonal and collective reactions that serve to "isolate," "treat," "correct," or "punish" individuals engaged in such behavior.[19]

A further perspective on the process of labeling was given by Howard Becker who referred to labelers as "moral entrepreneurs":

> Social groups create deviance by making rules whose infractions constitute deviance, and by applying those rules to particular people and labeling them as outsiders. From this point of view, deviance is not a quality of the act a person commits, but rather a consequence of the application by others of rules and sanctions to an "offender." The deviant is one whom the label has successfully been applied; deviant behavior is behavior that people so label.[20]

Labeling theorists contend that most youths commit acts that would constitute processing through the juvenile justice system and being labeled delinquent. However, the delinquent labeling of youths is differentially applied by those who control social power, such as lawmakers, law enforcement and related interests. Persons who occupy the lower end of the socioeconomic scale tend to have the least power to resist stigmatizing labels. This is evidenced by the lower class juveniles who are more likely to be arrested, prosecuted, given harsh sentences, and therefore labeled delinquent than their middle and upper class counterparts.[21]

Proponents of the labeling perspective also seek to discover the relationship between official labeling and a juvenile's self-perception of being a delinquent.[22]

Labeling theory is generally supported as a valid criminological theory. Yet like other theories, it is not without its weaknesses. Those most often noted are the narrowness of its approach and the inability of labeling theory to determine the circumstances that must be present before an individual or act is labeled deviant.

Radical Criminological Theories

Radical or critical theories focus their attention more on the relationship between capitalism and criminal and juvenile justice rather than explaining delinquent or criminal behavior. Critical theorists contend that the criminal laws primarily serve the greater interests of the ruling class (those who own the means of production), who use these laws to exploit, dominate and victimize the working and lower classes in order to perpetuate the economic and political system of capitalism. Because the laws are a product of the wealthy or capitalists, their socially harmful "crimes" (such as demoralization and exploitation) are generally not defined as crimes by the criminal justice system.[23]

Radical criminologists attribute the high rate of "street" or lower class crime to the economic functioning of the capitalist system which produces unemployment and under employment, resulting in conditions conducive to criminal and delinquent behavior. David Greenberg has posited this to be especially true for juveniles, which he suggests explains high delinquency rates. In applying a radical perspective to the causes of delinquency, Greenberg proposed three pressures adolescents face that account for most delinquent behavior in capitalist societies: (1) deprivation of employment opportunities necessary to finance the social activities stressed in peer norms; (2) stigmatizing, degrading school experiences by those who have a lesser stake in conformity (lower class and unemployed youths) resulting in hostile, rebellious responses; and (3) fear of failure in achieving adult male status positions, causing violent, status-defining behavior.[24]

The major faults with critical or radical criminology lie in its predictability, disregard for objective reality, and overstatement of its hypotheses. Nevertheless, radical theory must be considered sound in its overall interpretation of the capitalist system in relation to the criminal laws and definition of crime.

12. Familial Correlates
of Delinquent Behavior

THE ROLE OF THE FAMILY in delinquent behavior has been given much attention in the literature. Child rearing practices, child abuse, intergenerational criminality, disciplinary methods, and variables of family structure have all been shown to have varying levels of influence on both delinquent and nondelinquent behavior. Many experts believe that it is the interactants of family life that is the greatest predictor of adolescent delinquency.

Child Abuse

According to a number of sources, there are millions of children who are annually the victims of various types of child abuse ranging from physical battering to neglect to sexual abuse.[1] While experts disagree on the significance of this abuse with respect to adolescent antisocial behavior, there is solid evidence to associate child maltreatment to a high percentage of the delinquency and criminality of adolescents.

Brandt Steele cited research that found more than 80 of a group of adolescent offenders to be victims of abuse and neglect, with 43 percent recalling being knocked unconscious by a parent.[2] Martin Haskell and Lewis Yablonsky note that juvenile correctional facilities are filled with adolescents who were victims of family pathology and abuse.[3] In a study of 653 delinquents, D. Adams, H. Ishizuka, and K. Ishizuka found that 43 percent of the delinquents had been abused, neglected, or abandoned at some point in their lives.[4] According to James Garbarino:

> Many abused children and youth attempt to avoid or escape their parents. In doing so, they are likely to become involved in a variety of delinquent behaviors related to their status (unsupervised, uncared for minors), as well as their personal history (inadequate learning of social skills).[5]

The strong relationship between child abuse and delinquency prompted B. Schmitt and C. Henry Kempe to suggest that action on the problem of child abuse will prevent delinquency.[6]

133

Given the research in this area and the implications of child abuse with respect to delinquent and other aberrant adolescent behavior, it might be useful to cite some studies in specific areas of child abuse.

Child Sexual Abuse and Delinquency

Sexual abuse of juveniles has been associated with various adolescent delinquent behavior — particularly prostitution and sex crimes. The Huckleberry House project estimates that 9 out of 10 female prostitutes have been sexually violated during childhood by familial or nonfamilial perpetrators.[7] Female offenders were twice as likely to be abused as male offenders. In Mimi Silbert's study of prostitution and sexual assault, she found that nearly two-thirds of the sample were victims of incest and child abuse.[8] These findings correspond with studies on teenage runaways in several states.[9]

Violent Child Abuse and Violent Delinquency

The link between physical violence directed toward children and delinquency has been documented by a number of studies. H. Simmons suggested that "a brutal parent tends to produce a brutal child," and that the hostility a child feels toward a physically abusive parent manifests itself in delinquent behavior.[10] D. Lewis and J. Pincus reported that violent adolescents in their study had both witnessed and been victimized by severe physical violence.[11] In a study of chronically serious juvenile offenders, Jeanne Cyriaque advanced that "violence-dominated lifestyles [of] . . . sexually and physically abusing families, particularly characterize juvenile murderers and sex offenders."[12]

Child Abuse and Parental Abuse

Children who are abused tend to be more likely to abuse their parents than nonabused children. Researchers have estimated that upwards of 2.5 million parents are struck by their adolescent children each year in the United States, of which 900,000 are victims of severe violence.[13] Studies indicate that juvenile parent abusers are often the recipients of poor models of social behavior and highly stressful familial situations, which cause them to strike out as they have been directed or in the only way they know how.[14] A study of family violence by Suzanne Steinmetz held that abusive parents stand a 200 out of 400 chance of being abused by their children, compared to only a 1 in 400 chance for nonabusive parents.[15]

Intergenerational Cycle of Abuse and Delinquency

As we discussed in Chapter 9, there are some who advocate a generation-to-generation transmission of behavioral patterns. Much of this theory today is concerned not so much with genetic transference, but learned behavior and a cycle of social frustrations. Researchers have shown delinquency to be associated with parentage characterized by emotional disturbances, tension, stress, criminality, and delinquent behavior.[16] Vincent Fontana described the childhood history of abusive parents as being unloving, cruel, and brutal.[17] Through their study, Christopher Ounsted and associates concluded that abusing parents often come from families where violence has passed from generation to generation.[18] A similar observation was made by Norman Polansky and colleagues whose study of neglectful families revealed an intergenerational passage of "a lifestyle of neglect that comes from the sharing and passing on of family misfortunes."[19]

There is still much skepticism about the notion of intergenerational aberrant behavior. However, it is certainly more reasonable to assume its merits in the social and family interactant passage of such behavior than as a result of biological transmission.

A Critique of the Child Abuse Theory of Delinquency

There is sufficient evidence to indicate an important relationship between various types of child abuse and delinquent behavior. However, there are weaknesses to this approach, such as definitional problems with child abuse, lack of findings to actually show child abuse to cause delinquency, and the existence of delinquents who were not victims of child abuse. As told by Robert Weinback and associates:

> We would be both naive and grandiose if we were to assert that we can document a relationship of cause and effect when we attempt to associate delinquency and child abuse. . . . Furthermore . . . we cannot assume that all child abuse, as defined by rigid and perhaps culturally biased definitions, is motivated by sadism, frustration, or ignorance of human development.[20]

Disciplinary Practices

Parental disciplinary practices have been shown to be an important factor in delinquent behavior. More specifically, lax or inconsistent discipline as well as harsh discipline are seen as being more likely to result in juvenile delinquency than consistent, reasonable disciplinary practices. A number of longitudinal studies utilizing both self-report and official data have documented a strong predictive relationship between poor disciplinary practices of parents and eventual delinquent behavior of children.[21]

Extreme physical parental discipline has been associated with aggressive, destructive delinquency in studies by E. Deykin,[22] A. Buttons,[23] and M. Shore.[24] Ronald Flowers cites evidence in his study of children and criminality to indicate that lax or erratic discipline is correlated to delinquency.[25]

Several studies have explored parental discipline by its degree of measurement (consistency, fairness, and strictness) in relation to delinquent behavior. Walter Slocum and Carol Stone found that "fairness of discipline" was strongly related to conforming behavior of youths.[26] Sheldon Glueck and Eleanor Glueck reported that lax and erratic disciplinary practices resulted in a higher percentage of delinquents than did overly strict discipline and that firm, yet kind discipline was practiced considerably more often by the parents of nondelinquents than delinquents.[27] William McCord and associates found that consistent parental discipline, whether punitive or love-oriented, significantly reduced the incidence of delinquency.[28]

The major weaknesses of findings that relate discipline to delinquency are the inability to uniformly define what constitutes discipline or lack of, and differential perceptions of discipline by parents, delinquents or nondelinquents, which cannot be measured in terms of their reaction to such disciplinary practices. Nevertheless, the extremes of parental discipline can be seen as a strong influence in the potential for delinquent behavior.

Parental Affection

The presence of lack of parental affection has been cited in a number of studies as an important element of delinquency formation. The Gluecks found that every affectional pattern of the home (i.e., father-child, mother-child, child-parent) was significantly related to delinquency, with the most important being the father's affection for his son.[29] Studies by Robert Andry[30] and Walter Slocum and Carol Stone[31] support this assertion. Leo Davids noted the crucial role the father has in preventing delinquency by developing solid, meaningful relations with his children.[32]

Parental rejection has been found in studies by F. Ivan Nye[33] and William McCord and associates[34] to be closely associated with delinquency. The McCord study also linked the absence of maternal warmth with delinquent behavior. Another study found that the sons of rejecting parents frequently display aggressive behavior.[35]

Some research has examined both affection and discipline as it relates to delinquency. Kirson Weinberg cited the two variables as mutually critical in affecting children's personalities and predisposing them to deviant behavior.[36] Albert Bandura and Richard Walters found that parents of aggressive delinquents often denied the youths the opportunity to express dependency feelings. Parental discipline of these delinquents seeking dependency gratification, a form of parental rejection, was high compared to the nondelinquent control group and their parents.[37] Wesley Becker's review of relevant studies of parental rearing practices and their consequences was consistent with the research cited.[38]

Positive Parenting

Positive parenting—parenting that promotes interpersonal and communicative relations, academic, and professional skills; as well as encourages the development of normative values and positive behavioral standards in children—has been shown to be instrumental in preventing delinquent behavior. This positive interaction between parent and child is crucial in establishing a mutually reciprocal rapport and instilling appropriate behavioral characteristics in children.

Studies have found delinquents to be less interpersonally- and work-skilled and less responsive to normative values such as family and school than nondelinquents.[39] Longitudinal research has documented the predictive correlation between positive parenting techniques and delinquency. Nonpositive parenting (such as parental rejection, indifference, and noncommunication) has been shown through both self-report and official measurements to be associated with delinquent crimes against the person, property crimes, status offenses, nonstatus offenses, as well as recidivism and single acts of delinquency.[40]

Clearly positive parenting is an important factor in the onset or rejection of deviant or delinquent patterns in children and adolescents.

The Broken Home Factor

A good deal of attention has been devoted to the broken home or disrupted family setting as it relates to delinquency. "Broken home" generally refers to homes in which one or both parents are absent due to desertion, divorce, separation, or death—thus depriving the child of a complete, stable family life. Research in this area has produced mixed results. Clifford Shaw and Henry McKay's paper published in the early 1930s reported an insignificant relationship between delinquency and broken homes.[41] Their work was criticized as unrepresentative because of the lack of a control group. Other early studies utilizing control groups, notably H. Ashley Weeks and

Margaret Smith[42] and the Gluecks[43] found that the correlation between delinquency and broken homes was substantive. More recent studies have supported the broken home-delinquency relationship.[44]

However, in a review of 15 studies of the relationship between broken homes and male delinquency covering a 43-year period, Lawrence Rosen and Kathleen Neilson found broken homes to be only weakly associated with delinquency when race, age and social class were considered.[45] The Rosen and Neilson study may be mitigated somewhat since the most consistent finding of broken home research is that delinquent girls are more likely to be the product of a broken home than delinquent boys.[46] A number of reasons are attributed for this differential response to the broken home, including a greater effect on females of family disruption due to different socialization of girls and boys; more girls tend to run away from physically, sexually and emotionally abusive broken homes and are labeled as juvenile delinquents; and parents in disintegrated homes may refer the problems they encounter with delinquent daughters to the juvenile justice system more than with their delinquent sons. A longitudinal study by Rochelle Canter questioned the validity of assuming female delinquents come from broken homes more often than male delinquents. She found that the effect of a broken home was similar on both boys and girls, with male delinquents being more likely to come from broken homes where a lack of parental supervision or control was at issue.[47]

Overall, it seems as if the broken home is a solid factor in some delinquent behavior. However, it has not been shown to cause delinquency. Charles Browning took a stronger position in dismissing the relevance of the broken home in delinquency. In his study of legally and psychologically broken homes, he concluded that they were "ineffective and probably meaningless as an indicator of family disorganization and other characteristics of family life known to be associated with deviant behavior."[48]

Family Dissention

Family units that are unbroken yet characterized by discord, conflict, tension, and stress have also been shown to be contributory to delinquent behavior. Browning found that family solidarity had a significant relationship to truancy and auto theft, the two areas of delinquency he studied.[49] The Gluecks' study found that family incohesiveness was a factor considerably more often in the homes of the delinquent sample than the nondelinquent group.[50] In a study of delinquency and anomie, Lester Jaffe observed that family anomie, as measured by the amount of family disagreement on selected value questions, was related with a high score on a "delinquency proneness" scale.[51]

Some research has found delinquency to be more closely associated with family discord than social class. Beatrice Freeman's study of middle class male delinquents revealed that although the parents had never been in contact with law enforcement or social service agencies, their family lives were characterized by psychological problems, inconsistent child rearing practices, and in some cases, alcoholism, which was seen as a disruptive force in the family.[52] Other studies have suggested that emotional disturbances in parents may also result in emotionally disturbed delinquent children.[53]

Discord and familial conflict are seen as disrupting the practices of responsible discipline and positive parenting, which in turn increases the likelihood of delinquent behavior. There is indication that intact families beset by conflict and turmoil are more significant in delinquency formation than broken home families.[54]

Other Family Structural Dynamics

A number of other structural factors within the family have been studied with respect to adolescent delinquency. One such area examined has been the ordinal position of the child in the family. A study by J. Lees and L. Newson found that intermediates — children with older and younger siblings — were significantly overrepresented in a group of juvenile delinquents.[55] The researchers contended that parental attention accorded to the oldest and youngest children often "squeezes" the intermediates out of the family and into the gang.

Family size may also be significant in delinquent behavior. Both Nye[56] and the Gluecks[57] studies indicated that delinquents are more likely to come from large families. However, Nye found that this applied only to male delinquents. Albert Reiss found that psychiatric classifications (such as integrated, weak ego, superego) differentiated the delinquents according to family size. Delinquents with weak superegos were more likely to come from large families.[58]

Family structure has also been shown to be affected by sociodemographic factors such as unemployment, class, substance abuse — which is then related to personality and behavioral problems and delinquency.[59]

13. Law Enforcement
and the Adolescent Offender

JUVENILE ENTRY INTO the criminal or juvenile justice systems and to what extent is determined in large part by police personnel around the country. As the initial component of the justice system that juvenile offenders generally come into contact with, the police have wide discretionary powers on their subsequent fate, which could be nothing more than a reprimand or could ultimately result in imprisonment. The evidence indicates that the final disposition decision of police is nonuniformly administered with respect to variables such as race, gender, and class. This inconsistency has often led to charges of police discrimination. Juveniles rights have mitigated discriminatory police practices to some extent. However, police policies and decisions continue to be critical to the immediate and long term future of juvenile offenders.

Initiation of Police-Adolescent Contact

Police officers come to know of juvenile law violators through two primary means: citizen complaints and direct police observation of youths committing delinquent or otherwise suspicious acts. By far, the instigating force of the majority of police-juvenile offender contacts are citizen complaints. A study of 281 police encounters with adolescents in Chicago found that 72 percent were initiated by citizens, who mostly reported juvenile misconduct by telephone. The majority of these complaints (60 percent) involved minor offenses such as rowdiness and mischievious conduct; while only 5 percent concerned felonies.[1]

Disposition Decisions in Police-Juvenile Encounters

When police officers are advised of or observe juvenile violations or alleged violations of the law, there are several formal and informal options available to them in disposing of the matter. In general, these alternatives for what to do with the juvenile can be seen as follows:

- Outright release at the scene of the incident upon questioning.
- Admonish or reprimand on the street before releasing.
- Take the juvenile to the police station for questioning and release.
- Issue a citation to appear in the juvenile court at a future time, then release to family.
- Issue a citation and take directly to the juvenile court.
- Refer to a diversionary unit (such as a runaway center) with no court appearance or record of delinquency.
- Refer to the criminal court.

Research indicates that in most instances of police-juvenile contacts, no arrests are made; and that when arrests do occur, police decisions often result in dispositions other than referral to juvenile court. A study in Illinois reported that for every 100 juveniles arrested, only 40 ever reached the juvenile court. The study also found that youths were arrested in only 20 percent of the encounters in which law enforcement had sufficient grounds to make such arrests.[2]

Table 13-1 gives a breakdown of the disposition decisions of police regarding juveniles taken into custody in 1986. Of 1,173,715 arrests, more than 60 percent of the juveniles were referred to juvenile court jurisdiction, 29.9 percent were handled in the department and released, 5.5 percent were

Table 13-1. Police Disposition of Juvenile Offenders Taken into Custody, 1986 (1986 estimated population)

Population Group	Total[a]	Handled within department and released	Referred to juvenile court jurisdiction	Referred to welfare agency	Referred to other police agency	Referred to criminal or adult court
Total All Agencies: 8,646 agencies; population 164,816,000:						
Number	1,173,715	350,900	724,276	20,876	12,938	64,725
Percent[b]	100.0	29.9	61.7	1.8	1.1	5.5

[a]Includes all offenses except traffic and neglect cases.
[b]Because of rounding, the percentages may not add to total.
Source: U.S. Federal Bureau of Investigation, *Crime in the United States: Uniform Crime Reports 1986 (Washington, D.C., Government Printing Office, 1987), p. 240.*

referred to the criminal court, and 2.9 percent were referred to welfare agencies or other police agencies. Hence, when youths are actually arrested they are about twice as likely to be referred to the juvenile court than released with no court appearance.

Police Discretion

The ultimate resolution of a police-adolescent encounter is largely a matter of police discretion. This discretionary power or personal judgment is a reflection of not only the officer's own character, integrity, values, interpretations, prejudices, and experiences—but also of the citizenry and police agencies he or she represents. For instance, patrolmen confronting a situation must consider departmental objectives as well as community dictates in deciding which action would best satisfy those they must answer to. Yet even with these parameters, there is still broad latitude in police discretion. In the ideal world, such discretion is not simply the police officer's personal judgment, but the *best* judgment of the matter they are presented with without regard to incidental factors such as the neighborhood in which the police-suspect encounter takes place or the appearance of the person whose fate they will decide. Unfortunately, in the real world, police officers rarely can decide an issue without their judgment's overlapping into personal conflicts and feelings. Because the daily actions and discretionary dispositions of the police are rarely reviewed administratively or judicially, the results of this discretion more often than not is left solely to the officer's personal and individual discretion, for better or worse. This often results in differential application of police discretionary powers, as seen in the following section.

With respect to the juvenile, this discretion can mean diverting them from the claws of the juvenile or criminal justice systems and its stigmatizing labeling process or vice versa; creating a delinquent or criminal career or preventing one—in short, making a decision that could affect the juvenile for the rest of his or her life. Hence, police officers face an enormous burden in their use of discretionary powers, for they must at once balance the best interests of the juvenile, victim, community, laws, and enforcement of the laws.

Discretionary Law Enforcement and the Adolescent

The police officer-adolescent relationship is characterized largely by a cultural and generation gap. Few police can relate to the problems and lifestyle of the modern youth, particularly when racial or ethnic differences come into play. Police discretion in situations involving juveniles reflects a number of factors, however, few are as prominent as the officer's own background, prejudices, and attitudes. What follows are typical examples of two police-juvenile encounters and the disposition of them:

Police officers Johnson and Rogers, two white veterans of the police force in this midwestern city, received the call at 8:15 p.m. in this lower class, mostly black and Hispanic section of town, that a citizen had complained that someone was trying to break into a car in the huge Akers mall parking lot at 16th and Harlow. When the officers arrived minutes later, they observed a young black male walking away from several cars in the well-lit parking lot, whom they agreed looked suspicious with his strange haircut consisting of a lot on the top and little on the sides. His hands were in his pockets and he was walking briskly, as if in a hurry. Even though the officers had no trouble seeing him, they shone a bright spotlight in his face while they remained in the car and ordered him to halt.

Sixteen-year-old Dorian Romel complied with the order, and squinted in the blinding light not ten feet from him.

"What are you doing out here?" asked Officer Johnson.

"I'm goin' to the Crabtree," retorted the youth, referring to a popular arcade hangout in the mall.

"We just got a report that someone was trying to rip off a car. Know anything about it?"

"Do you see me with a car, man!" Dorian spat defiantly. "I don't know what you talkin' about."

"What's in your pocket?" asked the officer.

"Hey — you got eyes — my hands."

"Get them out . . . come on, up where we can see them, boy."

The officers got out of the car, guns drawn. They frisked the suspect and found two marijuana cigarettes.

"Well, what do we have here?" Officer Rogers said smugly.

The verbal exchange became more belligerent before the suspect was handcuffed and forcibly placed in the police car. The officers could find no signs of attempted forced entry into any cars in the lot. They took the youth into custody for drug possession and later referred him to the juvenile court.

Patrolman Ted Barkley, a young white officer in this mostly white northwest suburb, spotted the shaggy, blond-haired white male youth he guessed to be about 15, trespassing on private property, a bagged bottle in his hand. It was early evening. Barkley pulled his car up to the curb and honked to get the attention of the youth.

"Hey, don't you know this is private property?"

The boy looked around the area, almost as if in a daze. "No, officer," he smiled. "I didn't."

"What's in that bottle?"

"Just a beer — that's all."

"How old are you?"

"Eighteen."

Barkley looked at him suspiciously, but never asked for an I.D. "Where do you live?"

"Around the corner."

"I think you've had too much to drink," he admonished him. "Give me the bottle."

Reluctantly the juvenile complied.

"Now get the hell off this property before you do something we'll both regret."

He watched for a moment as the youth walked away before driving off.[3]

Determinants of Police Discretion

There are a number of factors that are influential in determining the outcome of police discretionary powers when dealing with an adolescent offender or suspect. The most significant relate to the severity of the offense, the citizen complainant; personal offender characteristics: gender, race/ethnicity, social class, offender background; the police-juvenile interaction; departmental policies; and community pressures.

The Severity of the Offense

The seriousness of an offense is the most important determining factor in police discretion involving juvenile offenders. Generally, broad police discretion is most applicable for minor status offenses. These types of offenses constitute the majority of those involving police-juvenile contact. Studies estimate that in 80 to 90 percent of such encounters, the police disposition tends to be nonofficial (such as a warning).[4] For more serious or violent crimes, police often are limited in their discretionary powers when encountering a juvenile suspect. The probability of juvenile arrest increases relative to the severity of the alleged crime.[5]

The Citizen Complainant

The complainant has been shown to have an important influence on the police disposition decision regarding an adolescent offender. In their study of Boston, Chicago, and Washington, D.C., police activity, Donald Black and Albert Reiss, Jr., found that when a citizen initiates a complaint, is present, and requests that a youthful offender be arrested, the police generally obliged. Conversely, when complainants suggested that no arrest was necessary, police tended not to arrest the juvenile.[6] Other studies have produced similar findings.[7]

Some research has found that the police disposition of a complaint is related to the race of the complainant. For example, one study showed that the police were more likely to make a disposition of arrest when the complainant was white.[8]

Overall, the probability of an adolescent being arrested is much greater as a result of a citizen initiated complaint than a police initiated encounter.[9]

Gender of the Adolescent Offender

Male juveniles are much more likely than female adolescents to be arrested and referred to the juvenile court for criminal violations of the law. In 1986, the male-female arrest ratio for persons under age 18 was 3.47. However, girls are more likely to be arrested and referred to juvenile court for status offenses that are inconsistent with traditional sex role expectations, such as running away, disobedience, and illicit sexual activity.[10] This double standard is a reflection of both complainants' attitudes and, to some degree, more chivalrous treatment of female youths by the criminal justice system and a tougher position with respect to male delinquents.

Race/Ethnicity of the Juvenile

Race and/or ethnicity of the adolescent appears to be prominent in police discretion in making disposition decisions. A number of studies have reached this conclusion. In a Philadelphia cohort study, Marvin Wolfgang, Robert Figlio and Thorsten Sellin found that the most important factor of police referral of a juvenile to the juvenile court jurisdiction rather than disposing of the case themselves was the juvenile being nonwhite.[11] Another study that compared the police and court disposition of adolescent arrestees found that there was a greater degree of racial bias by the police in requiring minority juveniles to appear before the court than there was in the court disposition of the youth.[12]

Some studies have contradicted the findings of racial bias in police decision making regarding juveniles, or offered an alternate reason why minority youths are disproportionately arrested compared to white youths. For example, Black and Reiss found that minority juveniles are arrested more often than their white counterparts, partly because the complainant (usually minority) was more likely than complainants of white juveniles (largely whites) to insist upon an arrest rather than merely a warning.[13]

The consensus of the available evidence indicates that race or ethnicity is a likely correlate of police disposition of juvenile matters.

Socioeconomic Status of the Adolescent

Similar to race and ethnicity influences in police discretion, socioeconomic factors are also seen as significant in the disposition of police-adolescent contacts. Many studies show that lower class youth are more likely to be arrested and referred to the jurisdiction of the juvenile court than middle or upper class youngsters.[14] There is some evidence that socioeconomic status may play a more important role in police discretion and discrimination than race or ethnicity.[15] Clemens Bartollas notes that law enforcement officers acknowledge more concern in "saving" middle and upper class youths from the juvenile justice system and the labeling process than lower class youths, justifying this bias by suggesting that such upper class youths' behavioral problems are more likely to be corrected due to the greater resources of their parents for psychotherapy or other services.[16]

Juvenile Offender Background and Related Factors

The background and related circumstances of the juvenile an officer is confronted with can also be influential in the disposition of the case. Prior arrest record, earlier offenses, age, family dynamics, parental attitudes, and peer group situations are all important elements the patrolman may weigh in his discretionary powers.[17] For example, a repeat or habitual offender is more likely to be referred to the juvenile court than a first time offender. Conversely, if the parents show real concern about the situation and seem as if they can control the youngster from here on, the officer may be more likely to release the juvenile into their custody with just a reprimand.

Police-Juvenile Interaction

The nature of the communication and interaction between a police officer and a juvenile suspect has been shown to be an important factor in police discretion. Irving Piliavin and Scott Briar pointed out that the adolescent who is polite and respectful to a police officer stands a much better chance of being given an informal disposition than the youth who is belligerent or otherwise disrespectful.[18] Similarly, Carl Werthman and Piliavin associated the scorn and hostility of black youth gang members toward law enforcement with their high rate of court referral.[19] Richard Lundman and colleagues found that where there was an absence of physical evidence tying a juvenile to a crime, the juvenile's demeanor becomes the most important determinant of the officer's disposition of the encounter.[20]

Personality clashes between the officer and the youth can also affect the action the officer takes. A confrontation involving an arrogant, prejudiced policeman who takes offense at the attitude of the juvenile, whom he may simply not like or be able to relate to, may result in a more formal disposition.

Departmental Policies

The policies, procedures, and precedents of a particular police department will largely determine the direction of police discretion. Generally speaking, the greater the degree of professionalism the department has, the more likely they are to dispose of a juvenile situation formally. James Wilson's study found that the more professional police departments referred greater numbers of adolescents to the juvenile court because they relied on discretion less than police departments with less professionalism.[21]

Department policies regarding juvenile offenders can vary considerably. Nathan Goldman's study of juvenile arrests in four Pennsylvania communities, revealed that the proportion of arrests ranged from 9 percent in one community to 71 percent in another.[22] In a study of 46 police departments in Southern California, Malcolm Klein reported that while in some departments 4 out of 5 juveniles were referred to the juvenile court, in other departments practically all police-juvenile contacts led to warning and release.[23]

Community Pressures

The various pressures that exist within the framework of the community (such as public attitudes, the media, departmental resources, and the status or stature of a complainant or victim) can also play a key role in police discretion. Because the police officer is in a sense an employee of the community he or she works in, and usually reflect the mandates and wishes of those they serve both professionally and personally, officers are likely to use their discretion involving a juvenile offender to make a disposition that most appropriately adheres to the pressures of the community forces.

Police Custody and Juvenile Rights

Whereas once upon a time juveniles taken into custody had little to no due process of law, and thus were often subjected to law enforcement conduct and abuses adults were legally protected from, court decisions have since given juveniles due process rights when in police custody. While most police departments have generally abided by these decisions, there are some that have been slow in granting juveniles their due process rights. Since juvenile cases are rarely appealed, police denial of the rights of juveniles are not often uncovered.

Search and Seizure

A number of key cases have granted juveniles the due process rights against search and seizure accorded adults in the 1961 decision of the U.S. Supreme

Court, *Mapp v. Ohio.*²⁴ One such case was a 1966 District of Columbia ruling that supressed evidence taken by police when they entered a juvenile's apartment without a warrant to arrest him. The court ruled that the United States Constitution's Fourth Amendment "is a protection designed to secure the homes and persons of young and old alike against unauthorized police searches and seizures."²⁵

Interrogation Practices

When a juvenile is taken into custody as a suspect in a violation of the criminal law, he or she is entitled to rights as established in *Miranda v. Arizona*²⁶ and *In re Gault.*²⁷ In the 1966 *Miranda v. Arizona* decision, the court held that individuals must be apprised of their rights before interrogation, particularly the right to remain silent and the right to have legal representation present during questioning. It was the 1967 *In re Gault* decision that made the constitutional right against self-incrimination and the right to counsel applicable to persons under 18.

The *Gault* ruling did not specify at what stage of the juvenile justice proceedings the juvenile must be advised of his or her rights. However, many lower court decisions have held that the full *Miranda* warnings must be advised to persons under 18 in custody during the investigatory questioning. A number of states also now require that *Miranda*-type rights be applied during juvenile interrogations.²⁸

The "totality of circumstances" also has been considered in Supreme Court cases with respect to juveniles and interrogation. In the 1948 decision, *Haley v. Ohio,* the court held that a confession during interrogation by a 15-year-old was inadmissible because of the absence of an attorney or parents, the length of the time the youth was questioned, the age of the defendant, and the approach taken by the police officers.²⁹ A similar finding emerged from the 1962 decision of *Gallegos v. Colorado.*³⁰

Fingerprinting Practices

Fingerprinting procedures involving juveniles vary from state to state. In some states, juvenile court statutes require approval of a judge in the fingerprinting of juveniles, judicial access to fingerprint records, and judicial provisions for having juvenile fingerprint records expunged under certain conditions.³¹ However, in many jurisdictions, police departments establish fingerprint policies. In some departments, juveniles taken into custody are routinely fingerprinted.

The most significant decision with respect to the fingerprinting of juveniles may be the Supreme Court reversal of a Mississippi ruling involving the confession of a black youth to rape and his being fingerprinted twice (the first time was along with 23 other black youths who, without arrest warrants, were taken to police headquarters, questioned, fingerprinted, and then released). The court ruled that the detention of the black youths at police headquarters was unauthorized by a judicial officer; the petitioner was unnecessarily required to be fingerprinted twice; and the petitioner was subjected to interrogation during the first fingerprinting session.[32]

Photographing Practices

The practice of photographing juveniles in custody also is inconsistently applied by states as well as controversial. Juvenile statutes in various states have specific guidelines pertaining to the photographing of juveniles.[33] The Uniform Juvenile Court Act recommended that juveniles not be fingerprinted or photographed unless it is relevant to proving the case; the Juvenile Justice and Delinquency Prevention Act recommended that such photographs of youths not be taken without a juvenile court judge's written consent.[34] Some states now require that a court order be obtained before photographing juveniles.

In most states, fingerprinting and photographing practices concerning the juvenile are considered a joint procedure rather than separate categories. However, there are some state statutes that do separate the two.[35]

Identification Practices

Placing juvenile suspects in lineups is also a controversial procedure. In 1967, *Wade v. U.S.* defined the standards of a proper lineup including the requirement of other persons in the lineup with similar physical characteristics to the suspect.[36] Although the case concerned an adult, the same due process applies to juveniles as well. However, because of the difficulty in arranging proper lineups when the suspect is a juvenile, given that the Wade decision requires the other parties in the lineup to be of similar physical characteristics, a one-on-one identification practice is more commonly used in juvenile cases. This involves a face-to-face encounter between the suspect and witness or the witness is permitted to observe the suspect singularly or in only a one-way contact, such as viewing photographs of only that person.

Several court rulings have decided against such practices. The Supreme Court held in *Stovall v. Denno,* that taking a handcuffed suspect before a victim in a one-on-one meeting was a violation of the principle of "fundamental fairness"[37]; while in *Simmons v. U.S.,* the Court similarly applied this principle to photo identifications.[38]

Police Violence and Adolescents

The use of excessive force and violence by police officers in situations involving juveniles is perhaps the most critical aspect of police-juvenile encounters. Although empirical evidence of police brutality against juveniles is lacking, several factors suggest that such misuse of power is occurring or has the potential to. One is the greater latitude law enforcement is being given these days due to more crime control legislation. Secondly, specialized juvenile officers have been reduced in recent years, meaning that less tolerant or understanding officers must deal with juvenile encounters. Third is the weak relationship between police forces who are mostly white and minority youths who are disproportionately involved in serious juvenile crime – always making for a potentially volatile situation in which police excessive force might be a quick or desired option. The same forces here apply for police encounters with many status offenders, suspects under the influence of substances, and mentally ill juveniles. Finally, lax or discriminatory departmental policies can, in effect, be a license to solve the problem any way possible.

In a society where violent and serious crimes by youth flourish, and many juveniles are ever defiant to authority, it is quite likely that police pressures and attitudes may result in more and more officers overstepping the line of proper conduct.

Adolescent Attitudes Toward Law Enforcement

Generally speaking, most adolescents have been shown to have positive attitudes about law enforcement. However, these attitudes can vary considerably among youth depending upon their police contacts and demographic variables such as gender, race, ethnicity, and class. Robert Portune's study of Cincinnati junior high school students revealed that whites tended to have more positive attitudes toward law enforcement than did blacks, females were more likely to have favorable attitudes than males, and middle and upper class students had more positive feelings toward the police than did lower class students. He also discovered that youth hostility toward law enforcement rose progressively between grades 7 and 9.[39] Donald Bouma and colleagues' self-report survey of 10,000 Michigan school juveniles attained results similar to Portune's major findings, while adding that most students viewed the police as "pretty nice" and indicated that they would cooperate in a police crime investigation involving a nonfriend.[40]

Some studies have found that adolescents with police contacts tend to have less positive attitudes toward police than juveniles without police contacts. In a study of students in 17 high schools, the researchers found that police contacts had a considerable influence on adolescents' attitudes concerning law enforcement. Negative contacts were shown to be more influential on such attitudes than race, gender, socioeconomic status, or residence.[41] Another study found that delinquent boys had more negative attitudes toward police officers than did nondelinquent boys.[42] Delinquent youth gangs have been shown to feel particular hostility toward law enforcement.[43]

In sum, we can say that the attitudes of today's youth toward the law and law enforcement is largely a reflection of their encounters with police, peer group attitudes, labeling status, and sociodemographic standing in society.

14. The Juvenile Court

THE CENTERPIECE OF THE JUVENILE justice system is the juvenile court. It is at this stage of the process of juvenile justice that the most critical decisions are made with respect to the adolescent offender. The juvenile court as we know it has undergone a series of changes since its creation, changes that have shifted some aspects of its philosophy. Some changes have come about as the result of court decisions giving juveniles more due process, while others are a reflection of pressures put upon the court by those dissatisfied with its handling (or lack) of various divisions of youth to come before it. On the whole, the juvenile court continues to maintain its place within the juvenile justice system and its objectives, despite mounting resistance. In this chapter, we will examine the history of the juvenile court, its present and future implications.

The Development of Juvenile Justice and the Juvenile Court

The development of juvenile justice in America is a relatively recent phenomenon. The notion of a "juvenile delinquent" as differentiating from an adult criminal in terms of intent, responsibility and the response taken, is innately tied to the modern conception of "childhood" and "adolescence" as developmental stages of life distinct from adulthood. It was in the nineteenth century that certain philanthropic groups, supported by the general reform movement, began to attribute the problems of American society to rapid industrialization and urbanization. The reformers decided that action must be taken to save the children of the lower classes and slums, who often labored in sweatshops, factories, and mines where ample, cheap, unskilled labor was in demand. Reformers regarded these conditions of the slums and work places as largely responsible for the rise in juvenile crime and delinquency and the general "immoral" behavior of lower class youths. In an effort to offset these debasing conditions, backers of the child-saving movement began to look at the treatment of juvenile offenders. At the time, juvenile offenders came before the same courts as adult offenders and received the same dispositions, including the sharing of incarceration facilities. These reformers played an important role in pressuring state legislators to establish separate hearings and detention facilities for juveniles from those of adults, and eventually to create juvenile courts.

Parens Patriae

Although the "juvenile court" is uniquely an American invention, in existence for less than a century, its roots can be traced to the English court of chancery, established in the thirteenth and fourteenth centuries. The chancery court was the first to provide special considerations to juveniles with respect to equity and protection. The court operated under the doctrine of *parens patriae,* or "father of his country," which basically meant that the king,

> acting through his representative, the chancellor of the court, could depart from the due process of law and, as a benevolent parent, not only exempt children from the penalties set for various criminal offenses, but also take control over children who had not committed crimes but were involved in vagrancy, idleness, incorrigibility, or association with undesirable persons. Under the concept of *parens patriae,* all children are regarded as subject to the benevolent protection of the courts.[1]

In England, the chancery court's *parens patriae* doctrine was principly concerned with disposing of or protecting the estates of children whose wealthy parents had passed away before the children reached the age of mandatory. It was in the late nineteenth century that some social philsophers, influenced by the concept of *parens patriae,* incorporated its philosophy into a new type of American court: one designed to respond only to the cases, behavior and needs of juveniles.

The Creation of the Juvenile Court

Near the turn of the century, a number of cities began establishing special courts and procedures for juveniles, this despite the view by many that such benevolence would only result in spoiling adolescents. The first formally created juvenile court was established in Cook County (Chicago), Illinois, in 1899. The Illinois Juvenile Court Act was a comprehensive child welfare law that reflected not only the earlier reforms in the treatment of juveniles, but in the creation of the juvenile court, applied the philosophy of *parens patriae* doctrine in extending the flexible rules and procedures of equity jurisdiction to juvenile delinquents, neglected and dependent children.[2]

The concept of the juvenile court was quick to catch on in other states. Within 12 years, juvenile court provisions had been adopted by 22 states; by 1925 every state but two had enacted legislation creating juvenile courts

As of 1945, every state had established a juvenile court jurisdiction (juvenile court statutes were already in effect when Alaska and Hawaii joined the Union).[3]

The early juvenile courts were most concerned with protecting children, particularly those of the lower class, from the undesirable influences believed to lead to delinquent behavior. This benevolent intent and the authority and enforcement power granted to juvenile courts in 1899 effectively stripped juveniles of their constitutional right to due process enjoyed by adults in criminal matters and was to, for the most part, remain that way until the mid-1960s. A number of offenses that had previously either been ignored or handled informally were brought before the newly created juvenile court.[4] Furthermore, the courts became responsible for a residual category of adolescent behavior such as incorrigibility, truancy, and vicious or immoral behavior. The courts, in their efforts to "straighten out children" and to promote "moral development" even went so far as to identify a group of "predelinquents" — juveniles who had done nothing deemed antisocial, but who were believed to be headed toward delinquency.[5]

To distinguish the juvenile court proceedings and philosophy from that of the criminal court, much of the language was changed. "Punishment" became "treatment"; a "criminal complaint" was reworded to a "juvenile court petition"; juvenile courts conducted "hearings" rather than "trials"; "arraignments" became "initial hearings"; young law violators were now "offenders" instead of "criminals"; "convictions" came to be known as "findings of involvement"; and "sentences" were renamed "dispositions." The purpose of this new language applied to the juvenile offender was to "restructure the proceedings [of the juvenile court] and to further the goal of investigation, diagnosis, and prescription of treatment rather than to adjudicate guilt or fix blame."[6]

Despite the juvenile court's withdrawal of the rights of juveniles brought before them for delinquency or other behavior which applied only to minors, the reform movement was responsible for a number of improvements in the handling of juveniles, including "highly secretive record keeping on children passing through the system, elimination of dual detainment and imprisonment with adult criminals, and more lenient dispositions than criminal sentences."[7] As we will note later in the book, not all these benevolent intentions hold true today.

The Legal Rights of Adolescents and Juvenile Justice

The issue of juvenile rights within the juvenile justice system made its greatest impact during the 1960s and 1970s when a series of landmark

United States Supreme Court decisions led to a shift in the juvenile court from a philosophy based on the doctrine of *parens patriae* to a new approach in court procedures and philosophy which gave equal consideration to guaranteeing juveniles their constitutional rights; responding to their need for treatment, guidance, rehabilitation, or punishment; and acting in the best interests of the community. The most important of these cases were *Kent v. United States* (1966), *In re Gault* (1967), *In re Winship* (1970), *McKeiver v. Pennsylvania* (1971), and *Breed v. Jones* (1975).

Kent v. United States

In 1966, *Kent v. United States* became the first case brought before the Supreme Court concerning the juvenile's right to due process of law in juvenile court proceedings. The case involved a 16-year-old youth, Morris Kent, who was charged with two counts of rape and three counts each of robbery and forcible entry into a Washington, D.C., apartment, where the alleged rape also took place. The juvenile judge decided to waive jurisdiction and transfer the case to the criminal court. This decision was made without holding a hearing on the waiver of jurisdiction, conferring with the youth, his mother, or counsel. Kent was eventually tried as an adult and received a sentence of 30 to 90 years imprisonment.

On appeal, the Supreme Court held that Kent was entitled to an evidential hearing, to be present when the court waived jurisdiction, and that the judge should have recorded a statement giving his reasons for the transfer. In the decision the court opined that

> the child involved in certain juvenile court proceedings was both deprived of constitutional rights and at the same time not given the rehabilitation promised under earlier juvenile court philosophy and statutes. . . . There is evidence, in fact, that there may be grounds for concern that the child receives the worst of both worlds; that he gets neither the protection accorded to adults nor the solicitous care and regenerative treatment postulated for children.[8]

Waivers of juvenile cases to adult court jurisdiction are presently allowed in most states.

In re Gault

In re Gault, decided in 1967, the Supreme Court went even further in recognizing the juvenile's constitutional rights, in rendering its first decision with respect to juvenile court procedure. The case involved Gerald Gault, a 15-year-old Arizona youth, who was taken into custody along with a friend for allegedly making an obscene phone call. Gault's parents were not notified of his arrest, nor was he advised of his right to counsel and the right to remain silent; further, the complainant was not required to be present at his hearings. Gault was committed to a state industrial school until age 21, or essentially 6 years (unless released sooner), for an offense that would have amounted to a maximum adult sentence of 2 months' imprisonment or a $50 fine.

In its decision on Gault's appeal, the Supreme Court ruled that he had not been granted due process and that juveniles were entitled to, at minimum, the following rights:

- The right to counsel.
- The right to early written notification of the charge.
- The right to confront and cross-examine their accuser.
- The right to remain silent.
- The privilege against self-incrimination.[9]

Hence, the Court upheld *In re Gault* the juvenile's right to due process and procedural safeguards during adjudication proceedings.

In re Winship

In the 1970 *In re Winship* case, the Supreme Court ruled that juveniles are entitled to the same "proof beyond a reasonable doubt" during adjudication proceedings as required in adult criminal proceedings. The Winship case concerned a 12-year-old New York boy who stole $112 from a women's purse and was committed to a state training school for 18 months or more. The commitment was based on the standard of proof required in juvenile court that at the time was the same as that required in civil law: "a preponderance of the evidence."

The Supreme Court, on appeal, held that when a juvenile is charged with an offense that would be criminal if perpetrated by an adult and to which he or she could be subject to confinement, the charge has to be proven beyond a reasonable doubt.[10] The decision both expanded on the ruling in *In re Gault* and reflected the Court's desire to protect juveniles during adjudicatory hearings as well as "maintain the confidentiality, informality, flexibility, and speed of the juvenile process in the prejudicial and postadjudicative states."[11]

McKeiver v. Pennsylvania

McKeiver v. Pennsylvania was decided in 1971 and was concerned with whether the due process clause of the Fourteenth Amendment that guaranteed the right to a trial by jury was applicable to the adjudication of a delinquency case in juvenile court. The issue involved Joseph McKeiver, age 16, who had been charged with robbery, larceny, and receiving

Table 14–1. Court Cases of Significance Pertaining to Adolescents and Due Process Rights

Case	Year Decided	Basis for Case	Decision
Ex parte Crouse	1838	Placement of a juvenile to a House of Refuge without a jury trial.	The Pennsylvania Supreme Court held that a trial was unnecessary, as the court in the role of a benevolent parent was acting in the child's best interests.
Haley v. Ohio	1948	Circumstances under which a minor may be questioned.	The U.S. Supreme Court held that a juvenile's confession was inadmissable as evidence due to circumstances related to the youth's questioning, including its length and the absence of counsel or parents.
In re Winburn	1966	A defense of insanity in the juvenile court.	A Wisconsin State Appeals Court held that a sanity defense was applicable in the juvenile court.
Stovall v. Denno	1967	One-on-one identification of suspect.	The Supreme Court held that the principle of "fundamental fairness" was violated when the suspect was brought before the victim in a one-to-one meeting while in handcuffs.
In re Patricia A.	1972	Differential maximum age limits for institution-alization of female and male juveniles.	A New York State Appeals Court ruled state law allowing such limits as unconstitutional because there were no factual disparities between females and males to justify this treatment.
Morales v. Turman	1974	The right to treatment.	A U.S. Court of Appeals held that involuntarily confined juveniles have a constitutional and statutory right to treatment.
Schall v. Martin	1984	Preventive juvenile detention.	The Supreme Court upheld a New York Family Court Act allowing detention prior to hearings of juveniles who are a serious risk to perpetrate another offense.
New Jersey v. T.L.O.	1985	Search of the persons and property of students by school officials.	A New Jersey State Appeals Court held that school officials have the right to search students' persons and property if there is probable cause to believe that a violation of the law has occurred.

stolen goods — all felonies under Pennsylvania law. McKeiver was adjudicated a delinquent at a juvenile court hearing and placed on probation following the denial of his request for a jury trial.

In its decision on the appeal, the Supreme Court upheld the juvenile's right to due process, but rejected the right of juveniles to a trial by jury, suggesting that the due process standard of "fundamental fairness" applied. The court's decision was aimed at preventing the juvenile court from becoming too similar to the adult court in its proceedings. It held that giving juveniles the right to jury trials would in effect "remake the juvenile proceeding into a full adversary process and will put an effective end to what has been the idealistic prospect of an intimate, informal protective proceeding."[12]

The McKeiver decision is seen by many as a step backwards in the juvenile acquisition of all the constitutionally guaranteed rights afforded adults. However there are some states that do allow jury trials for juveniles. Nevertheless, the Court's reluctance in the case to apply additional procedural safeguards for juveniles in juvenile court proceedings, particularly during preadjudicatory and postadjudicatory stages, is an indication that the role of the juvenile court is, at least in the eyes of constitutionalists, to remain unique in its function with respect to the welfare of juveniles.

Breed v. Jones

In *Breed v. Jones* (1975), the issue of transferring jurisdiction to the adult court, initially considered in the *Kent v. United States* case, was again looked upon in the Supreme Court's decision. The case concerned whether or not a juvenile could be prosecuted in the criminal court after receiving an adjudication hearing in the juvenile court. The matter involved Jones, then 17, who was charged with robbery and detained by the juvenile court in California. At his dispositional hearing, Jones was found to be unfit for treatment at the juvenile court level and was transferred to the adult court. At a preliminary hearing, he was bound over for a criminal trial, eventually tried and found guilty. His counsel argued that Jones was a victim of double jeopardy, but the defendant was committed to the California Youth Authority.

On appeal, the Supreme Court held that Breed's case was a matter of double jeopardy as a juvenile court cannot adjudicate a case and then transfer the same case to the adult criminal court for processing. The importance of the *Breed v. Jones* case is that prosecutors must decide before juvenile court adjudication of a juvenile offender whether or not they want to transfer the case to the adult court.[13]

Several other notable court decisions pertinent to the legal rights of adolescents are highlighted in Table 14-1.

Figure 14–1. The Juvenile Justice System

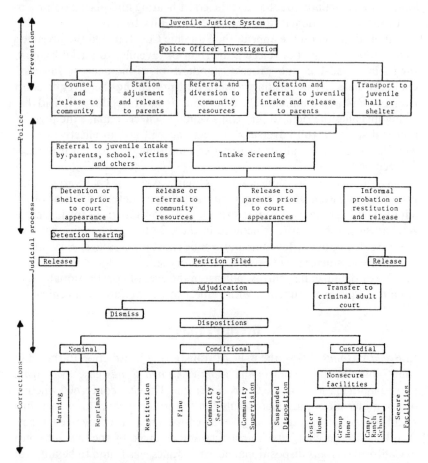

Source: Adapted from **National Advisory Committee on Criminal Justice Standards and Goals, Juvenile Justice and Delinquency Prevention** *(Washington, D.C.: Government Printing Office, 1976), p. 9.*

The Modern Juvenile Court

Today's juvenile court has taken on a facelift from that established in 1899. Court decisions have shifted the emphasis of the juvenile court from one of benevolence and assuming responsibility for the welfare of the child to one that has become increasingly more like the adult criminal court. The modern juvenile court is under constant pressure to remove status offenders and serious juvenile offenders from their jurisdiction for different reasons.

Additionally, the players in the juvenile court—judges, prosecutors, referees, defense attorneys, police—are not often coordinated, adequately trained, nor geared toward acting in the juvenile's best interest. Finally, juvenile courts are inconsistent in their staff, procedures, recognition of juvenile rights, dispositions, budgets, etc.—all of which result in differential treatment of youths from court to court. The future direction of the juvenile court is still far from established.

The Juvenile Court Process

Although there is variation in the juvenile justice system, the path a juvenile will take from state to state and differences in the juvenile court process itself from one court to another, a general model of the key decision points in the juvenile justice system process and juvenile court procedures is provided in Figure 14-1.

The police officer usually begins the process through investigating a complaint or observing a youth committing an act of misconduct. The officer then has several options, including counseling and releasing the juvenile, making a station adjustment, issuing a citation and referring to the juvenile court, and taking the youth directly to a detention center. Other sources may also refer the juvenile to the juvenile court, such as parents, victims, schools, and probation officers.

Cases referred to juvenile courts are screened by intake workers. The intake worker or prosecutor may opt to detain the juvenile, at which point a detention hearing is scheduled to review the detainment decision. In some states the prosecutor, upon reviewing the case, may choose to remove it from the jurisdiction of the juvenile court and file the case in the criminal court, provided it meets with the legislative criteria set forth for such a transfer. The prosecutor or intake officer may also decide to dismiss the case due to lack of legal sufficiency or to dispose of the matter on an informal basis (such as referral to a social agency for counseling or informal probation).

If the evidence is sufficient to warrant proceeding, the intake officer may recommend to the prosecutor that the case be formally handled by filing a petition and placing on the court calendar for an adjudicatory or waiver hearing. If the request is for a waiver hearing, the judge is asked to consider whether or not the juvenile should be waived to the adult court for prosecution. If there is an adjudication hearing, the case may be dismissed, continued in consideration of dismissal, or the juvenile could be adjudicated delinquent or as needing of supervision (such as a status offender) in which the case moves to a dispositional hearing.

At the dispositional stage of the court proceedings, the judge, upon reviewing the probation officer's report and dispositional proposals decides

Figure 14–2. Delinquency Status Offense Cases disposed by United States Juvenile Courts in 1983

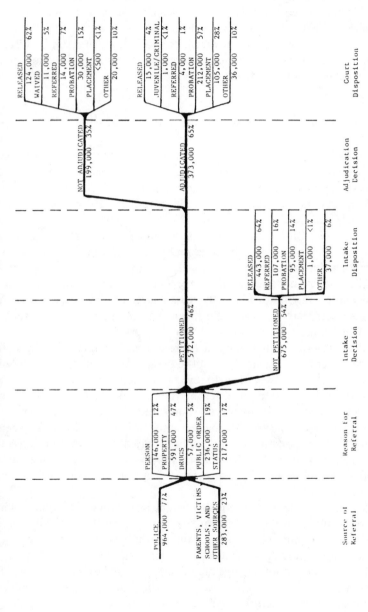

Source: Adapted from National Center for Juvenile Justice, Delinquency in the United States 1983 (Pittsburgh: National Council of Juvenile and Family Court Judges, 1987), p. 11.

the most appropriate disposition. The alternatives at the disposal of the court may include commitment to a juvenile correctional facility, placement in a residential treatment facility, probation, or imposition of some form of restitution.

Depending upon the dispositional outcome, the adolescent will either continue on with the next phase of the juvenile justice system (such as incarceration) or be given the opportunity (such as paying a fine) to return to society.

Sources of Juvenile Court Referral

The vast majority of the referrals to juvenile courts come from law enforcement agencies. Figure 14–2 illustrates the general case flow breakdown for delinquency and status offense cases disposed by the nation's juvenile courts in 1983. As indicated, law enforcement agencies accounted for 77 percent of the total referrals, while other sources such as parents, victims, and schools were responsible for 23 percent of the cases.

Property crime cases were referred most often, at 47 percent of the aggregate delinquency and status offense cases. Public order and status offense cases were the second and third most common reasons for referral at 19 and 17 percent respectively. The figure also provides an interesting look at the distribution of decisions at various stages of the juvenile court proceedings.

The Nature of Juvenile Court Referrals

The reasons for which adolescents are referred to juvenile courts can be seen in Table 14–2. According to the U.S. Department of Justice's *Report to the Nation on Crime and Justice,* property crime accounts for nearly half the juvenile court referrals of adolescents; followed by status offenses at 20

Table 14–2. Percentage Distribution of Reasons for Juvenile Referral to Juvenile Court, by Offense Category

Percent Offense Category	*Reason for Referral*	*Percent Breakdown*
11%	**Crimes Against Persons**	
	Criminal homicide	1%
	Forcible rape	2%
	Robbery	18%
	Aggravated assault	22%

Percent Offense Category	Reason for Referral	Percent Breakdown
	Simple assault	52%
	Other	5%
		100%
49%	**Crimes Against Property**	
	Burglary	26%
	Larceny	41%
	Motor vehicle theft	9%
	Arson and vandalism	12%
	Stolen property offenses	5%
	Trespassing	4%
	Other	3%
		100%
15%	**Offenses Against Public Order**	
	Weapons offenses	10%
	Sex offenses	6%
	Drunkenness	12%
	Disturbing the peace	22%
	Escape, contempt, probation, parole	19%
	Other	32%
		100%
6%	**Drug Offenses**	
	Narcotics	9%
	Nonnarcotics	91%
		100%
20%	**Status Offenses**	
	Runaway	27%
	Truancy	12%
	Curfew	7%
	Ungovernable	18%
	Liquor	28%
100% Total all	Other	8%
Offenses		100%

Percents may not add to 100 because of rounding.
Source: U.S. Department of Justice, Bureau of Justice Statistics, Report to the Nation on Crime and Justice (Washington, D.C.: Government Printing Office, 1983), p. 60.

percent; offenses against public order represents about 15 percent of the juvenile court cases; 11 percent are for crimes against persons; and drug offenses constitute some 6 percent of the reasons why juveniles are referred to the juvenile court. As for specific offense reasons, by category, the following offenses reflect the greatest frequencies of juvenile court referrals: simple assault, larceny, narcotics, disturbing the peace, and liquor law violations.

Trends in Juvenile Court Cases

Overall, juvenile court cases have shown a decline in recent years, as shown in Table 14–3. Between 1975 and 1983, the estimated number of delinquency and status offense cases disposed by juvenile courts dropped 11 percent. A 6 percent decline occurred for the five-year period, 1979–1983, while cases processed by juvenile courts nationally decreased 4 percent between 1982

Table 14–3. Juvenile Cases Disposed by Juvenile Courts, 1975–1983

Year	Estimated Number of Cases (thousands)	Juvenile Population at Risk (millions)[a]	Percent Distribution of Delinquency and Status Cases Disposed			Rate[b]		
			Delinquency	Status	Total	Delinquency	Status	Total
1975	1,406	31.1	75	25	100	34	11	45
1976	1,397	30.7	78	23	100	35	10	46
1977	1,356	30.0	79	21	100	36	9	45
1978	1,341	29.6	76	24	100	35	11	45
1979	1,307	29.0	80	20	100	36	9	45
1980	1,345	28.5	81	19	100	38	9	47
1981	1,348	28.1	82	18	100	39	9	48
1982	1,296	27.4	83	17	100	39	8	47
1983	1,247	26.9	83	17	100	38	8	46

[a]Juvenile population at risk refers to the number of children age 10 to upper age limit of juvenile court jurisdiction, as defined by each state (usually age 15 to 17).
[b]Rate is based on the number of cases disposed annually per 1,000 children at risk.
Source: Adapted from Howard N. Snyder and Terrence A. Finnegan, Delinquency in the United States 1983 (Pittsburgh: National Center for Juvenile Justice, 1987), p. 8.

and 1983. Much of the drop in the cases disposed by the courts from 1975 to 1983 can be attributed to the substantial reduction in the number of status offense cases processed. Status offense cases decreased by 39 percent over the period, while delinquency cases rose 2 percent. The drop in status offense cases handled by juvenile courts reflects a shift in court philosophy toward relinquishing its jurisdiction over status offenders and transferring the responsibility to child welfare agencies.

Hence, in 1983, delinquency cases comprised a greater proportion of the juvenile court caseload than in 1975, as indicated by the percent and rate distributions. During this period, the delinquency offense case rate rose by 13 percent, while the rate for status offense cases dropped by 30 percent.

To some degree, the aggregate decrease in juvenile court cases between 1975 and 1983 correlate with the decline in the size of the population of juveniles at risk during the period. Nevertheless, there is a clear indication that the juvenile court is moving toward an emphasis on handling cases in which juveniles violated laws that apply to adults as well.

The Waiver of Juvenile Cases to the Criminal Court

Where the juvenile justice system has come under the most fire is with respect to its inability to adequately handle violent and chronic juvenile offenders. To many, the traditional philosophy of the juvenile court simply cannot work when dealing with adolescents who murder, rape, rob, deal in drugs, and are otherwise vicious or habitual in their antisocial behavior. Increasingly, the response to serious juvenile offenders is to transfer their cases to the adult criminal courts where the sentence can presumably more appropriately fit the crime.

Every state presently permits juveniles to be tried as adults in the criminal court system under varying circumstances. In some states, youths accused of serious felony crimes are automatically under the jurisdiction of the criminal court, irregardless of age; while in other states in which there is "concurrent jurisdiction," prosecutors can choose to file charges against a juvenile in either juvenile court or the criminal court. In a few states, juveniles accused of crimes can request a trial in the adult criminal court. The most common means in which cases involving juveniles come before criminal courts is through the waiver of original jurisdiction by the juvenile court, usually after a hearing. There are 10 states that do not specify the minimum age limit in which youths accused of crimes can be transferred to adult courts. However, for those states with a minimum age limit, it usually ranges from age 14 to 16.[14]

There is some question as to whether juveniles tried in adult courts actually receive sentences parallel to adult offenders. The implication is that in most instances the sentence is much less severe, which suggests that even in criminal courts juvenile offenders are still looked upon as not quite as responsible for their actions as adult criminals. Yet thus far no better alternatives have surfaced as to what to do with the adolescent criminal who has outgrown the juvenile justice system but may not belong in the criminal justice system either.

15. The Institutionalization of Adolescent Offenders

ONE OF THE MOST CONTROVERSIAL aspects of the criminal and juvenile justice systems pertains to the incarceration of juvenile law violators. Many believe that institutionalizing youths does far more harm than good, for it treats them as criminals rather than minors in need of treatment and protection; deprives them of normal familial and environmental settings that relate to proper and optimal emotional development; affixes them with the stigmatizing effects of labeling; and often socializes them to delinquent and criminal habits. Further, there are the differential and harmful patterns of detaining status offenders with delinquent or adult offenders, and juveniles with adult criminals. Evidence exists as well that detention practices discriminate against minority youths.

Yet there are a great deal of supporters who favor placing adolescents in correctional facilities—particularly habitual and violent delinquent offenders—for both punishment and as a deterrent to teenage crime. Generally, the juvenile justice system's objective is to treat most juvenile offenders in a noninstitutionalized manner whenever possible. This is evidenced by the fact that only about 5 percent of the juvenile cases disposed by juvenile courts in a given year result in the institutionalization of youths.[1] Nevertheless, the implications of any such imprisonment are complex and of grave concern. In this chapter we will look at the dynamics of institutional commitment of adolescent offenders. The following chapter will examine noninstitutional juvenile treatment methodologies.

Adolescents in Adult Correctional Facilities

Jailed Juveniles

The jailing of juveniles may be the worst example of the failings of the justice and correctional systems. According to the *Annual Survey of Jails,* fewer than 1 percent of the country's jail population in 1986 were juveniles.

This survey estimated that on June 30, 1986, there were 1,708 juveniles in adult jails nationwide.[2] However, since most youths brought to jails are detained for only a short time, the actual number of juvenile jail inmates over the course of a year is substantially higher. It is estimated that as many as 600,000 juveniles serve time in adult jails yearly.[3] The explanation for why so many youths are housed in police lockups and county jails is that in roughly 93 percent of the juvenile court jurisdictions, including some 2,800 cities and counties nationwide, they are forced to use such facilities for detaining juvenile offenders because of inadequate juvenile correctional institutions and funding.[4]

Adolescents in jails reflect youthful offenders in society in their demographic makeup: that is, most are male, white, older teenagers, and of lower income backgrounds. Minority youths are disproportionately represented in the jail population. Female juveniles in jails and prisons constitute a smaller proportion of the prisoner population than they do in juvenile correctional institutions, whereas there are proportionately more minorities in jails or prisons than in juvenile custody facilities.[5] Although most of the juveniles put in jails across the country are older teens, many are young adolescents, and some are under age 10.[6]

Most of the youths forced to spend time in adult jails are detained for minor or status offenses. A study of adolescent jail inmates in 18 states revealed that more than 40 percent were arrested for status offenses.[7] The Children's Defense Fund survey of juveniles in jails in nine states found that under 20 percent had been confined due to a violent crime.[8] Another study of juveniles in Wisconsin county jails showed that only 21 percent were jailed for violent or property offenses.[9] The minor significance of most adolescent misbehavior is reflected in their brief period of jail confinement. One study found that 70 percent of the juvenile inmates were in jail for two days or less, and 80 percent were returned home or placed within the community upon release.[10] In a study of juveniles held in Minnesota jails in 1975, it was found that the average length of detainment was 1.9 days, but half the youths were confined only 14 hours. The study also demonstrated the wide variation in jail stays depending upon the county, with the mean length of confinement ranging from 8 hours to 6.9 days.[11]

Many juveniles held in adult jails are subjected to physical or sexual abuse, and have a rate of suicide seven times greater than that of juvenile inmates in juvenile institutional facilities.[12] Sometimes the abuse begins before the juvenile even reaches the jail. Sexual abuse of adolescents in vans transporting prisoners to jails and prisons in Philadelphia has been shown to occur at a high rate.[13] Health problems are also a likely occurrence in the jail setting, as items the juvenile may have taken for granted at home such as soap, toothbrushes, and clean towels and sheets are in short supply. Mistreatment of juvenile jail inmates can further be seen in the jail conditions they must endure — "conditions . . . which . . . are often like something out of Dickens. Small, dark cells. Little human contact. Hours of boredom and depression."[14]

The Juvenile Justice and Delinquency Prevention Act has led to some decline in recent years in placement of juveniles in jails in many states.[15] However, the fact remains that thousands upon thousands of youths are still finding their way into a jail cell and the misery and peril accompanying it.

Imprisoned Juveniles

The percentage of juvenile offenders incarcerated in adult correctional institutions is fairly low — frustrating some, but still too many to others. Although most such youths are presumed to be the perpetrators of serious and violent crimes, a federally funded 1982 survey found that more than 60 percent of the juveniles tried in adult courts were charged with less severe or nonpersonal crimes.[16] Recent statistics of state prisoners nationwide showed that approximately 9 percent were age 18 and under.[17] The American Corrections Association reported that there were 6,392 juvenile prisoners in adult correctional institutions nationwide in 1984.[18] That number is likely a large underestimation since three states and the District of Columbia did not respond to the survey, and further, many states record juvenile offenders who have been tried in adult courts as adults.

Despite the conception that juvenile offenders tried in adult courts receive sentences parallel to adult offenders convicted of the same crime, the evidence does not support this. For instance, a New York law enacted in 1978, which gave adult courts jurisdiction over juveniles age 13 to 15 who were arrested for such crimes as murder, rape, and robbery, resulted in fewer than 8 percent of the first 3,898 juveniles arrested receiving sentences comparable to adults had they committed the same crime.[19] The majority of the cases were either referred to the juvenile court or dismissed on legal grounds.

Adolescent offenders in adult prisons have a sociodemographic makeup similar to juveniles in jails. They also face many of the same physical and sexual abuses, poor living conditions, and limited opportunity to better themselves.

Adolescents in Juvenile Corrections Institutional Settings

As of 1985, there were some 3,040 public and private juvenile correctional facilities in the United States, confining more than 83,300 juvenile offenders. These facilities consist of short and long term institutions, and are further classified as institutional and open environment settings. Short term facilities include detention centers, shelter homes, and reception and diagnostic centers.[20] Long term institutions include training schools; ranches, forestry camps, and farms; and halfway houses and group homes. The approximate distribution of juveniles housed in these facilities can be seen in Table 15-1 and Figure 15-1.

Table 15-1. Percentage Distribution of Adolescents in Juvenile Custody, by Type of Facility

Type of Facility	Percent Distribution
Training schools	61.5
Ranches, forestry camps, or farms	11.4
Detention centers	8.9
Group homes or halfway houses	7.3
Special security and treatment centers	6.1
Separate centers	4.8
Total Juvenile Correctional Facilities	100

Source: 1986 Corrections Yearbook, Criminal Justice Institute.

Figure 15-1. Percentage Distribution of Residents of Public and Private Juvenile Correctional Institutions, by Type of Facility

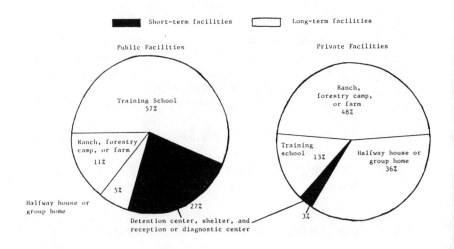

Source: Adapted from Todd R. Clear and George F. Cole, American Corrections (Monterey: Brooks/Cole Publishing Company, 1986), p. 512.

Short-Term Juvenile Institutions

Detention Centers

Detention centers, also known as juvenile halls, are secure custody facilities that detain juveniles on a temporary basis, usually ranging from a few hours to as much as 90 days. Juveniles are placed in detention by the police prior to juvenile court referral, by order of court intake workers, and through judicial decisions which can occur before, during, or after adjudication or the final disposition of the case. Youths who are detained while awaiting juvenile court hearings generally fall into three categories: (1) those who are deemed too risky to release because of the nature of their delinquency (such as violent offenders or running away), (2) those whose home environment is unacceptable because of possible child abuse, parental abandonment, etc., and (3) youths in need of physical or mental treatment. Other juveniles are temporarily held in detention centers after having been adjudicated delinquent and while awaiting a court ordered placement in an institutional or residential facility. A typical example of the adolescent juvenile hall detainee can be seen in the section immediately below.

Detention facilities can range from local jails and police lockups to secure detention centers built specifically for juvenile offenders to the more recent use of shelter care facilities — nonsecure facilities that provide a nonsecure detention setting for status offenders and minor delinquent offenders.

One Adolescent's Journey to Juvenile Hall

Los Angeles' Central Juvenile Hall is one of the largest juvenile detention facilities in the world. This is where Janice, 15, was recently placed by the juvenile court for two months before being transferred for a longer stint of up to three years to a group home for delinquent girls. Her crime was the robbery of a small clothing store. Also figuring in her detention was a history of delinquency, including drug abuse.

The process which landed Janice in Juvenile Hall began when she robbed the clothing store of $118 with her 18-year-old sister as her accomplice. Fifteen minutes later they were questioned at their home by police, before eventually being identified by the store owner and two witnesses and placed under arrest. Handcuffed, Janice was brought to the police station and detained in a cell while her mother was contacted and her prior arrest record investigated (her sister was referred to the adult court jurisdiction). "I sat alone in a jail cell for about five hours," she recalls. "I was glad to finally have the handcuffs off because my wrists hurt."

Hours later, a probation officer came to the jail cell and met Janice. This person's disposition of the matter would be based on Janice's history, the severity of the crime, her family setting, and other factors. Said the probation officer: "It became clear that she was living in a home essentially without supervision. . . . It was very clear that Janice did not understand the seriousness of her crime."

Ultimately the probation officer decided she was to be held in juvenile hall while her case went through the juvenile justice process.

A detention hearing was the next step, to review the merits of the detention decision, and thus establish whether or not the accused should be held until the case came to trial. Because of the nature of Janice's crime and her apparent unwillingness to follow the law, the judge determined after the detention and juvenile court hearings that she would spend 2 months in juvenile hall enroute to her longer institutionalization in a group home.

Los Angeles' Central Juvenile Hall is coed and spread over 20 acres. The girls

> live in groups of 20. Each living unit has 16 individual rooms, each with a bed, small sink, and toilet. The toilet has no seat. The narrow institutional bed with its steel frame is purely functional — there is no decoration. The walls are blank and the single window is enclosed with a thick metal screen. . . . Each group of 20 girls will stay together all day, at school, meals, and during recreation time.[21]

Janice's day as a confined delinquent starts at 6:30 a.m. with a shower, cleaning of her room, and a silent line march to breakfast. At 8:30 the march resumes, this time to school, which they attend for five periods. Amidst classes ranging from art to math is a recreational period. Dressed in their prison "uniform" of sweatshirts, jeans, and tennis shoes, the girls are watched each minute of the day by guards.[22]

Shelter Care Facilities

Shelter care facilities, or shelter homes, are short-term facilities that primarily house dependent or neglected children and, as indicated, status offenders. Delinquent youths, mostly minor offenders, are also placed in shelter homes when there are no other detention centers available, when a juvenile is transferred from a detention center due to positive behavior, or when a judge decides against detaining a juvenile in a county jail. The length of shelter home detention generally varies from an overnight stay to several days, but can lap over into weeks through delays in juvenile court hearings or problems in scheduling court-ordered family therapy sessions. Unlike detention center placements, which are usually through police or juvenile court referrals, juveniles in shelter care facilities can be referred there by parents, the welfare department, or other social agencies.

Reception and Diagnostic Centers

In some states, juveniles who have received a disposition of institutionalization are referred to reception and diagnostic centers, where they are evaluated through psychological, medical and aptitude testing to determine the best treatment plan for them as well as the best institutional placement. These evaluations generally take four to six weeks to complete. In states where there are no reception and diagnostic centers or where the referrals arc to private institutions, the juvenile court judge determines at the disposition hearing the particular placement the youth will receive.

Long-Term Juvenile Institutions

Training Schools

Most juvenile offenders in correctional institutions are placed in training schools. Training schools represent the most secure long-term juvenile detention facility and, hence, house the most serious, dangerous, and chronic juvenile offenders. The majority of the training schools are in the public sector and are penitentiary like in their organizational philosophy and environment with respect to the care of the inmates (such as clothing, food, and programs). Physically, the structures vary from fortress-type facilities to open dormitory settings to small, homey cottages – depending to some degree on whether they are maximum, medium, or minimum security training schools.

The terms or sentences of juveniles placed in training schools usually last only until they reach the age of majority – the age in a given state in which the juvenile justice system no longer has jurisdiction over the person.

Ranches, Forestry Camps, and Farms

Ranches, forestry camps, and farms contain the second highest percentage of institutionalized youthful offenders. These institutions generally serve as minimum security facilities for minor delinquent offenders and first-time offenders. Juvenile residents of these institutions tend to have more freedom, a closer relationship with staff, and contact with the outside community than those in training schools. Because these type facilities are nonsecure, escapes are an easy and regular occurrence – and a problem correctional officials have yet to adequately deal with in their attempt to maintain such environments and detain the inmates at the same time.

Halfway Houses and Group Homes

Group homes and halfway houses are small facilities, usually housing anywhere from 12 to 25 juvenile offenders. Mostly privately run, these facilities serve several functions including an alternative to secure detention institutions, short-term community placement, a "halfway" setting to enable youths to ease their way back into society, and as a "halfway-out" setting for delinquents prepared to return to the community but who have not yet established an appropriate home placement. Group homes often cater to minimum risk juvenile offenders; many such facilities, however, particularly those in urban areas, contain youths with chronic or violent delinquent backgrounds. Group homes usually only have limited security, making it fairly simple for youths to run away if they so choose.

Distributional Characteristics
of Institutionalized Adolescent Offenders

Regional and State Confinement of Juveniles

Table 15-2 reflects the distribution of juvenile confinement in public institutions by region and state in 1985. The largest regional population of confined juveniles is concentrated in the West, followed by the South, Midwest, and Northeast. California housed by far the most juvenile inmates in public facilities in 1985 with 12,524, with Ohio confining the second greatest number at 3,058, followed by Texas with 2,209, and Florida at 2,179.

The West had the highest regional rate of juveniles in public facilities per 100,000 juvenile residents, followed by the Midwest, South, and Northeast. The District of Columbia had the highest rate of juvenile confinement to public institutions (461), with California second (430), followed by Nevada (425), and Alaska (314).

Demographic Characteristics of Juveniles in Custody

Demographic data and adjudication status for adolescents held in public and private juvenile confinement facilities in 1983 is presented in Table 15-3. Of the 80,091 juvenile detainees, 48,701 or 60.8 percent were confined to public facilities compared to 31,390 or 39.2 percent in private facilities. Males accounted for 80.4 percent of the juveniles in custody, while females constituted 19.6 percent. By race, white youths comprised approximately 64 of the juvenile custody population, blacks 33 percent, and other racial groups 3 percent. The ethnic distribution shows that Hispanic represented

Table 15-2. Juvenile Population and Confinement Rate for Public Correctional Facilities by Region and State, 1985

Region and State	Number of Juveniles 1985	Number of Juveniles in Custody per 100,000 Juveniles in the Population[a] 1985
United States, Total	49,322	185
Northeast[b]	5,015	99
Connecticut	202	74
Maine	242	167
Massachusetts	187	32
New Hampshire	152	127
New Jersey	1,508	166
New York	1,516	98
Pennsylvania	1,060	76
Rhode Island	148	133
Midwest	11,382	166
Illinois	1,534	126
Indiana	1,334	193
Iowa	399	112
Kansas	651	233
Michigan	1,733	170
Minnesota	634	125
Missouri	815	158
Nebraska	269	140
North Dakota	94	111
Ohio	3,058	230
South Dakota	193	222
Wisconsin	668	112
South	14,905	162
Alabama	680	133
Arkansas	274	93
Delaware	190	264
District of Columbia	281	461
Florida	2,179	189
Georgia	1,053	161
Kentucky	609	130
Louisiana	1,188	200
Maryland	1,377	263
Mississippi	410	114
North Carolina	798	142
Oklahoma	314	80
South Carolina	647	175
Tennessee	1,128	195

Region and State	Number of Juveniles 1985	Number of Juveniles in Custody per 100,000 Juveniles in the Population[a] 1985
South (continued)		
Texas	2,209	125
Virginia	1,456	218
West Virginia	112	45
West	18,020	327
Alaska	201	314
Arizona	905	244
California	12,524	430
Colorado	581	156
Hawaii	149	123
Idaho	118	87
Montana	204	198
Nevada	451	425
New Mexico	511	275
Oregon	702	222
Utah	170	73
Washington	1,342	260
Wyoming	162	231

Note: Data are for February 1 of each year.
[a]Juveniles in the population are persons 10 years old through the statutorily defined maximum age subject to juvenile court authority in each state.
[b]Vermont did not operate any public juvenile facilities.
Source: U.S. Department of Justice, Public Juvenile Facilities, 1985, **Children in Custody** (Washington, D.C.: Government Printing Office, 1986), p. 2.

9.8 percent of the juveniles in custody compared to a non–Hispanic population of 80.2 percent.

The 14 to 17 age group accounted for 79.7 percent of the adolescents in juvenile facilities in 1982, followed by those 10 to 13 representing 10.6 of the confined juvenile population, with juveniles under 10 making up less than 1 percent of the total. Juvenile correctional facilities also held 7.4 percent persons age 18 and over. The average age of persons confined in juvenile corrections was 15.2.

Committed (postadjudication) juveniles comprised 74 percent of the juveniles in custody, with 18 percent detained (preadjudication), and 8 percent representing voluntary admissions (without adjudication).

Table 15–4 compares the demographic makeup and adjudication distribution of juveniles confined in public juvenile facilities in 1983 and 1985. There is little variation between the two census counts. The male population rose by 1 percent (to 86 percent) in 1985, while females in confinement jumped 4 percent. On February 1, 1985, roughly 82 percent of the

Table 15-3. Demographic Characteristics and Adjudication Status of Juveniles Held in Public and Private Juvenile Facilities, 1983[a]

Demographic Characteristics	Public and Private Facilities	Public Facilities	Private Facilities
TOTAL	80,091	48,701	31,390
Sex			
Male	64,424	42,182	22,242
Female	15,667	6,519	9,148
Race			
White	50,182	27,805	22,377
Black	25,842	18,020	7,822
Other[b]	2,020	1,104	916
Not reported	2,047	1,772	275
Ethnicity			
Hispanic	7,844	5,727	2,117
Non-Hispanic	72,247	42,974	29,273
Age			
9 years & under	661	42	619
10-13 years	8,523	3,104	5,419
14-17 years	63,808	39,571	24,237
18-20 years	5,890	4,804	1,086
21 years & over	115	86	29
Not reported	1,094	1,094	0
Average age	15.2 years	15.4 years	14.9 years
Adjudication Status			
Committee	59,590	35,178	24,412
Detained	14,376	13,156	1,220
Voluntarily admitted	6,125	367	5,758

[a]*February 1, 1983.*
[b]*American Indians, Aleuts, Asians and Pacific Islanders.*
Source: U.S. Department of Justice, Children in Custody: 1982/83 Census of Juvenile Detention and Correctional Facilities (Washington, D.C.: Government Printing Office, 1986), p. 5.

Table 15-4. Demographic Characteristics and Adjudication Status of Juveniles Held in Public Juvenile Facilities, 1983 and 1985

	Number of Juveniles	
Characteristics	1983	1985
TOTAL	48,701	49,322
Sex		
Male	42,182	42,549
Female	6,519	6,773

Characteristics	Number of Juveniles	
	1983	*1985*
Race[a]		
White	27,805	29,969
Black	18,020	18,269
Other[b]	1,104	1,084
Ethnicity[a]		
Hispanic	5,727	6,551
Non-Hispanic	41,202	42,771
Age on Census Date		
9 years and under	42	60
10-13 years	3,104	3,181
14-17 years	39,571	40,640
18-20 years	4,804	5,409
21 years and over	86	32
Not reported	1,094	0
Adjudication Status		
Detained	13,156	14,474
Committed	35,178	34,549
Voluntarily admitted	367	299

Note: Data are for February 1 of each year.
[a]Excludes 1,772 cases for which race and ethnicity were not reported in 1983.
[b]American Indians, Alaskan natives, Asians and Pacific Islanders.
*Source: U.S. Department of Justice, Public Juvenile Facilities, 1985, **Children in Custody** (Washington, D.C.: Government Printing Office, 1986), p. 3.*

juveniles in public facilities fell between the ages of 14 and 17. Seventy percent of the inmates had been committed, 29 percent detained, and 1 percent voluntarily admitted.

Reasons for Adolescent Detention

Adolescents are detained in or committed to juvenile custody facilities for three reasons: (1) they have been charged with or adjudicated delinquent due to acts in violation of criminal laws, (2) they have been charged with or found to have perpetrated status offenses (offenses applicable only to juveniles), or (3) they have been placed in such facilities as a result of dependency, abuse, neglect, or other reasons. A percentage distribution of the specific reasons why juveniles are held in custody can be seen in Figure 15-2, based on 1983 findings. Property crimes accounted for by far the greatest percentage of adolescents in confinement at 34.6 percent, more than twice the 17.1 percentage of juveniles held for violent crimes, which represented the second most common reason for juvenile detention. Only 11.3 percent of the confined juveniles were being held for status offenses, a significant decline from recent years. Other reasons for confinement

Figure 15–2. Reasons Why Adolescents Are Held in Juvenile Custody

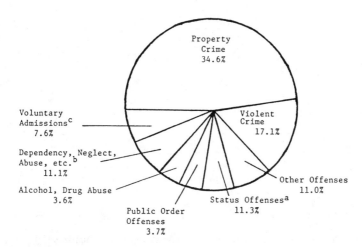

[a]*Acts that would not be criminal if committed by adults, such as running away and refusing to attend school.*
[b]*Those who are emotionally or mentally disturbed, or who have been neglected or abused by parents or guardians.*
[c]*Referrals by courts, parents, schools, social agencies, as well as youths who ask for admission.*
Source: U.S. Department of Justice, Children in Custody: 1982/83 Census of Juvenile Detention and Correctional Facilities (Washington, D.C.: Government Printing Office, 1986), p. 7.

include alcohol and drug offenses, public order offenses, and voluntary admissions, which combined accounted for less than 15 percent of the total.

Table 15–5 reflects the number and percentage of juveniles held in public and private juvenile facilities by reason held in 1983. We see that

Table 15–5. Juveniles Held in Public and Private Facilities by Reason Held, 1983

	Number and Percent of Juveniles in:					
	Public and Private Facilities		Public Facilities		Private Facilities	
Reason Held	Number	Percent	Number	Percent	Number	Percent
Total	80,091	100.0	48,701	100.0	31,390	100.0
Delinquents[a]	56,063	70.0	45,351	93.1	10,712	34.1
Violent offenders	13,687	17.1	12,164	25.0	1,523	4.9
More serious[b]	9,617	12.0	8,901	18.3	716	2.3
Less serious	4,070	5.1	3,263	6.7	807	2.6
Property offenders	27,720	34.6	22,624	46.5	5,096	16.2
More serious[c]	19,516	24.4	16,644	34.2	2,872	9.1
Less serious	8,204	10.2	5,980	12.3	2,224	7.1

	Number and Percent of Juveniles in:					
	Public and Private Facilities		Public Facilities		Private Facilities	
Reason Held	Number	Percent	Number	Percent	Number	Percent
Alcohol/drug offenders	2,850	3.6	2,239	4.6	611	1.9
Public order offenders	2,981	3.7	2,582	5.3	399	1.3
Other offenders	8,825	11.0	5,742	11.8	3,083	9.8
Nondelinquents[d]	17,903	22.4	2,983	6.1	14,920	47.5
Status offenders	9,042	11.3	2,390	4.9	6,652	21.2
Nonoffenders	8,861	11.1	593	1.2	8,268	26.3
Voluntary admissions[e]	6,125	7.6	367	0.8	5,758	18.3

[a]Delinquents are those whose offense would be a criminal offense for adults.
[b]Includes those held for murder, forcible rape, robbery and aggravated assault.
[c]Includes those held for burglary, arson, larceny-theft and motor vehicle theft.
[d]Status offenders are those whose offense would not be a criminal offense for adults (runaways, truants, incorrigibles, etc.). Nonoffenders are those held for dependency, neglect, abuse, emotional disturbance and mental retardation.
[e]Voluntary admissions are those who are admitted without adjudication.
Source: U.S. Department of Justice, Children in Custody: 1982/83 Census of Juvenile Detention and Correctional Facilities (Washington, D.C.: Government Printing Office, 1986), p. 7.

7 out of every 10 juveniles in custody were detained or committed as delinquents. Public facilities were more likely to contain delinquent offenders (93 percent), whereas private facilities were more likely to hold nondelinquents (47.5 percent), and voluntary admissions (18.3 percent). Over half the delinquents in custody were held for violent and property crimes. Nondelinquents confined were almost equally divided between status offenders and nonoffenders.

A further examination of the reasons for adolescent detention can be seen in Table 15-6, which distributes juvenile correctional detainees in public facilities in 1985 by gender and reasons held. The data are consistent

Table 15-6. Juveniles Held in Public Juvenile Facilities, by Reason Held, 1985

	Number of Juveniles		
Reason Held	Total	Male	Female
TOTAL	49,322	42,549	6,773
Juveniles detained or committed for:			
Delinquent acts[a]	46,086	40,929	5,157
Violent	12,245	11,214	1,031
Murder, forcible rape, robbery, and aggravated assault	8,656	8,096	560
Other	3,589	3,118	471

Reason Held	Number of Juveniles Total	Male	Female
Property	22,020	19,978	2,042
Burglary, arson, larceny-theft, and motor vehicle theft	16,129	14,948	1,181
Other	5,891	5,030	861
Alcohol/drug offenses	2,660	2,319	341
Public order offenses	1,936	1,505	431
Probation violations	4,557	3,652	905
All other offenses[b]	2,668	2,261	407
Status offenses[c]	2,293	1,096	1,197
No Offenses[d]	644	364	280
Juveniles voluntarily admitted	299	160	139

Note: Data are for February 1, 1985.
[a] Acts that would be criminal if committed by adults.
[b] Includes unknown and unspecified offenses.
[c] Acts that would not be criminal for adults such as running away, truancy, and incorrigibility.
[d] Those held for dependency, neglect, abuse, emotional disturbance, or mental retardation.
Source: U.S. Department of Justice, Public Juvenile Facilities, 1985, **Children in Custody** (Washington, D.C.: Government Printing Office, 1986), p. 4.

with that we have already reviewed, in that the vast majority of juveniles in public custody (93 percent) were detained or adjudicated for delinquent acts, specifically violent and property crimes; and confined juveniles were predominantly male (86 percent). Despite accounting for only 14 percent of all juvenile public facility inmates, female juveniles constituted 52 percent of the total juveniles in custody for status offenses. A greater percentage of males than females (96 percent to 76 percent) were detained or committed for delinquent acts.

Adjusting to the Realities of Adolescent Institutional Confinement

Adolescents who enter juvenile institutional facilities must adjust to a number of painful realities and methods of survival. Foremost is the loss of freedom. Residents are subject to strict rules and regulations including locked doors, restricted movement, strip searches, and solitary confinement. Furthermore, institutionalized adolescents must regularly contend with the stresses and strains associated with prisoner societies, structural conditions in the institutional setting, exploitation, physical and sexual assaults, and other forms of victimization. Discriminatory practices and racism can also be an unpleasant but very likely reality in most juvenile institutional facilities. It is common for residents to experience depression, fear, frustration, low self-esteem, and other negative reactions to their confinement. Few adolescents can spend time in a secure juvenile facility without some scars remaining with them upon returning to society.

Violence and Victimization in Juvenile Institutions

The spectre of violence and victimization in the institutional setting is a problem in most juvenile facilities, and can involve both intraresident situations and resident-staff confrontations. Studies of violent and aggressive behavior by residents of secure facilities have related these patterns of behavior to a deprivation theory or a cultural importation theory. The deprivation approach views inmate aggression as a response to the grim conditions, deprivation, and degradation of institutional life. Contrastingly, the cultural importation theory assumes that inmate violent and aggressive behavior is more a product of values and patterns of behavior the inmate possessed before entering the institution and which is then used to the inmate's advantage in terms of material gain, power, respect, etc. In a study of aggressive behavior by adolescents in four juvenile institutions of various organizational structures and programming, a history of aggressive behavioral patterns was found to be the most significant variable in explaining institutional inmate aggression.[23]

Adolescent victimization and exploitation in the juvenile correctional setting was examined by Clemens Bartollas, Stuart Miller, and Simon Dinitz. They found that at least 90 percent of the subjects studied were participants in the victimization-exploitation game. Race was the single most important sociodemographic variable. In a reversal of the traditional white-black racial order in American society, black inmates generally occupied the upper echelon of the institutional hierarchy, and were the dominant group with respect to sexual assaults of white inmates. Other major findings were that:

• Most victimizations relate to property appropriation.
• The stronger and more aggressive inmates dominate the weaker inmates.
• Lower-class youths disproportionately victimize lower-middle and upper class inmates.
• Staff members are victimized through "con games"; and are exploitative of inmates (such as using inmates to maintain order).
• Inmates respond to severe victimization through running away, drug use, and attempted suicide.[24]

Modes of Adaptation to the Institutional Setting

Adolescents confined to juvenile facilities develop various modes of adaptation to their situation, depending on their background, values, and the circumstances they encounter in the institutional setting. The mode of adaptation most commonly used is to make the most of the institutional stay, including meeting one's needs in the best way possible with minimum unpleasantries. Other residents take a "playing it cool" mode of adaptation, and learn to control their emotions while doing whatever is necessary to make their stay as short as possible. A third adaptation to institutional life is rebellion, whereby inmates rebel against authority through threats, intimidation, violence, protests, and instigation of other inmates to riot. These youths often are leaders of the inmate subculture and exercise much power within the correctional institution. A fourth mode of adaptation is by withdrawing, such as running away and the use of drugs.

Some studies have identified other adolescent inmate modes of adaptation including conformists, innovators, ritualists, and retreatists[25]; and toughs, con artists, quiet types, bushboys, and scapegoats.[26] In all, the confined adolescents' survival as well as very sanity may hinge on their ability to adequately adapt to the conditions with which they find themselves in.

The Rights of Institutionalized Adolescents

Interest in the rights of juveniles in the juvenile corrections has come about largely as a result of similar concerns regarding the rights of adult prisoners. Juveniles in confinement presently have won through court decisions rights in two major areas: right to treatment and the right of freedom from cruel and unusual punishment.

Right to Treatment

The right to treatment for juveniles held in juvenile correctional institutions came about through a series of court decisions. In *White v. Reid* (1954), the court held that juveniles could not be confined in institutions that did not allow for their rehabilitation.[27] Similar decisions emerged in *Inmates of the Boy's Training School v. Affect* (1972)[28] and *Nelson v. Heyne* (1974).[29]

It was the 1974 *Morales v. Turman* court decisions that is most extensive with respect to the juvenile's right to treatment.[30] In this case, the United States District Court for the Eastern District of Texas ordered the closure of two Texas facilities because of their lack of treatment of inmates and the harsh and cruel punishment inmates were forced to endure, including beatings, exposure to crowd-control chemicals, and overly long solitary confinement. The court held that various criteria must be met by the state of Texas to ensure proper treatment of institutionalized juveniles, including minimum standards for providing medical and psychiatric care, and minimum standards for establishing humane institutional conditions.

The decision was eventually overturned on procedural grounds by the Fifth Circuit Appeals Court. Their decision was then reversed by the United States Supreme Court, who remanded the case. The outcome of any further proceedings on this case could well set the trend for the rights adolescents will have in the future to treatment.[31]

Right of Freedom from Cruel and Unusual Punishment

Court decisions have also guaranteed confined adolescents the right to be free from cruel and unusual punishment. In *Pena v. New York State Divison for Youth,* the court decided that the use of hand restraints, tranquilizers, and isolation violated the Eighth Amendment right of freedom from cruel and unusual punishment and the Fourteenth Amendment right to treatment.[32] In the decision on *Inmates of the Boy's training School v. Affect,* the court condemned such practices as strip cells and solitary confinement, inadequate educational programs, and established minimum standards for confined juveniles.[33] Federal courts have also held that long periods of solitary confinement and the use of such drugs as Thorazine as a method of control constitute cruel and unusual punishment.[34]

16. Noninstitutional Approaches to Juvenile Corrections

COMMUNITY-BASED AND DIVERSIONARY correctional programs represent an alternative philosophy to the institutionalization of youthful offenders. Noninstitutional corrections are seen as more effective in treating and rehabilitating juvenile offenders, more humane, and more cost-efficient than placing juveniles in training schools and adult institutions. Although a variety of noninstitutional treatment programs are in existence, they basically fall under five areas: probation, diversion, residential, non-residential, and aftercare.

Probation

Probation, which refers to a juvenile court disposition imposed upon an adjudicated delinquent by a judge, is the most common disposition of juvenile cases disposed by the juvenile court. In 1983, nearly 60 percent of the juvenile court cases were handled in this manner.[1] Moreover, a study by Frank Scarpitti and Richard Stephenson of 1,210 male youths who received juvenile court dispositions over a recent three-year span, revealed that 78 percent had been given probation.[2] Probation enables juvenile offenders to remain within the community under the official supervision of a probation officer. The probation is contingent upon the youth following certain restrictions and conditions imposed by the juvenile court. Typical examples of general conditions include obeying their parents, attending school, obeying laws, and often restitution in some form to the victim.

Probation, as a facet of the juvenile justice system, reflects several different themes. First it is a legal court placement of a juvenile adjudicated delinquent. This placement may come about as a result of a "suspension of the imposition of the disposition," which refers to the suspension of a disposition of institutional commitment, whereby the youth is put on probation; or as an "order of probation," which is a dispositional issuance of

185

probation by a juvenile court judge. Secondly, probation is a dispositional alternative to institutionalization. Thirdly, it is a component of the system of juvenile justice. Lastly, probation is a process that at once involves the juvenile delinquent, the juvenile court, and the community.

The intake officer who usually is a probation officer,[3] occupies the key decision point in the juvenile justice process. He or she, acting as a screening agent for the intake department (or probation department[4]), must determine whether or not the youth brought to the intake unit, usually by police but also by parents and others, is to be moved further along the official judicial process (such as detention pending a detention hearing) or informally handled. An informal disposition may consist of an unofficial or informal probation in which the juvenile and his or her parents agree to a voluntary supervision arrangement as opposed to official processing of the case.

For youths who are adjudicated delinquent, probation officers must prepare a report on the social history of the juvenile to assist the judge in deciding the proper disposition. The adolescent sentenced to probation is often at this point explained the ramifications of the disposition by the probation officer (such as when to report to the probation officer and the importance of compliance with the conditions set forth for probation). One study found that juveniles were most receptive to assistance during this stage of their probation than during any other time.[5]

The length of juvenile probation varies depending upon the state. In some states, a youth may be on probation until reaching the age of mandatory within a given state (usually 16 or 17); other states place a limit on how long an offender can be placed on probation (for instance, in California it is six months).[6]

Supervision of probationers consists of casework management, surveillance, and treatment. The particulars will depend on the youth, their history, their risk to society and other factors.

Presently there are those who are disenchanted with the probation system. Some police and probationers themselves view probation as something they "get off with," reflecting an attitude by many of a juvenile justice system too soft on adolescent offenders. Others regard probation as an infringement of the legal rights of juveniles, while still others question the fine line probation personnel tread between rehabilitation and control of probationers, as described by R. Emerson:

> The formal goal of probation is to improve the delinquent's behavior—in short, to "rehabilitate" him. This goal is short-circuited, however, by a pervading preoccupation with control. Reflecting insistent demands that the court "do something" about recurrent misconduct, probation is organized to keep the delinquent "in line," to prevent any further disturbing and inconveniencing "trouble." The ultimate goal of permanently "reforming" the

delinquent's personality and conduct becomes subordinated to the exigencies of maintaining immediate control. Probationary supervision consequently takes on a decidedly short-term and negative character; probation becomes an essentially disciplinary regime directed toward deterring and inhibiting troublesome conduct.[7]

Diversionary Programs

Diversionary programs are another commonly used noninstitutional alternative for dealing with juvenile delinquents. The major impetus for juvenile diversion arose during the late 1960s when the President's Commission on Law Enforcement and Administration of Justice recommended that dispositional alternatives be established in treating juvenile offenders that circumvent the formal juvenile justice system and its stigmatization of youth.[8] Since that time, diversionary programs have proliferated and taken on a array of typologies. Juveniles are diverted from the juvenile justice system by police, the courts, and agencies outside the system.

Police discretion accounts for the vast majority of all juvenile diversion. As the first official line of contact with juvenile offenders, police officers frequently release juveniles they encounter with little more than questioning or admonishment—thus bypassing formal processing that could well be justified. Of the 1,173,715 youths taken into custody by police in 1986, more than one-third were handled informally.[9] Police diversion programs consist of predelinquent intervention and actual diversion of juvenile offenders. Police predelinquent programs include courses in secondary schools discussing alcohol and drug abuse, city government, and juvenile delinquency. Police diversionary referrals are commonly to such social agencies as youth service bureaus, child welfare departments, and mental health agencies.

Informal probation is the form of diversion most often used by the juvenile court. In 1983, 14 percent of the juveniles referred to intake units were placed on informal probation, while 64 percent were released.[10] There is some indication that the rights of juveniles are commonly denied through this informal handling. The courts also divert juvenile offenders to various diversionary alternatives such as substance abuse clinics, shoplifters' programs, and crisis intervention programs.

Youth Service Bureaus (YSBs), also called Youth Assistance Programs and Youth Resource Bureaus, were established in the late 1960s as a result of the President's Commission on Law Enforcement and Administration of Justice's call for such agencies to work with troubled youths outside the formal process of the juvenile court.[11] Today, YSBs are a major diversionary option commonly utilized by law enforcement to refer youthful offenders to. Youth Service Bureaus operate services ranging from drop-in centers and school outreach programs to crisis intervention hotlines and programs for pregnant teens. The YSBs have been criticized in recent years for, among other reasons, their coercive measures, discriminatory practices, and being too dependent upon the juvenile justice system to be effective in their aims.

Other types of diversionary programs include runaway shelters and alternative schools. Despite the success of diversion in limiting the penetration of juvenile offenders into the web of the system of juvenile justice, such juveniles are still subject to the juvenile court if they fail to participate satisfactorily in diversionary programs or otherwise continue to commit delinquent acts.

Residential Treatment Programs

Residential treatment programs such as foster care placement and group homes are 24-hour-a-day, community-based corrections for youthful offenders. For many of these youths, such residential treatment becomes necessary due to inappropriate, insufficient, or perilous conditions at home that threaten the welfare of the youth (such as sexual abuse, family dysfunction, or substance abuse).

Foster care refers to juvenile placement in a residential setting other than his or her own home, where other adults take the place of parents. Foster parents are subsidized by local or state governments to provide food, care and shelter to abused, neglected, or delinquent children. Ideally, the foster home is a setting were there is love, trust, affection, communication—or as close to a natural parent-child relationship as possible.

Although foster care is generally more favorable for youths removed from their homes than group home placement or institutionalization, in some instances the adolescent may be worse off in a foster home, as they may be subjected to abuse, sexual molestation, and other mistreatment.

Group home placement is generally used as residential treatment for adolescents who have experienced behavioral problems or otherwise were unsuccessful with foster care, or those who need more intensive treatment and supervision than foster parents are able to provide. Also, some youths appear to adjust better to life in a group setting in which they are usually among peers, as opposed to a traditional family setting of foster care.

Group homes are generally larger than foster homes—averaging anywhere from 10 to 25 youths—and offer 24-hour residential and treatment staff members. The staff works in shifts and cannot live at the treatment facility full-time. It is estimated that more than 6,000 adolescents are placed in group homes annually.[12] (See also Chapter 15.)

Nonresidential Day Treatment Programs

Nonresidential or day treatment programs are informal correctional programs that juvenile offenders attend during standard school hours and return home in the evenings and, in some instances, on weekends. Day treatment programs are often reserved for adolescents on probation who are unable to adjust to the latitude present in probation supervision. The rationale behind such community-based programs is that they provide a tightly structured setting that enables adolescents to participate in educational and training programs needed to enhance their development into mature and productive adults.

During the 1970s, nonresidential day treatment programs became extremely popular as a community-based correctional alternative because of their economic feasibility (for instance, they do not have the burden of supplying living quarters for juvenile participants), more successful participation of parents, requirement of fewer staff members, and less punishment-oriented and coercive measures than residential treatment programs.

Nonresidential programs typically treat male adolescents, although there are programs for female juveniles and a number of coeducational programs. New York's STAY programs and Chicago's United Delinquency Intervention Service are examples of two successful day treatment programs.

Aftercare

Aftercare is the juvenile justice system's synonym for parole and refers to the release of juveniles from the institutional setting and the support and supervisory services accompanying the youth's reinsertion into the community. Since mandatory sentencing is rarely used, and only the state of Washington uses determinate sentencing, the predominant means of juvenile release from custodial facilities is through the aftercare program.

Once a juvenile is adjudicated delinquent and committed to a state training school, the state usually retains jurisdiction pending the inmate's release. However, in a number of states, juvenile court judges have the power to remove youths from institutions. The authority to release juvenile detainees to aftercare status is usually granted to institutional staff, although in some states other agencies or boards have the power to make this decision. Usually the institutional staff monitors the progress of each inmate at various intervals; once release is recommended, the recommendation must be reviewed by a board consisting of institutional staff members. Upon the concurrence of the board, the recommendation must then be approved by an institutional coordinator at the youth commission or youth authority. The factors taken into consideration by cottage staffs before recommending the release of an inmate include a review of his or her total institutional adjustment (such as school performance, peer relationships, and attitude), a risk assessment in returning the youth to the community, cottage work detail performance, and personal hygiene.

Once an adolescent is paroled, he or she comes under the responsibility and supervision of an aftercare officer who provides the parolee with a list of conditions or rules which he or she must abide by. These are similar to those required of a probationer such as obeying parental authority, being home at a certain time each night, and avoidance of other delinquents or drug use. Violation of the conditions of release could lead to a return to an institution. Placement of the youth into the community may be in his or her home or, if unacceptable, an alternate setting such as a group or foster home. In most cases, aftercare status of a juvenile lasts one year or more.

Opponents of aftercare complain about its ineffectiveness (for example, returning a youth to the community where they initially got into trouble) and the too lenient policies of the aftercare system pertaining to serious adolescent offenders.

17. Adolescent Crime and Delinquency in Other Countries

ANTISOCIAL BEHAVIOR BY YOUTHS is believed by many to be primarily a product of the American culture. The basis for this assumption, to a great extent, is the vast body of research and theories devoted to the study of juvenile crime and delinquency in the United States compared to the rest of the world. Hence, most of our knowledge about the nature and incidence of juvenile misconduct and all its generalities have been derived from what we know (or believe that we do) about American delinquency. One reason why so much attention has been given to juvenile deviance in this country is that its characteristics with respect to creating conditions conducive to adolescent misbehavior (such as social disorganization, disrespect for law and order, and subcultural systems) seem unique among countries. Only somewhat recently have we begun to learn about juvenile delinquency outside the United States.

In this chapter, we will address adolescent misbehavior as an issue on a global scale. However, as such research is still fairly limited, of various methodology, and in some instances of questionable reliability, it might be best not to think in terms of close comparative examination or even accuracy. One should also keep in mind that cultural differences may result in different definitions of juvenile delinquent behavior.

Adolescent Criminality: A Worldwide Problem

There are a number of studies to suggest that juvenile delinquency is a serious and rising problem throughout the world.[1] Researchers have attributed much of this to the urbanization, industrialization, modernization and other elements of social change and affluence that has taken place in many countries since World War II. Ruth Cavan and Jordan Cavan focused on a social structural perspective in noting the rise in juvenile crime in Mexico, England, Soviet Union, and several other European countries.[2] T.C.N. Gibbens and R. Ahrenfeldt give evidence of this increase in delinquent behavior among youth in Canada, Japan, Belgium, Soviet Union and other countries.[3] Jackson Toby has placed much emphasis on the rise in juvenile misbehavior in other countries as it relates to economic deprivation, social control, and affluence.[4]

An indication of the recent juvenile participation in crime around the world can be seen in Table 17-1. We see that the percentage of juvenile crime relative to total crime varies considerably from country to country and offense to offense. For instance, in Japan juveniles are responsible for

Table 17-1. Adolescent Crime Globally[a]

| | Percent of All Crimes Committed by Juveniles[b] | | | | | | |
Country	Murder	Rape	Assault	Car Theft	Drug Use	Robbery	All Crimes
Australia	5%	15%	13%	49%	9%	28%	27%
Canada	5%	N/A	8%	32%	7%	14%	23%
Chile	7%	7%	4%	8%	4%	12%	8%
Finland	8%	14%	20%	66%	20%	38%	23%
France	6%	15%	8%	27%	9%	24%	11%
West Germany	5%	7%	12%	24%	7%	19%	13%
Israel	1%	16%	15%	44%	9%	18%	13%
Italy	4%	11%	N/A	14%	4%	11%	6%
Japan	4%	38%	34%	62%	7%	33%	39%
Nigeria	.1%	N/A	2%	.5%	.4%	1%	1%
Sweden[c]	4%	13%	6%	94%	12%	11%	13%
Syria	23%	23%	18%	4%	11%	N/A	19%
United States	7%	16%	13%	36%	12%	26%	17%
Zambia	N/A	14%	4%	1%	3%	3%	5%

[a]As official definitions of criminal offenses are not uniform from country to country, it is best not to view this data too stringently for comparative purposes.
[b]Crimes reported to or detected by the police.
[c]Data refer only to ages 15 to 17.
Source: International Criminal Police Organization (INTERPOL), St. Cloud, France.

approximately 38 percent of the rapes, or more than twice that in the United States; while in West Germany only 7 percent of the rapes are attributable to juveniles. In Sweden, 94 percent of the car thefts are believed to be committed by juveniles, compared to less than 1 percent in Nigeria.

When considering all offenses, the lowest percentage of juvenile involvement is 1 percent of the crime in Nigeria, whereas the highest is in Japan where youths commit 39 percent of the total criminality. In the United States, 17 percent of the crime is estimated as being perpetrated by juveniles. The data, as provided by the International Criminal Police Organization (INTERPOL), presents an interesting comparative study of serious juvenile delinquency on a global scale. However, again, caution should be exercised before drawing any inferences or strict comparisons.

United Kingdom

After the United States, the most research done on juvenile delinquency has taken place in the United Kingdom. Researchers have found that delinquency in Great Britain parallels that in the United States in many ways: male youths are far more involved in delinquencies than female youths (the male-female ratio of delinquents in England, in fact, has been shown to be greater than in the United States); most delinquency is committed by older adolescents; loosely structured juvenile delinquent gangs can be found in large cities; and adolescent antisocial behavior is most common in deteriorating and working class communities.[5] Further, juvenile delinquents in Great Britain are often "drawn from the group of alienated, uncommitted, working class youths who are involved in the pursuit in short-run, hedonistic pleasures. Most of them do not show a marked sense of status frustration."[6]

Juvenile delinquency in Britain has risen sharply since World War II. More recently, the rate of juvenile crime there upsurged by 16 percent from 1975 to 1985. Almost half of all offenders known to the police in Britain fall between the ages of 15 and 19. Seventy percent of the adolescents jailed return there within two years of their release. Nearly one-fourth of all British males are convicted for some type of offense before they reach the age of 20.[7] Correctional programs for youths in the United Kingdom vary from social worker supervision of offenders aged 10 to 17 to detention center or youth custody placement of juvenile delinquents ages 18 to 20. The number of male juveniles placed in long-term youth custody facilities has climbed recently by 16 percent, while the number of female adolescent long-term detainees has grown by 22 percent.[8]

Soviet Union

Some research has yielded surprising information about juvenile crime in the U.S.S.R. Mark Field, based on his examinations of mass media comments on crime in the Soviet Union, concluded that juvenile delinquency has become a problem of epidemic proportions there, most notably that of drunkenness and the periodic formation of youth gangs. He also contended that adolescent misbehavior is essentially encouraged by Russian adults due to their indifference shown towards it. Field noted the emergence of a group of youthful offenders—the jeunesse dorée—consisting primarily of the children of powerful, wealthy, and successfully intellectual members of Soviet society. These youths were reported as engaging in crime, debauchery, and dissipation.[9]

Similar observations of juvenile crime in the Soviet Union were made by Walter Connor, Paul Hollander, and Cavan and Cavan. Connor postulated that adolescent crime in the Soviet Union is predominantly a problem of the lower class, urban male youths who have low educational attainment and weak prospects for social and economic mobility. Property crimes, as in America, seems to be the most frequently committed juvenile act of delinquency.[10]

Cavan and Cavan posited that since World War II juvenile delinquency has become common throughout the socioeconomic strata of the Soviet Union. "Working-class youths, from slum areas sometimes become *stilyagi,* or 'hooligans,' dressing in American-style clothing, listening to popular music, and engaging in antisocial conduct in the form of public drunkenness and rebelliousness. Among the children of the socially elite, some become 'guilded youths' and get caught up in drinking and wild parties."[11] According to the researchers, juvenile deviance among Soviet youths is a reflection of their desire to break away from the repressive and boring conditions of life in the Soviet Union.

Paul Hollander further supports the contention that delinquency in the U.S.S.R. has increased since World War II. He linked this rise to the blandness and uniformity of Soviet life, in addition to economic dysfunction, broken homes, low socioeconomic status, and truancy.[12]

With adolescent crime in the Soviet Union reaching dangerously high levels, the list of informers is also on the rise, such as teachers who look for indications of a "deviant attitude" among youths. The records of juveniles who are labeled as "crime prone" are passed on to a Commission for Minors' Affairs which is empowered to impose "measures of influence" on such juveniles. These measures include after school programs of recreation and regular visits from adults who monitor the youth's school behavior and work.

Soviet youths aged 14 to 17 can end up in court if they perpetrate actual criminal offenses. In the court, a social worker as well as the juvenile's teacher function as the judge's advisors. A serious crime could result in an 11- to 18-year-old youth serving time in a juvenile labor colony, where the majority of the prisoners are confined from 6 to 12 months. In the labor colony, the youths continue their education in addition to performing "socially useful labor."[13]

Juveniles in the Soviet Union have little to no defense against charges of misconduct. The interpretation of who is delinquent is almost entirely up to the discretion of the teacher or principal. Notes an expert on Soviet delinquency: "There is no sense of due process in Soviet schools. What constitutes a serious offense varies from school to school — and even from one classroom to another."[14]

Parents of delinquent Soviet youth may also be liable for their behavior. Officials in the children's department of the Soviet militia closely monitor parents who have been labeled "antisocial" or "immoral." Those determined to be "bad" parents with "crime-prone" children may be forced to attend meetings to learn how to change their child's behavior.

Sweden

As in other European countries, Sweden has seen a significant increase in its juvenile crime since World War II. Research indicates that the majority of Sweden's crime is being committed by youths aged 14 to 16. A 1985 study reported that 61 percent of all sudden, violent attacks in Sweden were perpetrated by males under age 19.[15] Many of the Swedish delinquents are repeat offenders. More than 60 percent of the 11- to 13-year-old youths are recidivists within 5 years of the initial offense; while 75 percent of Swedish adolescents committing the most crimes are never able to lead a normal life, absent of criminal involvement.[16]

The inexplicable wave of juvenile crime in Sweden is somewhat baffling considering that the country is, as one source put it, "healthy, wealthy, and slumless."[17] Hence, such behavior cannot be readily attributed to unemployment, low income, deprivation, undereducation and other sociodemographic factors frequently associated with delinquency in the United States and other countries. A Swedish authority on juvenile crime referred to it as "a type of *affluence* criminality."[18]

Experts point towards two prime reasons in explaining the delinquency of Swedish youths. One is that their upwardly mobile status (i.e., access to cars, drugs, and alcohol) gives them greater opportunities to commit crimes than youths in poor, downwardly mobile societies. Secondly, adequate discipline and control of youths by parents and grandparents are lacking in Swedish society. Notes an official of the National Swedish Council for Crime Prevention: "The absence of clear standards of upbringing has a close connection with juvenile criminality."[19]

Carl-Gunnar Janson, who has studied the rise in Swedish juvenile criminality since World War II, blamed it on the decline in *expressive patience* — or a pattern of deferred gratification. He advanced that the sweeping economic stability in Sweden has caused many youths to "abandon expressive patience, postponement of gratification, and success striving in favor of hedonistic pleasure seeking."[20]

The Swedish juvenile justice system is more concerned with rehabilitating than punishing delinquent youth. Most juvenile offenders under age 15 are handled directly by the social welfare authorities. Police investigation of juvenile delinquent acts is limited to serious crimes such as murder. Dependent upon the offense, the disposition can vary from a counseling session to foster care placement. Only in rare instances are youths placed in reformatories — and usually only upon parental approval. For delinquents aged 15 to 20, punishment for an offense may comprise of a fine, probation, and/or suspended sentence.

France

Little research is available on juvenile crime in France. A comprehensive study has noted the presence and nature of gang delinquency in Paris. Edmund Vaz, who interviewed correctional officials, social scientists, and educators in Paris, found that delinquent youth gangs in the city were loosely organized and participated in a range of offenses including sex crimes, robbery, assault, vandalism and drinking. He observed that in contrast to American youth gangs, drug addiction, gang warfare, and structural associations between adolescent and adult criminal gangs are virtually nonexistent among Parisian juvenile gangs. However, similar to gang delinquency in the United States and England, Vaz found that most Parisian juvenile gang criminality takes place in neighborhoods characterized by slum conditions, low income, poor housing, family dysfunction, limited recreational outlets, and other weak systems.[21]

Refer also to Table 17-1, which gives some perspective on the nature of juvenile crime in France relative to other countries.

Argentina

Adolescent crime in Argentina has been examined in a few studies. Two, in particular, have compared the delinquency of Argentinian and American youth. Lois DeFleur found delinquency in the two countries to be comparable in terms of the male-female ratio (around five boys are referred to court for delinquent acts in Argentina for every female), age (Argentinian delinquents are 15 to 16 years old on average), and the type of offense most common among youthful offenders (property crimes).

However, she found cultural differences between Argentina and the United States in some areas of delinquent behavior. For example, female sex offenders are relatively rare in Argentina, reflecting a greater tolerance of sexual experimentation there than in the United States. Male youth sex offenses generally relate to child molestation. Drug use, auto theft, and vandalism were also shown to be infrequent among Argentinian youthful offenders compared to American delinquents.[22]

Pedro David and Joseph Scott's comparison study of juvenile court cases in Rosario, Argentina, and Toledo, Ohio, revealed that the majority of the delinquency cases in both cities involved youths from predominantly lower socioeconomic class areas, although the rate of delinquency was significantly higher among the Toledo adolescents. The researchers did point to a difference in delinquency definitions between the two countries. Argentinian juvenile court statutes do not include prohibitions against status offenses, which may account for some of the differential in rates of delinquency.[23]

Delinquency in Other Nations

Information about delinquent conduct in many other nations is particularly scarce. Some research of delinquency in Africa and Asia has shown it to be somewhat similar to the United States in terms of gender and age characteristics, the nature of offenses (such as runaways), family dynamics, social class, and status frustration.[24] Demographic data on Australian youthful offenders has found them to be disproportionately male, urban, of lower socioeconomic status, and unemployed.[25]

Obviously there is still much to be learned about the extent and nature of adolescent crime and delinquency in various parts of the world. Since one culture cannot act as a representative of every society, it is important that researchers branch out across the globe in order to enhance our knowledge, theories, and directions on juvenile criminality as a worldwide issue.

18. Directions in Adolescent Crime Control and Delinquency Prevention

As we head into the 1990s, it is still quite apparent that we face a number of issues with respect to adolescent crime and delinquency and the systems of juvenile and criminal justice. In some instances minors continue to be unduly penalized for acts that were they committed by adults, would not be subject to the whim of the justice system. In other cases, juveniles are literally getting away with murder because of their legal status. Yet some adolescent offenders are being treated as adults, including serving time in adult penitentiaries. There is also strong evidence that discriminatory practices are being administered throughout the system of justice. Further concerns relate to a persistent wave of adolescent crime, ineffective crime control policies, budgetary and administrative weaknesses in the juvenile and criminal justice systems, and inadequate contributions in fighting and preventing juvenile delinquency from supplementary sources: parents, schools, community, social services, researchers.

In this chapter we will address what has been done in recent years towards alleviating some of these issues and what needs to be in future years.

The "Big D's" of Juvenile Justice

During the 1960s and 1970s four trends were established in the juvenile justice system's handling of adolescent offenders. Referred to as the "Big D's" of juvenile justice, these include: due process, diversion, decriminalization, and deinstitutionalization.

Due Process

Due process may have had the greatest impact on the justice system and its treatment toward juvenile offenders. The due process rights' explosion in

198

juvenile justice came on the strength of a number of United States Supreme Court decisions in the 1960s and 1970s that applied constitutionally guaranteed rights to due process to juveniles during various stages in the juvenile justice system process. Among the most important rights extended to juveniles are the right to counsel, the right to notification of charges, the right of confrontation and cross examination, the privilege against self-incrimination, the right to be proven guilty beyond a reasonable doubt, the right against illegal search and seizure, and the right to treatment when in confinement. Despite some setbacks in the due process drive for juveniles, the implication is that in the future the juvenile will draw closer to the adult in terms of their constitutionally guaranteed rights.

Diversion

Diversionary programs began in the late 1960s as a means to limit the juvenile's penetration into the juvenile justice system and its resultant stigmatization and negativity by diverting youthful offenders from the system into informal programs such as probation and youth service bureaus. Although diversion has been shown to reduce recidivism, other research has found that diversion has been unsuccessful in achieving their prevention objectives.[1] In recent years the concept has fallen into disfavor by many. The charges leveled against diversionary programs include their widening of the scope of the juvenile justice system, disregard for the due process rights to juveniles, stigmatization of program participants, and establishment of new legal entities.

Decriminalization

Decriminalization, or removal from the criminal law jurisdiction offenses deemed as nondangerous or illegal, primarily relates to status offenses with respect to juveniles. Through much of the 1970s the decriminalization movement was in force nationwide. Status offenders were in many instances handled differently than delinquent or criminal offenders, placed in different facilities, and generally looked upon as deviant but noncriminal. Nevertheless, status offenders were to remain under the juvenile court's scope of jurisdiction. Today decriminalization of status offenders still receives solid public support. However, it seems unlikely that the juvenile justice system will ever relinquish total control over juvenile status offenders.

Deinstitutionalization

The deinstitutionalization, or decarceration, movement began in the late 1960s and was concerned with humanizing the treatment of juvenile offenders through normalization techniques, which included placing youths into community-based correctional care and eliminating the involuntary confinement of adolescent offenders in the structured environment of large long-term correctional institutions. It was in Massachusetts, under the guidance of youth commissioner Jerome Miller, that the concept of juvenile deinstitutionalization established its major prominence.[2] Miller, who sought to force communities to take responsibility for their own delinquency problems, closed most of the state's juvenile instutions in the early 1970s, placing youths in small group homes and utilizing existing community-based corrections and private facilities to house delinquents. Juvenile detainees were given much more responsibility in decision-making (such as wearing their own clothes and self-governing) in an attempt to counteract the negative aspects of the prisoner subculture.

Some other states followed suit during the 1970s.[3] An additional element of the decarceration movement was an attempt to remove status offenders from training schools. In the early 1970s, 70 to 80 percent of the female training school inmates were status offenders and as many as 30 percent of the males. Deinstitutionalization seems to have been effective in this area since, by the late 1970s, the numbers of youths placed in institutions for status offenses had dropped sharply.[4]

However, in general, support for residential community-based correctional programs has waned since the late 1960s and early 1970s with more support being given to "get tough policies" in dealing with juvenile delinquents. There is, in fact, indication that some states are starting a reinstitutionalization process.[5] Nevertheless, the influence of deinstitutionalization can still be seen in statistics that suggest that the training school inmate population has declined since the early 1970s.[6]

Federal Legislative Strides

Federal legislation has been enacted in recent years to respond to some of the key issues related to juvenile delinquency and juvenile justice. The most important of this legislative reform are the Juvenile Justice and Delinquency Prevention Act, the Child Abuse Prevention and Treatment Act, the Protection of Children Against Sexual Exploitation Act, the Runaway and Homeless Youth Act, the Missing Children Act, and the National Center for Missing and Exploited Children.

Juvenile Justice and Delinquency Prevention Act

The Juvenile Justice and Delinquency Prevention Act was enacted in 1974 and amended in 1980. Its purpose was to identify dependent and neglected children and status offenders and to divert them from institutionalization facilities shared by delinquents and adult offenders. The act required (1) a comprehensive assessment of the effectiveness of the existing system of juvenile justice, (2) the impetus for development and implementation of innovative alternatives in delinquency prevention and diversion of status offenders from the juvenile justice system, and (3) use of juvenile justice system resources to deal more effectively with adolescent delinquent offenders.

The Juvenile Justice and Delinquency Prevention Act required that for states to receive federal funds they must

> provide within two years after submission of the plan that juveniles who are charged with or who have committed offenses that would not be criminal if committed by an adult, shall not be placed in juvenile detention or correctional facilities, but must be placed in shelter facilities.[7]

Child Abuse Prevention and Treatment Act

The Child Abuse Prevention and Treatment Act was enacted in 1974 and amended in 1978 as a response to increasing public concern about the incidence of child abuse and neglect. The Act provided for several programs aimed at protecting all juveniles in the United States from maltreatment, including:

> (1) the establishment of a National Center on Child Abuse and Neglect, (2) increasing public awareness on child maltreatment, detection, and reporting, (3) assisting states and local communities in developing more effective mechanisms for delivery of services to families, (4) providing training and technical assistance to state and local communities in dealing with the problems of child abuse and neglect, and (5) supporting research into causal and preventative measures in child victimization.[8]

In order to qualify for federal funds, states were required to meet the following criteria: a uniform, comprehensive definition of child abuse and neglect; investigation of child abuse reports; an assurance of confidentiality of records; and the appointment of guardians ad litem for juveniles involved in abuse or neglect court proceedings. The importance of this legislation can be seen in the strong link documented between child victimization and adolescent delinquency.

Protection of Children Against Sexual Exploitation Act

The Protection of Children Against Sexual Exploitation Act of 1978 emerged after extensive hearings in both the House and Senate. Its objective was to help fill the gaps existing in federal statutes aimed at protecting children from sexual exploitation. The law hoped to halt the production and dissemination of child pornography by prohibiting the interstate transportation of persons under the age of 18 for purposes of sexual exploitation. Furthermore, the act extended the federal government's power to prosecute both producers and distributors of child pornography. In specific,

> the law provides punishment for persons who use, employ, or persuade minors to become involved in the production of visual or print materials that depict sexually explicit conduct if the producers know or have reason to know that the materials will be transported in interstate or foreign commerce or mailed. Punishment is also specifically provided for parents, legal guardians, or other persons having custody or control of minors and who knowingly permit a minor to participate in the production of such material.[9]

The Sexual Exploitation Act also mandated stiff penalties against sexual exploiters of children. Further federal legislation in the fight against child pornography occurred in 1983 when the United States Supreme Court upheld the constitutionality of a New York law that prohibited the dissemination of child pornography irregardless of whether or not it is judged legally obscene. The ruling, in effect, upheld similar laws in 20 other states.[10]

Runaway and Homeless Youth Act

The Runaway and Homeless Youth Act, enacted in 1978, authorized what presently is the Secretary of Health and Human Services to provide assistance to local organizations for operating temporary shelter homes for runaways.[11] The act addresses the serious implications of children who run away (such as prostitution, child abuse, delinquency) and the need to curtail the problem. The legislation made grants available for the establishment and maintenance of runaway houses by states, localities, and nonprofit organizations. To qualify for federal funding for a runaway house, criteria to be met included: (1) an accessible location to runaways, (2) a maximum capacity of 20 children, (3) a sufficient staff-juvenile ratio, (4) adequate plans for contacting parents or relatives of the juvenile and providing for the runaway's safe return home, and (5) the maintenance of sufficient statistical recordkeeping profiling runaways and their parents.

The 1980 amendment to the Runaway and Homeless Youth Act included the following: (1) recognition that many "runaways" are actually "throwaways" — that is, thrown out of their homes by parents or others, (2) clarification of the requirements that shelter services be provided to the families of runaways and homeless youth in addition to the juveniles themselves, and (3) the addition of program authorities for the establishment of model programs designed to aid habitual runaways.[12]

Missing Children Act

The Missing Children Act was enacted in 1982 in direct response to the increasing numbers of missing children nationwide due to parental abduction, nonrelative kidnapping, running away, or some other means.[13] The act was created to establish a national clearinghouse of information designed to identify deceased persons and help locate missing ones, particularly children. It provided parents, guardians, or next-of-kin of missing children "confirmation" of an entry into the FBI's National Crime Information Center computer to which some local law enforcement agencies have access. Such a clearinghouse would assist local police departments in identifying and finding missing children and parents who know that their missing children are registered across the country, thereby increasing the chances of being found. Furthermore, the legislation allows for FBI intervention upon proof of kidnapping.

National Center for Missing and Exploited Children

The continued and growing interest in the tragedy of missing and exploited children nationwide and a demand that something be done about it led to the United States Congress mandating by law the establishment of a permanent National Center for Missing and Exploited Children.[14] The Center was established to initiate a national effort to try to halt the epidemic of missing and exploited juveniles and to provide assistance in curbing the problems of sexual exploitation of children, child pornography, and juvenile prostitution. The Center was also designed to serve as a central contact point for parents of missing children and people who think they have information on such children. Other key features of the National Center include providing assistance and expertise in education, legislation, advocacy, public awareness, and improving the criminal justice system.

To further focus attention on the serious issue of missing children, on May 25, 1984, the United States began observing National Missing Children's Day.

State Legislative Progress

Before 1977, state legislation pertaining to youthful offenders was generally vague. However, with the recent passage of important federal legislation addressing various aspects of child maltreatment and juvenile delinquency, states have been quick to implement similar statutes. Today most states have enacted new or have revised existing criminal legislation addressing juvenile crime and crime against juveniles.

Other strides on the state level can be seen in a greater slant toward viewing the adolescent status offender as a noncriminal and recognizing the serious nature of some violent and chronic juvenile offenders when establishing policies.

Law Enforcement Progress

Law enforcement agencies are addressing juvenile crime and delinquency in the late 1980s by placing greater emphasis on specialized juvenile and gang units, putting more officers on the street in especially high crime areas, arming themselves with weaponry better suited to deal with violent juvenile offenders, and developing a better rapport with other police forces, social agencies, and the community in fighting adolescent delinquency.

Juvenile Corrections' Progress

The last two decades have seen great strides in the philosophy and direction of the juvenile corrections system. No longer is the training school seen as the only answer in dealing with troubled youths. A variety of community-based treatment programs have emerged through diversionary and deinstitutionalization approaches. Greater attention is also being given in the late 1980s to rehabilitative techniques and better preparing the confined youth for a return to society.

Local and National Progress

In the 1980s, many local and national groups and organizations have joined in the fight against juvenile delinquency and juvenile victimization. Neighborhood watch groups, shelters, hotlines, counseling services, referral services, media coverage, and other responses to adolescent crime have sprung up across the country. Many organizations rely on community resources while others depend heavily on grants and funding through federal, state and private sources. Examples of organizations that have established themselves as important resources in dealing with the issues of juvenile delinquency, child abuse and exploitation include the Juvenile Justice Clearinghouse in Rockville, Maryland; the National Coalition for Children's Justice in Shelburne, Vermont; the National Child Safety Council in Jackson, Michigan; Children in Crisis in New York; Children of the Night in Los Angeles; and the National Crime Prevention Council in Washington, D.C.

Implications for Addressing Adolescent Crime and Delinquency in the 1990s

In spite of some positive direction taken in various levels of society in dealing with the issues pertaining to the adolescent offender, there still remains serious concerns as we head into the 1990s. How can we improve upon our efforts to reduce juvenile crime, ensure that juveniles' rights are being upheld, make the various stages of the juvenile justice system more effective, and better respond to research needs in addressing adolescent criminality? What follows are recommendations.

Reduction of Juvenile Crime

- Communities must better incorporate youths in community organizations and functions.
- More positive role models are needed on the local level to counteract negative role models for youths.
- The police must play a less hostile, more active role in communities in which they work, including speaking at schools and participating in local functions.
- Schools and parents must place greater emphasis on discussing the elements of delinquency and crime with elementary and junior high school students.
- Jobs and positive activities (such as sports and community functions) must be made available to youth, particularly in lower-class areas.
- Urban schools need to broaden their range of study for students, improve upon course materials, develop greater incentives for learning and higher education, and establish a better rapport with students.
- Juvenile gangs need to be better understood and communicated with by neighborhood residents, teachers, law enforcement; and emphasis should be placed on getting youth gangs to interact and redirect their goals into more positive and, possibly, joint directions.
- Drug and alcohol abuse by youths needs to be dealt with through more innovative means, such as student forums and school coursework.
- The criminal and juvenile justice systems must put more resources into controlling juvenile crime through more sophisticated deterrent methodologies, more severe penalties against hardened and violent youthful offenders, more patrol officers and specialized juvenile officers, and joint efforts by juveniles and criminal justice employees in addressing the issues of concern to them.

The Legal Rights of Adolescents

- More watchdog efforts are needed at the various stages of federal, state, and local governments as well as with the system of justice to ensure that juveniles rights are not violated when brought into the system.
- The juvenile court needs to become more uniform in its processes and procedures nationwide when dealing with juvenile cases.
- Greater education is needed by personnel in law enforcement agencies, the courts, and correctional systems to more fully understand the due process rights of juveniles and adults.
- Legal challenges must continue in an effort to grant juveniles more of their constitutional rights.

The Juvenile Justice System

- Administrators must implement new policies aimed at making the juvenile justice system more efficient and responsive to the needs of both juveniles and society.
- Accusations of discriminatory or brutal justice system treatment against particular groups need to be better investigated and acted upon accordingly.
- More minority and female personnel are needed in all stages of the criminal and juvenile justice systems.
- Higher education must become a required prerequisite for all staff in the various levels of the juvenile justice system to better reflect new research and techniques aimed at understanding juveniles, their problems and concerns, as well as gaining a broader grasp of other subject matter relevant to a changing culture.
- The correctional philosophy needs to focus more on community-based programs and treatment for juvenile offenders.
- Juvenile corrections need to develop more improved rehabilitative techniques and broaden educational and occupational training.
- Detention facilities need to be established for violent and chronic juvenile offenders, separating them from status and minor offenders as well as adult offenders.
- Juvenile offenders should not be confined in adult jails or prisons.
- Status offenders need to be removed completely from the jurisdiction of the juvenile court.

Juvenile Delinquency Research

- More empirical study is needed on addressing juvenile delinquency with respect to sociodemographic characteristics such as race, gender, and age correlates and their interrelationship.
- More sophisticated research is needed on theories of delinquency and the interactional dynamics of delinquent behavior.
- The hidden delinquency of the middle and upper classes should be more comprehensively examined.
- The role of discrimination relative to race, class, and gender must be explored more closely.
- Greater attention needs to be devoted amongst criminological researchers on preventative theories and research.
- Researchers should place more attention on examining the future of adolescent crime.
- Juvenile delinquency researchers need to incorporate more in their studies on possible dynamics of delinquency rarely addressed such as the role of siblings, television, the media, authority figures, racism, and free will in juvenile misbehavior.

- More literature is needed in which juveniles and delinquents give their views on crime, delinquency, background correlates, concerns, etc.

The most substantive trends in juvenile justice in recent years have been the advances made through due process, diversion, decriminalization, and deinstitutionalization. As we move toward the 1990s, due process and decriminalization figure to be issues that will remain most prominent in shaping juvenile justice policies. Diversion and deinstitutionalization are less popular these days, but also should play some role in the future direction taken in crime and delinquency control.

Federal legislation in the 1970s and 1980s has paved the way for state and local laws designed to more effectively deal with juvenile delinquency and child abuse, neglect, and exploitation. Juvenile justice system practices and local and national efforts to fight juvenile crime and victimization also reflect federal efforts as well as a growing awareness of adolescent rights, delinquency, violence by youths, and victimized and exploited youth. Innovative and aggressive moves are necessary in the 1990s to continue progress in the areas of reducing adolescent crime and improving juvenile justice.

Chapter Notes

Chapter 1. Measurement and Characteristics

1. Amended Ch. 1748, Stats. 1971.
2. Amended Ch. 1748, Stats. 1971.
3. Task Force on Juvenile Justice and Delinquency Prevention, *Juvenile Justice and Delinquency Prevention* (Washington, D.C.: U.S. Government Printing Office, 1977), p. 297.
4. U.S. Department of Justice, Bureau of Justice Statistics.
5. Donna Hamparian et al., *Youth in Adult Courts: Between Two Worlds* (Columbus, Ohio: Academy of Contemporary Problems, 1983), p. 24.
6. Ronald B. Flowers, *Children and Criminality: The Child as Victim and Perpetrator* (Westport, Conn.: Greenwood Press, 1986), p. 119.
7. Ibid., p. 118.
8. Donald J. Black and Albert J. Reiss, Jr., "Police Control of Juveniles," *American Sociological Review* 35 (1970): pp. 63–67.
9. William B. Sanders, *Juvenile Delinquency: Causes, Patterns and Reactions* (New York: Holt, Rinehart and Winston, 1981), p. 5.
10. Paul A. Strasberg, Violent Delinquents: A Report to the *Ford Foundation from the Vera Institute of Justice* (New York: Monarch, 1978), p. 41.
11. Federal Bureau of Investigation, *Crime in the United States: Uniform Crime Reports 1986* (Washington, D.C.: U.S. Government Printing Office, 1987), p. 183.
12. Ibid., p. 186.
13. Howard N. Snyder and Terrence A. Finnegan, *Delinquency in the United States 1983* (Pittsburgh: National Center for Juvenile Justice, 1987); Department of Justice, *Report of the National Juvenile Justice Assessment Centers* (Washington, D.C.: U.S. Department of Justice, 1981, p. 144.
14. Marc LeBlanc, "Delinquency as an Epiphenomenon of Adolescence," in Raymond R. Corrado, Marc LeBlanc, and Jean Trepanier, eds., *Current Issues in Juvenile Justice* (Toronto: Butterworths, 1980), pp. 31–35.
15. Peter C. Kratcoski and Lucille Dunn Kratcoski, *Juvenile Delinquency,* 2nd ed. (Englewood Cliffs, N.J.: Prentice-Hall, 1986), p. 11.
16. Gary Jensen and Raymond Eve, "Sex Differences in Delinquency, An Examination of Popular Sociological Explanations," *Criminology* 13 (1976): pp. 427–448.
17. Martin Gold and David J. Reimer, "Changing Patterns of Delinquent Behavior Among Americans 13 Through 16 Years Old: 1967–72," *Crime and Delinquency* 7 (1975): pp. 483–517.
18. Department of Justice, Office of Juvenile Justice and Delinquency Prevention, *Juvenile Justice Before and After the Onset of Delinquency* (Washington, D.C.: U.S. Government Printing Office, 1980), pp. 12–13.
19. Steve Cernkovich and Peggy Giordano, "A Comparative Analysis of Male and Female Delinquency," *Sociological Quarterly* 20 (1979): pp. 131–145.

20. Calvin J. Larson, *Crime, Justice and Society* (Bayside, N.Y.: General Hall, 1984), p. 201.

21. Department of Justice, *Criminal Victimization in the United States, 1985: A National Crime Survey Report* (Washington, D.C.: U.S. Government Printing Office, 1987), pp. 5, 38, 42.

22. American Correctional Association, "Juveniles Commit One-Fourth of Violent Personal Crimes," *On the Line* 42, 7 (1981): pp. 11–12.

23. Department of Justice, *Report to the Nation on Crime and Justice: The Data* (Washington, D.C.: Bureau of Justice Statistics, 1983), p. 32.

24. Kratcoski and Kratcoski, *Juvenile Delinquency*, p. 17.

25. *Uniform Crime Reports*, p. 169.

26. *Report to the Nation on Crime*, p. 33.

27. Peter Applebome, "Juvenile Crime: The Offenders Are Younger and the Offenses More Serious," *New York Times* (February 3, 1987), p. A16.

28. Charles H. Shiremen and Frederic G. Reamer, *Rehabilitating Juvenile Justice* (New York: Columbia University Press, 1986), p. 20.

29. Edwin W. Sutherland and Donald R. Cressey, *Criminology*, 10th ed. (Philadelphia: J.B. Lippincott, 1978), p. 29.

30. Flowers, *Children and Criminality*, p. 23.

Chapter 2. Violent Offender

1. Pat Murkland, "Girl's Confession to Killing: 'We Wanted to Go Out and Celebrate'," *Sacramento Bee* (July 30, 1983): p. A12.

2. U.S. Federal Bureau of Investigation, *Crime in the United States: Uniform Crime Reports 1986* (Washington, D.C.: Government Printing Office, 1987), p. 180.

3. Ibid., p. 154.

4. Peter Applebome, "Juvenile Crime: The Offenders Are Younger and the Offenses More Serious," *New York Times* (February 3, 1987): p. A16.

5. *Uniform Crime Reports*, pp. 176, 178.

6. Ibid., p. 183.

7. Ibid., p. 186.

8. Isabel Wilkerson, "Crime-jaded Detroiters Jolted by Surge in Teen Violence," *Sacramento Bee* (May 9, 1987): p. A2.

9. Richard Herrnstein as quoted in Wilkerson.

10. Lynn A. Curtis, *Criminal Violence* (Lexington, Mass.: Lexington Books, 1974), pp. 20–24, 28–36.

11. U.S. Department of Justice, Bureau of Justice Statistics, *Report to the Nation on Crime and Justice: The Data* (Washington, D.C.: Government Printing Office, 1983).

12. U.S. Department of Justice, *Criminal Victimization in the United States, 1985: A National Crime Survey Report* (Washington, D.C.: Government Printing Office, 1987), p. 5, 38, 43.

13. Jeff Coplon, "Young, Bad & Dangerous," *Ladies' Home Journal* 103 (1986): p. 166.

14. Peter C. Kratcoski, "Perspectives on Intrafamily Violence," *Human Relations* 37, 8 (1984): pp. 443–454.

15. See, for example, James M. Sorrells, "Kids Who Kill," *Crime and Delinquency* 23, 2 (1977): pp. 312–320; Ronald B. Flowers, *Children and Criminality: The Child as Victim and Perpetrator* (Westport, Conn.: Greenwood Press, 1986).

16. Marvin E. Wolfgang and Franco Ferracuti, *The Subculture of Violence: Toward and Integrated Theory in Criminology* (London: Tavistock, 1967); Franco Ferracuti and Marvin Wolfgang, *Violence in Sardinia* (Rome: Bulzoni, 1970), p. 71.

17. Robert Mawson, "Aggression, Attachment, Behavior, and Crimes of Violence," in Travis Hirschi and Michael Gottfredson, eds., *Understanding Crime* (Beverly Hills: Sage, 1981), p. 12.

18. Donna Hamparian et al., *The Violent Few* (Lexington, Mass.: Lexington Books, 1978), p. 210.

19. As cited in Glenn Collins, "The Violent Child: Some Patterns Emerge," *New York Times* (September 27, 1982).

20. Jonathan Pincus as quoted in Collins.

21. D. Sargeant, "Children Who Kill — A Family Conspiracy?" in J. Howells, ed., *Theory and Practice of Family Psychiatry* (New York: Brunner-Mazel, 1971).

22. L. Bender and F. J. Curran, "Children and Adolescents Who Kill," *Journal of Criminal Psychopathology* 1, 4 (1940): p. 297.

23. C. H. King, "The Ego and the Integration of Violence in Homicidal Youth," *American Journal of Orthopsychiatry* 45 (1975): pp. 134–145.

24. Richard Gelles as quoted in "Parental Abuse," *USA Today* (March 18, 1983): p. A6.

25. Flowers, *Children and Criminality,* pp. 52–53.

26. Carol A. Warren, "Parent Batterers: Adolescent Violence and the Family," paper presented at the annual meeting of the Pacific Sociological Association, Anaheim, Calif. (April, 1978): pp. 3–5.

27. P. Hellsten and O. Katila, "Murder and Other Homicide, by Children Under 15 in Finland," *Psychiatric Quarterly Supplement* 39, 1 (1965): pp. 54–74; R. Campbell, "Violence in Adolescence," *Journal of Analytical Psychology* 12, 2 (1967): pp. 161–173.

28. Suzanne K. Steinmetz, "The Use of Force for Resolving Family Conflict: The Training Ground for Abuse," *Family Coordinator* 26 (1977): p. 19.

29. Murray A. Straus, Richard J. Gelles, and Suzanne K. Steinmetz, *Behind Closed Doors: Violence in the American Family* (Garden City, N.Y.: Doubleday/Anchor, 1979).

30. Wolfgang Pindus, quoted in "Kids, Crime and Punishment," *U.S. News & World Report* (August 24, 1987): p. 50.

31. David Dunlap, quoted in Mary Jordan, "More Juveniles Being Tried as Adults," *Washington Post* (December 30, 1984): p. A6.

32. Mark Moore, quoted in Ibid.

Chapter 3. Property Crime

1. J. F. Short, Jr., *Gang Delinquency and Delinquent Subcultures* (New York: Harper & Row, 1968), p. 79.

2. Howard N. Snyder and Terrence A. Finnegan, *Delinquency in the United States* (Pittsburgh: National Center for Juvenile Justice, 1987), p. 7.

3. "Jake" (the name has been changed) is a profile of a case study done by Cheryl Carpenter, Barry Glassner, Bruce D. Johnson, and Julia Loughlin, *Kids, Drugs, and Crime* (Lexington, Mass.: Lexington Books, 1988), pp. 121–133.

4. The Evan profile is based on my interview with an inmate in the California correctional system.

5. U.S. Federal Bureau of Investigation, *Crime in the United States: Uniform Crime Reports 1986* (Washington, D.C.: Government Printing Office, 1987), pp. 176, 178.

6. Ibid., p. 28.

7. Ibid., pp. 29, 31.

8. Ibid., p. 24.

9. C. E. Pope, *Crime-Specific Analysis: An Empirical Examination of Burglary Offense and Offense Characteristics* (Washington, D.C.: U.S. Government Printing Office, 1977).

10. C. E. Pope, *Crime-Specific Analysis: An Empirical Examination of Burglary Offender Characteristics* (Washington, D.C.: U.S. Government Printing Office, 1977).

11. Ibid.

12. *Uniform Crime Reports,* pp. 33, 180.

13. Carpenter, Glassner, Johnson, and Loughlin, *Kids, Drugs, and Crime,* p. 83.

14. *Uniform Crime Reports,* p. 36; M. Karter, "Fire Losses in the United States During 1981," *Fire Journal* **76** (1982): pp. 68–86.

15. *Uniform Crime Reports,* p. 37.

16. Ibid., p. 38.

17. E. Robbins and L. Robbins, "Arson with Special Reference to Pyromania," *New York State Journal of Medicine* **2** (1964): pp. 795–798; J. Boudreau, Q. Kwan, W. Faragher, and G. Denault, *Arson and Arson Investigation* (Washington, D.C.: U.S. Government Printing Office, 1977).

Chapter 4. Status Offender

1. President's Commission on Law Enforcement and Administration of Justice, *Task Force Report: Juvenile Delinquency and Youth Crime* (Washington, D.C.: U.S. Government Printing Office, 1967).

2. American Bar Association, *Juvenile Justice Standards Project* (Chicago, American Bar Association, 1979); Don C. Gibbons and Marvin D. Krohn, *Delinquent Behavior,* 4th ed. (Englewood Cliffs, N.J.: Prentice-Hall, 1986), p. 23.

3. Gibbons and Krohn, *Delinquent Behavior,* p. 23.

4. Charles P. Smith et al., *A Preliminary National Assessment of the Status Offender and the Juvenile Justice System: Role Conflicts, Constraints, and Information Gaps* (Washington, D.C.: U.S. Department of Justice, 180), p. 30.

5. Ted H. Rubin, "Retain the Juvenile Court? Legislative Developments, Reform Directions and the Call for Abolition," *Crime and Delinquency* **25** (1979): p. 283.

6. Howard N. Snyder and Terrence A. Finnegan, *Delinquency in the United States 1983* (Pittsburgh: National Center for Juvenile Justice, 1987), pp. 3–4, 18–19.

7. "PINS May Be Placed in State Training Schools," *Juvenile Court Digest* **6**, 13 (1975): p. 418; James C. Latina and Jeffrey L. Schembera, "Volunteer Homes for Status Offenders: An Alternative to Detention," *Federal Probation* **40**, 4 (1976): p. 45.

8. U.S. Federal Bureau of Investigation, *Crime in the United States: Uniform Crime Reports 1986* (Washington, D.C.: Government Printing Office, 1987), pp. 176, 178.

9. Snyder and Finnegan, *Delinquency in the United States 1983,* p. 20.

10. Ibid., p. 25.

11. Ibid., p. 1.

12. Ibid., p. 1.

13. Ronald B. Flowers, *Children and Criminality: The Child as Victim and Perpetrator* (Westport, Conn.: Greenwood Press, 1986) p. 131–134; Michael Satchel, "Kids for Sale," *Parade Magazine* (July 20, 1986): pp. 4–6.

14. Tim Brennan, *The Social Psychology of Runaways* (Toronto: Lexington Books, 1978), p. 5.

15. *Uniform Crime Reports,* pp. 176, 178.

16. C. J. English, "Leaving Home: A Typology of Runaways," *Society* **10** (1973): pp. 22–24.

17. "'Runaways,' 'Throwaways,' 'Bag Kids'—An Army of Drifter Teens," *U.S. News & World Report* (March 11, 1985): p. 53.

18. "'Rat Pack' Youth: Teenage Rebels in Suburbia," *U.S. News & World Report* (March 11, 1985): p. 54.

19. Robin Lloyd, *For Money or Love: Boy Prostitution in America* (New York: Ballantine, 1976), pp. 58–72.

20. June Bucy as quoted in Dotson Rader, "I Want to Die So I Won't Hurt No More," *Parade Magazine* (August 18, 1985): p. 4.

21. Rader, pp. 5–6.

22. Patricia Hersch, "Coming of Age on City Streets," *Psychology Today* (January, 1988): p. 34.

Chapter 5. Prostitution and Pornography

1. Michael Satchel, "Kids for Sale," *Parade Magazine* (July 20, 1986): p. 4.

2. Ronald B. Flowers, *Children and Criminality: The Child as Victim and Perpetrator* (Westport, Conn.: Greenwood Press, 1986), pp. 80–81.

3. Cited in Sam Meddis, "Teen Prostitution Rising, Study Says," *USA Today* (April 23, 1984): p. 3A.

4. See, for example, Flowers, *Children and Criminality;* Satchel, "Kids for Sale"; Frances Newman and Paula J. Caplan, "Juvenile Female Prostitution as a Gender Consistent Response to Early Deprivation," *International Journal of Women's Studies* 5, 2 (1981): pp. 128–137.

5. Ellen Hale, "Center Studies Causes of Juvenile Prostitution," *Gannett News Service* (May 21, 1981).

6. Paul H. Hahn, *The Juvenile Offender and the Law,* 3rd ed. (Cincinnati: Anderson, 1984), p. 125.

7. U.S. Federal Bureau of Investigation, *Crime in the United States: Uniform Crime Reports 1986* (Washington, D.C.: Government Printing Office, 1987), pp. 176, 178; Enablers, *Juvenile Prostitution in Minnesota: The Report of A Research Project* (St. Paul: The Enablers, 1978), p. 102.

8. Ronald B. Flowers, *Minorities and Criminality* (Westport, Conn.: Greenwood Press, 1988); Sol Gordon, *The Sexual Adolescent* (North Scituate, Mass.: Duxbury Press, 1973), p. 83.

9. *Uniform Crime Reports,* p. 178; D. Kelly Weisberg, *Children of the Night: A Study of Adolescent Prostitution* (Lexington, Mass.: Lexington Books, 1985), pp. 86–87.

10. Jennifer James, *Entrance into Juvenile Prostitution* (Washington, D.C.: National Institute of Mental Health, 1980), p. 17.

11. *Uniform Crime Reports,* p. 178.

12. James, *Entrance into Juvenile Prostitution,* p. 29; Enablers, *Juvenile Prostitution,* p. 52; Weisberg, *Children of the Night,* p. 94.

13. Sparky Harlan, Luanne L. Rodgers, and Brian Slattery, *Male and Female Adolescent Prostitution: Huckleberry House Sexual Minority Youth Services Project* (Washington, D.C.: U.S. Department of Health and Human Services, 1981), p. 7.

14. Enablers, *Juvenile Prostitution,* p. 18.

15. James, *Entrance into Juvenile Prostitution,* p. 19.

16. Ibid., p. 19; Enablers, *Juvenile Prostitution,* p. 18; Mimi H. Silbert, *Sexual Assault of Prostitutes: Phase One* (Washington, D.C.: National Institute of Mental Health, 1980), p. 10.

17. James, *Entrance into Juvenile Prostitution,* p. 10; Silbert, *Sexual Assault,* p. 10.

18. Dorothy H. Bracey, *"Baby-Pros": Preliminary Profiles of Juvenile Prostitutes* (New York: John Jay Press, 1979), p. 19; Diana Gray, "Turning Out: A Study of Teenage Prostitution," *Urban Life and Culture* 1, 4 (1973): p. 405.

19. Silbert, *Sexual Assault,* p. 15.

20. James, *Entrance into Juvenile Prostitution,* p. 18; Jennifer James, *Entrance into Juvenile Prostitution: Progress Report, June 1978* (Washington, D.C.: National Institute of Mental Health, 1978), p. 53.

21. Maura G. Crowley, "Female Runaway Behavior and Its Relationship to Prostitution," Masters thesis, Sam Houston State University, Institute of Contemporary Corrections and Behavioral Sciences, 1977, p. 63.

22. James, *Entrance into Juvenile Prostitution,* p. 88.

23. Harlan, Rodgers, and Slattery, *Male and Female Adolescent Prostitution,* p. 14.

24. Ibid., p. 15.

25. Diana Gray, "Turning Out: A Study of Teenage Prostitution," Masters thesis, University of Washington, 1971, p. 25.

26. Crowley, "Female Runaway Behavior," pp. 73–74.

27. See, for example, Newman and Caplan, "Juvenile Female Prostitution", p. 131. Katherine MacVicar and Marcia Dillon, "Childhood and Adolescent Development of Ten Female Prostitutes," *Journal of the American Academy of Child Psychiatry* 19, 1 (1980): pp. 148–149.

28. Flowers, *Children and Criminality;* Ronald B. Flowers, *Women and Criminality: The Woman as Victim, Offender, and Practitioner* (Westport, Conn.: Greenwood Press, 1987); Joseph J. Peters, "Children Who Are Victims of Sexual Assault and the Psychology of Offenders," *American Journal of Psychotherapy* 30 (1976): pp. 398–421.

29. Harlan, Rodgers, and Slattery, *Male and Female Adolescent Prostitution,* p. 21.

30. Ibid., p. 15; Crowley, "Female Runaway Behavior," p. 63.

31. James, *Entrance into Juvenile Prostitution,* p. 68.

32. Bracey, *"Baby-Pros,"* p. 23.

33. Enablers, *Juvenile Prostitution,* p. 57.

34. Bracey, *"Baby-Pros,"* p. 23.

35. Enablers, *Juvenile Prostitution,* p. 70; Silbert, *Sexual Assault,* p. 60; Weisberg, *Children of the Night,* pp. 96–97, 105–106.

36. Enablers, *Juvenile Prostitution,* p. 20; James, *Entrance into Juvenile Prostitution,* pp. 78–79.

37. Weisberg, *Children of the Night,* p. 107.

38. Ibid., pp. 101–103; V. W. Wilson, "A Psychological Study of Juvenile Prostitutes," *International Journal of Social Psychiatry* 5, no. 1 (1959): p. 69.

39. James, *Entrance into Juvenile Prostitution,* p. 68.

40. Ibid., p. 80; Silbert, *Sexual Assault,* p. 56.

41. Bracey, *"Baby-Pros,"* p. 23.

42. Allen M. Mistiak, quoted in Ellen Hale, "Center Studies."

43. "Prostitutes: The New Breed," *Newsweek* (July 12, 1971): p. 78.

44. As quoted in Clemens Bartollas, *Juvenile Delinquency* (New York: John Wiley & Sons, 1985), p. 342.

45. James, *Juvenile Prostitution: Progress Report.*

46. Weisberg, *Children of the Night,* pp. 117–119; Enablers, *Juvenile Prostitution,* p. 89; Silbert, *Sexual Assault,* p. 48.

47. Weisberg, *Children of the Night,* p. 118.

48. Crowley, "Female Runaway Behavior," p. 80; Harlan, Rodgers, and Slattery, *Male and Female Adolescent Prostitution,* pp. 22–23.

49. Enablers, *Juvenile Prostitution,* p. 75.

50. Ibid.; Flowers, *Children and Criminality,* pp. 81–82; Bracey, *"Baby-Pros."*

51. Flowers, *Women and Criminality;* Bracey, *"Baby-Pros,"* pp. 61–62; Silbert, *Sexual Assault,* p. 62.

52. Flowers, *Children and Criminality;* Flowers, *Women and Criminality;* Kenneth Wooden, *Weeping in the Playtime of Others* (New York: McGraw-Hill, 1976); Peter C. Kratcoski, "Differential Treatment of Delinquent Boys and Girls in Juvenile Court," *Child Welfare* 53, 1 (1984): pp. 16–22.

53. Robin Lloyd, *For Love or Money: Boy Prostitution in America* (New York: Vanguard, 1976), p. 211.

54. Weisberg, *Children of the Night,* p. 19.

55. Ibid., p. 40.

56. Hilary Abramson, "Sociologists Try to Reach Young Hustlers," *Sacramento Bee* (September 3, 1984): p. A8.

57. Cited in Tamar Stieber, "The Boys Who Sell Sex to Men in San Francisco," *Sacramento Bee* (March 4, 1984): p. A22.

58. Weisberg, *Children of the Night,* p. 61.

59. Harlan, Rodgers, and Slattery, *Male and Female Adolescent Prostitution,* p. 22.

60. Donald M. Allen, "Young Male Prostitutes: A Psychosocial Study," *Archives of Sexual Behavior* 9, 5 (1980).

61. Weisberg, *Children of the Night,* p. 58.
62. D. Sweeney, cited in Stieber, "The Boys Who Sell Sex to Men."
63. Weisberg, *Children of the Night,* pp. 124–128.
64. Ibid., p. 75.
65. Patricia Hersch, "Coming of Age on City Streets," *Psychology Today* (January, 1988), p. 37.
66. Cited in Ronald B. Flowers, "Violent Women: Are They Catching up to Violent Men or Have They Surpassed Them?," an unpublished article, June, 1988.
67. Ibid.
68. Quoted by Trudee Able-Peterson, director of an outreach program in New York in Hersch, "Coming of Age," p. 35.
69. Hersch, "Coming of Age," pp. 28–37.
70. Flowers, *Children and Criminality,* p. 81; Shirley O'Brien, *Child Pornography* (Dubuque, Iowa: Kendall/Hunt, 1983), p. 15; Judianne Densen-Gerber, "Child Prostitution and Child Pornography: Medical, Legal, and Societal Aspects of the Commercial Exploitation of Children," in *Sexual Abuse of Children: Selected Readings* (Washington, D.C.: U.S. Department of Health and Human Services, 1980).
71. O'Brien, *Child Pornography,* p. 19; M. Guio, A. Burgess, and R. Kelly, "Child Victimization: Pornography and Prostitution," *Journal of Crime and Justice* 3 (1980): pp. 65–81.
72. Flowers, *Children and Criminality,* p. 82.
73. Ibid.
74. Ibid.

Chapter 6. Delinquency of Females

1. U.S. Federal Bureau of Investigation, *Crime in the United States: Uniform Crime Reports 1986* (Washington, D.C.: Government Printing Office, 1987), p. 178.
2. Ibid., pp. 176, 178.
3. Howard N. Snyder and Terrence A. Finnegan, *Delinquency in the United States 1983* (Pittsburgh: National Center for Juvenile Justice, 1987), pp. 18, 20.
4. Ibid., p. 21.
5. Ronald B. Flowers, *Minorities and Criminality* (Westport, Conn.: Greenwood Press, 1988).
6. Suzanne S. Ageton, "The Dynamics of Female Delinquency, 1976–1980," *Criminology* 21 (1983): pp. 577–578; Stephen A. Cernokovich and Peggy C. Giordano, "A Comparative Analysis of Male and Female Delinquency," *Sociological Quarterly* 20 (1979): p. 142.
7. Cernkovich and Giordano, "A Comparative Analysis," pp. 142–143.
8. Stephen A. Cernkovich and Peggy C. Giordano, "Delinquency, Opportunity, and Gender," *Journal of Criminal Law and Criminology* 70 (1979): p. 150.
9. Nancy Wise, "Juvenile Delinquency Among Middle-Class Girls," in *Middle Class Juvenile Delinquency* (New York: Harper & Row, 1967).
10. F. Ivan Nye and James F. Short, "Scaling Delinquent Behavior," *American Sociological Review* 22 (1958): pp. 326–332.
11. Cernkovich and Giordano, "A Comparative Analysis," pp. 131–145.
12. Peter C. Kratcoski and John E. Kratcoski, "Changing Patterns in the Delinquent Activities of Boys and Girls: A Self-Reported Delinquency Analysis," *Adolescence* 10, 37 (1975): pp. 38–91.
13. Ageton, "The Dynamics of Female Delinquency," pp. 555–584; Ronald B. Flowers, *Demographics and Criminality: The Characteristics of Crime in America* (Westport, Conn.: Greenwood Press, 1989).

14. See, for example, J. R. Williams and Martin Gold, "From Delinquent Behavior to Official Delinquency," *Social Problems* 20 (1972): p. 213; Rachelle J. Canter, "Family Correlates of Male and Female Delinquency," *Criminology* 20, 2 (1982): pp. 149–167.

15. Cited in Clemens Bartollas, *Juvenile Delinquency* (New York: John Wiley & Sons, 1985), p. 335; Patricia J. Miller, "Gender, Delinquency and Social Control," mimeographed.

16. Martin Gold and David J. Reimer, *Changing Patterns of Delinquent Behavior Among Americans 13 to 16 Years Old, 1967–1972* (Ann Arbor, Mich.: Institute for Social Research, 1974).

17. Illinois Institute for Juvenile Research, *Juvenile Delinquency in Illinois* (Chicago: Illinois Department of Mental Health, 1972).

18. Darrell J. Steffensmeier and Renee Hoffman Steffensmeier, "Trends in Female Delinquency: An Examination of Arrest, Juvenile Court, Self-Report, and Field Data," *Criminology* 18 (1980): pp. 22–23.

19. Ageton, "The Dynamics of Female Delinquency," pp. 555–584.

20. Flowers, *Demographics and Criminality.*

21. Freda Adler, *Sisters in Crime: The Rise of the New Female Criminal* (New York: McGraw-Hill, 1975), p. 15.

22. Ibid., p. 106.

23. See, for example, Flowers, *Demographics and Criminality;* Eileen B. Leonard, *Women, Crime, and Society: A Critique of Theoretical Criminology* (New York: Longman, 1982).

24. Steffensmeier and Steffensmeier, "Trends in Female Delinquency."

25. Leonard, *Women, Crime and Society;* Joseph G. Weis, "Liberation and Crime: The Invention of the New Female Criminal," *Crime and Social Justice* 6 (1976): pp. 17–27; Laura Crites, "Women Offenders: Myth vs. Reality," in Laura Crites, ed., *The Female Offender* (Lexington, Mass.: Lexington Books, 1976), pp. 36–39.

26. *Uniform Crime Reports 1986;* U.S. Federal Bureau of Investigation, *Crime in the United States: Uniform Crime Reports 1960* (Washington, D.C.: Government Printing Office, 1961).

27. Ibid.; Flowers, *Demographics and Criminality.*

28. Cernkovich and Giordano, "A Comparative Analysis," p. 139.

29. Flowers, *Demograhics and Criminality;* Ronald B. Flowers, *Children and Criminality: The Child as Victim and Perpetrator* (Westport, Conn.: Greenwood Press, 1986), pp. 117–129.

30. Rita Simon, *Women and Crime* (Lexington, Mass.: D.C. Heath, 1975), p. 42.

31. See Ronald B. Flowers, *Women and Criminality: The Woman as Victim, Offender, and Practitioner* (Westport, Conn.: Greenwood Press, 1987), pp. 102–103; George W. Noblit and Janie M. Burcart, "Women and Crime, 1960–1970," *Social Science Quarterly* 56 (1976): pp. 656–657.

32. Flowers, *Women and Criminality; Uniform Crime Reports 1986,* pp. 169, 178.

33. *Uniform Crime Reports 1986; Uniform Crime Reports 1960.*

34. Michael Hindelang, "Age, Sex, and the Versatility of Delinquency Involvement," *Social Problems* 18 (1971): p. 533.

35. Kratcoski and Kratcoski, "Changing Patterns in the Delinquent Activities of Boys and Girls," p. 88.

36. Gary J. Jensen and Raymond Eve, "Sex Differences in Delinquency," *Criminology* 13, 4 (1976): pp. 427–448.

37. Ibid.

38. Suzanne S. Ageton and Delbert S. Elliot, *The Incidence of Delinquent Behavior in a National Probability Sample of Adolescents* (Boulder, Colo.: Behavioral Research Institute, 1978).

39. Williams and Gold, "From Delinquent Behavior to Official Delinquency."

40. See Table 6-1; Flowers, *Children and Criminality;* Anne Campbell, *Girl Delinquents* (New York: St. Martin's Press, 1981).

41. Cited in Flowers, *Children and Criminality*, p. 139.

42. Cheryl Carpenter, Barry Glassner, Bruce D. Johnson, and Julia Loughlin, *Kids, Drugs, and Crime* (Lexington, Mass.: Lexington Books, 1988), p. 140.

43. D. Hoffman-Bustamante, "The Nature of Female Criminality," *Issues in Criminology* **8** (1973): pp. 117–136.

44. Campbell, *Girl Delinquents*, p. 127.

45. Ibid., p. 131.

46. Cesare, Lombroso, *The Female Offender* (New York: Appleton, 1920).

47. T. C. N. Gibbens, "Female Offenders," *British Journal of Hospital Medicine* **6** (1971): pp. 279–286.

48. J. Cowie, B. Cowie, and E. Slater, *Delinquency in Girls* (London: Heinemann, 1968).

49. R. Barri Flowers, "Violent Women: Are They Catching up to Violent Men or Have They Surpassed Them?" on microfiche with *ERIC Clearinghouse for Social Studies/Social Science Education;* K. Dalton, "Menstruation and Crime," *British Medical Journal* **2** (1961): pp. 1752–1753; R. M. Carney and B. D. Williams, "Premenstrual Syndrome: A Criminal Defense," *Notre Dame Law Review* **59** (1983): pp. 253–269.

50. William I. Thomas, *The Unadjusted Girl: With Cases and Standpoint for Behavior Analysis* (New York: Harper & Row, 1923).

51. Sigmund Freud, *New Introductory Lectures on Psychoanalysis* (New York: W. W. Norton, 1933); Sigmund Freud, *An Outline of Psychoanalysis in James Strachey,* trans. (New York: W. W. Norton, 1949).

52. Cited in Flowers, *Women and Criminality*, p. 94.

53. Gisela Konopka, *The Adolescent Girl in Conflict* (Englewood Cliffs, N.J.: Prentice-Hall, 1966).

54. See, for example, Clyde Vedder and Dora Somerville, *The Delinquent Girl* (Springfield, Ill.: Charles C. Thomas, 1970); Emily Werner and Ruth S. Smith, *Kauai's Children Come of Age* (Honolulu: University Press of Hawaii, 1977).

55. Sheldon Glueck and Eleanor T. Glueck, *Five Hundred Delinquent Women* (New York: Alfred A. Knopf, 1934).

56. Otto Pollak, *The Criminality of Women* (Philadelphia: University of Pennsylvania Press, 1950).

57. Susan K. Datesman, Frank R. Scarpitti, and Richard M. Stephenson, "Female Delinquency: An Application of Self and Opportunity Theories," *Journal of Research in Crime and Delinquency* **12** (1975): p. 120.

58. Cernkovich and Giordano, "Delinquency, Opportunity, and Gender."

59. Adler, *Sisters in Crime.*

60. Rita Simon, *The Contemporary Woman and Crime* (Washington, D.C.: Government Printing Office, 1975).

61. Carol Smart, "The New Female Criminal: Reality or Myth," *British Journal of Criminology* **19** (1979): pp. 50–59.

62. Crites, "Women Offenders."

63. Weis, "Liberation and Crime."

64. Flowers, *Demographics and Criminality;* Ilene H. Nagel and John Hagan, "Gender and Crime: Offense Patterns and Criminal Court Sanctions," in Michael Toury and Norval Morris, eds., *Crime and Justice: An Annual Review of Research,* vol. 4 (Chicago: University of Chicago Press, 1983), pp. 91–144.

65. See, for example, Steven Schlossman and Stephanie Wallach, "The Crime of Precocious Sexuality: Female Juvenile Delinquency in the Progressive Era," *Harvard Educational Review* **48** (1978): pp. 65–94; Media Chesney-Lind, "Juvenile Delinquency: The Sexualization of Female Crime," *Psychology Today* **8** (1974): pp. 43–46; Etta A. Anderson, "The Chivalrous Treatment of the Female Offender in the Arms of the

Criminal Justice System: A Review of the Literature," *Social Problems* **23** (1976): pp. 350–357; Kenneth Wooden, *Weeping in the Playtime of Others* (New York: McGraw-Hill, 1976).

66. Kristine Olson Rodgers, "For Her Own Protection . . . Conditions of Incarceration for Female Offenders in the State of Connecticut," *Law and Society Review* **7** (1972): pp. 223–246; Gordon H. Baker and William T. Adams, "Comparison of the Delinquencies of Boys and Girls," *Journal of Criminal Law, Criminology, and Police Science* **53** (1972): pp. 470–475.

67. Peter C. Kratcoski and Lucille Kratcoski, *Juvenile Delinquency*, 2nd ed. (Englewood Cliffs, N.J.: Prentice-Hall, 1986) pp. 143–144.

Chapter 7. Substance Use

1. Cited in Ken Barun, "How to Help Your Children Stay Off Drugs," *Parade Magazine* (May 1, 1988): p. 15.

2. U.S. Federal Bureau of Investigation, *Crime in the United States: Uniform Crime Reports 1986* (Washington, D.C.: Government Printing Office, 1987), pp. 176, 178.

3. Ronald B. Flowers, *Minorities and Criminality* (Westport, Conn.: Greenwood Press, 1988).

4. Howard N. Snyder and Terrence A. Finnegan, *Delinquency in the United States 1983* (Pittsburgh, PA: National Center for Juvenile Justice, 1987), p. 25.

5. U.S. Federal Bureau of Investigation, *Crime in the United States: Uniform Crime Reports 1960* (Washington, D.C.: Government Printing Office, 1961).

6. Lloyd D. Johnson, Jerald G. Bachman, and Patrick M. O'Malley, *Highlights from Student Drug Use, 1975-80,* National Institute on Drug Abuse (Washington, D.C.: Government Printing Office, 1981), p. 22–24.

7. Lloyd D. Johnson, Jerald G. Bachman, and Patrick O'Malley, *Student Drug Use, Attitudes and Beliefs, National Trends, 1975-1982* (Washington, D.C.: Government Printing Office, 1983), pp. 24, 26, 28.

8. Cited in Martin R. Haskell and Lewis Yablonsky, *Juvenile Delinquency,* 3rd ed. (Boston: Houghton Mifflin, 1982), p. 337.

9. National Institute on Alcohol Abuse and Alcoholism, "Information and Feature Service Publication," 102 (December 1, 1982).

10. Cited in Paul W. Haberman and Michael M. Baden, *Alcohol, Other Drugs and Violent Death* (New York: Oxford University Press, 1978), pp. 18–19.

11. U.S. Department of Health, Education and Welfare, *The Special Report to the U.S. Congress on Alcohol and Drugs* (Washington, D.C.: Government Printing Office, 1978).

12. Peter C. Kratcoski and John E. Kratcoski, "Changing Patterns in the Delinquent Activities of Boys and Girls: A Self-Reported Delinquency Analysis," *Adolescence* **10**, 37 (1975): p. 87.

13. There is a gray area in the legal use of alcohol by adults since the legal drinking age varies between ages 18 and 21, depending upon the state; meaning that some persons who are adults in every other sense are unable by law to purchase or consume alcohol.

14. Haskell and Yablonsky, *Juvenile Delinquency,* p. 337.

15. Thomas D. Elias, "Law Would Park Teens at Midnight," *Cincinnati Post* (May 3, 1983).

16. Paul H. Hahn, *The Juvenile Offender and the Law,* 3rd ed. (Cincinnati: Anderson, 1984), p. 109.

17. Ibid., pp. 109–110.

18. Ibid.

19. "How to Stop Teen Drug Use," *Consumer's Research* **70**, 1 (1987): p. 27.

20. Ibid.

21. Barun, "How to Help Your Children Stay off Drugs"; U.S. Department of Health and Human Services, *A Drug Retrospective: 1961-1980* (Washington, D.C.: Government Printing Office, 1980).

22. Lloyd Johnson, Jerald G. Bachman, and Patrick M. O'Malley, *Drugs and the Nation's High Schools* (Rockville, Md.: U.S. Department of Health, Education and Welfare, 1979), pp. 23-30.

23. U.S. Department of Health, Education and Welfare, *Marijuana and Health: Sixth Annual Report to the U.S. Congress* (Washington, D.C.: Government Printing Office, 1977); U.S. Department of Health, Education and Welfare, *Marijuana and Health: Eighth Annual Report to the U.S. Congress* (Washington, D.C.: U.S. Government Printing Office, 1980).

24. Quoted in "Crack: A Cheap and Deadly Cocaine Is a Spreading Menace," *Time* **127** (June 2, 1986): p. 16.

25. Ibid., pp. 16-17.

26. "Cocaine Survey Shows Poorer, Younger Users," *Jet* (July 15, 1985): p. 31.

27. "Crack: A Cheap and Deadly Cocaine," p. 17.

28. Barun, "How to Help Your Children Stay off Drugs."

29. "Crack: A Cheap and Deadly Cocaine," p. 18.

30. Kratcoski and Kratcoski, "Changing Patterns in the Delinquent Activities," p. 87.

31. Nechama Tec, *Grass Is Green in Suburbia* (Roslyn Heights, N.Y.: Libra Publishers, 1974), p. 46.

32. See, for example, Hahn, *The Juvenile Offender,* pp. 110-111; Cheryl Carpenter, Barry Glassner, Bruce D. Johnson, and Julia Loughlin, *Kids, Drugs, and Crime* (Lexington, Mass.: Lexington Books, 1988); D. Kelly Weisberg, *Children of the Night: A Study of Adolescent Prostitution* (Lexington, Mass.: Lexington Books, 1985).

33. James Thorton, *Delinquency and Justice* (Glenview, Ill.: Scott Foresman and Co., 1982), p. 296.

34. Carpenter, Glassner, Johnson, and Loughlin, with Erica Wood, "Drug Selling and Dealing Among Adolescents," *Kids, Drugs, and Crime,* pp. 39-59.

35. Ibid., p. 39; Bruce D. Johnson, *Marijuana Users and Drug Subcultures* (New York: Wiley, 1973).

36. Bruce D. Johnson, Eric Wish, and David Huizinga, "The Concentration of Delinquent Offending: The Contribution of Serious Drug Involvement to High Rate Delinquency," in Bruce D. Johnson and Eric Wish, eds., *Crime Rates Among Drug Abusing Offenders* (New York: Interdisciplinary Research Center, 1986), pp. 106-143.

37. Carpenter, Glassner, Johnson, and Loughlin, *Kids, Drugs, and Crime,* pp. 44, 220-221.

38. Ibid., p. 42.

39. Quoted in Clemens Bartollas, *Juvenile Delinquency* (New York: John Wiley & Sons, 1985), p. 341.

40. Cited in Curtis J. Sltomer, "Drugs, Drink and Youth Crime," *Christian Science Monitor* (November 18, 1985): p. 3.

41. Carpenter, Glassner, Johnson, and Loughlin, *Kids, Drugs, and Crime;* Johnson, Wish, and Huizinga, "The Concentration of Delinquent Offending"; Ronald B. Flowers, *Children and Criminality: The Child as Victim and Perpetrator* (Westport, Conn.: Greenwood Press, 1986).

42. Carpenter, Glassner, Johnson, and Loughlin, *Kids, Drugs, and Crime,* p. 221; Johnson, Wish, and Huizinga, "The Concentration of Delinquent Offending."

43. Flowers, *Children and Criminality.*

44. Carpenter, Glassner, Johnson, and Loughlin, *Kids, Drugs, and Crime,* pp. 87-100.

45. Ibid., p. 62; Nicholas J. Kozel and Robert L. DuPont, *Criminal Charges and*

Drug Use Patterns of Arrestees in the District of Columbia (Rockville, Md.: National Institute on Drug Abuse, 1977); Ronald B. Flowers, *Demographics and Criminality: The Characteristics of Crime in America* (Westport, Conn.: Greenwood Press, 1989).

46. Carpenter, Glassner, Johnson, and Loughlin, *Kids, Drugs, and Crime*, p. 85.

47. Weisberg, *Children of the Night*, pp. 58–59, 117–119.

48. Flowers, *Children and Criminality*, pp. 81, 97, 134–137.

49. Ibid., p. 97.

50. See, for example, Enablers, *Juvenile Prostitution in Minnesota: The Report of a Research Project* (St. Paul: The Enablers, 1978); Mimi H. Silbert, *Sexual Assault of Prostitutes: Phase One* (Washington, D.C.: National Institute of Mental Health, 1980).

51. Flowers, *Children and Criminality*, p. 51.

52. Ibid., pp. 88, 97.

53. Ibid., p. 88; Jerry P. Flanzer, *The Many Faces of Family Violence* (Springfield, Ill.: Charles C. Thomas, 1982), pp. 36–38.

54. "Student Discipline," *Ohio Schools* 55, 11 (September 2, 1977): p. 15.

55. Kenneth Polk and Steven R. Burkett, "Drinking As Rebellion: A Study of Adolescent Drinking," in Kenneth Polk and Walter E. Schafer, eds., *Schools and Delinquency* (Englewood Cliffs, N.J.: Prentice-Hall, 1972), pp. 125–126.

56. Flowers, *Demographics and Criminality*.

57. "War on Alcohol Abuse Spreads to New Fronts," *U.S. News & World Report* 97 (December 24, 1984): p. 63.

58. "A 'Rite of Passage' More Young People Avoid," *Scholastic Update* 117 (May 10, 1985): pp. 14–15.

Chapter 8. Gang Delinquency

1. Frederick Thrasher, *The Gang* (Chicago: University of Chicago Press, 1927), p. 57.

2. Walter B. Miller, *Violence by Youth Gangs and Youth Groups as a Crime Problem in Major American Cities* (Washington, D.C.: Government Printing Office, 1975).

3. Lewis Yablonsky, *The Violent Gang* (Baltimore: Penguin Books, 1962).

4. John Quicker, "The Chicano Gang: A Preliminary Description," a paper presented to the Pacific Sociological Association, San Jose, California, 1974.

5. Yablonsky, *The Violent Gang*, p. 227.

6. Peter C. Kratcoski and Lucille Dunn Kratcoski, *Juvenile Delinquency*, 2nd ed. (Englewood Cliffs, N.J.: Prentice-Hall, 1986), p. 105.

7. Miller, *Violence by Youth Gangs;* Walter B. Miller, "Gangs, Groups and Serious Youth Crime," in David Schichor and Delos H. Kelly, eds., *Critical Issues in Juvenile Delinquency* (Lexington, Mass.: Lexington Books, 1980).

8. Miller, *Violence by Youth Gangs*, p. 17.

9. Ibid., pp. 21–23.

10. Peggy C. Giordano, "Girls, Guys, and Gangs: The Changing Social Context of Female Delinquency," *Journal of Criminal Law and Criminology* 69 (1978): p. 130.

11. Waln K. Brown, "Black Female Gangs in Philadelphia," *International Journal of Offender Therapy and Comparative Criminology* 21 (1970): pp. 221–229.

12. Miller, *Violence by Youth Gangs*.

13. Freda Adler, *Sisters in Crime: The Rise of the New Female Gang* (New York: McGraw-Hill, 1975), p. 99.

14. Anne Campbell as quoted in "On the Wild Side: Women in Gangs," *New York Times* (January 2, 1985): p. C8.

15. Ronald B. Flowers, *Children and Criminality: The Child as Victim and Perpetrator* (Westport, Conn.: Greenwood Press, 1986), pp. 148–149.

16. Ronald B. Flowers, *Minorities and Criminality* (Westport Conn.: Greenwood Press, 1988).

17. Ibid.; Miller, *Violence by Youth Gangs.*

18. Jim Morris, "Gangs at War in L.A. Streets," *Sacramento Bee* (October 19, 1986): Al; Peter Hecht, "1,000 Police Added to L.A.'s War on Gangs," *Sacramento Bee* (April 5, 1988): p. A12.

19. Morris, "Gangs at War."

20. Ibid.

21. Howard L. Myerhoff and Barbara G. Myerhoff, "Field Observation of Middle Class 'Gangs'," *Social Forces* **42** (1964): pp. 328–336.

22. Dale G. Hardman, "Small Town Gangs," *Journal of Criminal Law, Criminology and Police Science* **60**, 2 (1969): pp. 176–177.

23. Walter B. Miller, "White Gangs," in James F. Short, Jr., *Modern Criminals* (Chicago: Aldine, 1970), pp. 57, 60, 64.

24. Amy Chance, "New Tack in War on Gangs," *Sacramento Bee* (April 10, 1988): p. A26.

25. Robert Reinhold, "When Gang Violence Leaves the Ghetto," *Sacramento Bee* (February 8, 1988): p. A3.

26. Steve Valdivia, as quoted in Ibid.

27. Valdivia as quoted in Hecht, "1,000 Police Added to L.A.'s War on Gangs."

28. Flowers, *Minorities and Criminality.*

29. Robert Ruchhoft as quoted in Morris, "Gangs at War."

30. Ibid.

31. Albert K. Cohen, *Delinquent Boys: The Culture of the Gang* (New York: Free Press, 1955).

32. Ibid., pp. 36–44.

33. Albert K. Cohen and James F. Short, Jr., "Research on Delinquent Subcultures," *Journal of Social Issues* **14**, 3 (1958): pp. 20–37.

34. Richard A. Cloward and Lloyd E. Ohlin, *Delinquency and Opportunity: A Theory of Delinquent Gangs* (New York: Free Press, 1960).

35. Ibid., p. 80.

36. Ibid., p. 148.

37. Walter B. Miller, "Lower-Class Culture as a Generating Milieu of Gang Delinquency," *Journal of Social Issues* **14** (1958): pp. 5–19.

38. Ibid.

39. See, for example, Travis Hirschi, *Causes of Delinquency* (Berkeley: University of California Press, 1969).

40. Yablonsky, *The Violent Gang.*

Chapter 9. Biological Approaches

1. Cesare Lombroso and William Ferrero, *Criminal Man* (Montclair, N.J.: Patterson Smith, 1972). Originally titled *L'Uomo Delinquente* in its 1876 publication.

2. Charles Goring, *The English Convict: A Statistical Study* (Montclair, N.J.: Patterson Smith, 1972).

3. Ernest A. Hooton, *Crime and the Man* (Cambridge, Mass.: Harvard University Press, 1939).

4. William H. Sheldon, *Varieties of Temperament* (New York: Harper & Row, 1942).

5. Sheldon Glueck and Eleanor T. Glueck, *Physique and Delinquency* (New York: Harper & Row, 1956).

6. J. B. Cortes and F. M. Gatti, *Delinquency and Crime: A Biopsychosocial Approach* (New York: Seminar Press, 1972).

7. Richard Louis Dugdale, *The Jukes: A Study in Crime, Pauperism, and Heredity* (New York: Putnam, 1877).

8. Henry H. Goddard, *Feeblemindedness, Its Causes and Consequences* (New York: Macmillan, 1914).

9. Johannes Lange, *Crime as Destiny* (London: George Allen & Unwin, 1931). Originally published as *Vebrechen als Sochicksal* in 1928.

10. Karl O. Christiansen, "A Preliminary Study of Criminality Among Twins," in Sarnoff A. Mednick and Karl O. Christiansen, eds., *Biosocial Bases of Criminal Behavior* (New York: Gardner Press, 1977); Karl O. Christiansen, "Seriousness of Criminality and Concordance Among Danish Twins," in R. Hood, ed., *Crime, Criminology and Public Policy* (London: Heinemann, 1977).

11. Hans J. Eysench, *The Inequality of Man* (San Diego: Edits Publishers, 1973), p. 167.

12. Odd S. Dalgaard and Einar Kringlen, "A Norwegian Twin Study of Criminality," *British Journal of Criminology* 16 (1976): pp. 213-233.

13. F. Schulsinger, "Psychopathy: Heredity and Environment," *International Journal of Mental Health* 1 (1972): pp. 190-206.

14. Bernard Hutchings and Sarnoff A. Mednick, "Registered Criminality in the Adoptive and Biological Parents of Registered Male Criminal Adoptees," in R. R. Fiene, D. Rosenthal, and H. Brill, eds., *Genetic Research in Psychiatry* (Baltimore: John Hopkins University Press, 1975).

15. S. A. Mednick, W. F. Gabrielli, and B. Hutchings, "Genetic Influences in Criminal Convictions: Evidence from an Adoption Cohort," *Science* 234 (1984): pp. 891-894.

16. See, for example, A. A. Sandberg, G. F. Koepf, T. Ishiara and T. S. Hanschka, "An XYY Human Male," *Lancet* 262 (1961): pp. 488-489.

17. Herman A. Witkin et al., "XYY and XXY: Criminality and Aggression," in Sarnoff A. Mednick and Karl O. Christiansen, eds., *Biosocial Bases of Criminal Behavior* (New York: Gardner Press, 1977), pp. 165-187.

18. Ronald B. Flowers, *Minorities and Criminality* (Westport, Conn.: Greenwood Press, 1988).

19. Vicki Pollock, Sarnoff A. Mednick and William F. Gabrielli, Jr., "Crime Causation: Biological Theories," in Sanford H. Kadish, ed., *Encyclopedia of Crime and Justice*, Vol. 1 (New York: Free Press, 1983).

20. Ibid.

21. Harold R. Holzman, "Learning Disabilities and Juvenile Delinquency: Biological and Sociological Theories," in C. R. Jeffrey, ed., *Biology and Crime* (Beverly Hills: Sage, 1979), pp. 77-86; Charles A. Murray, The Link Between Learning Disabilities and Juvenile Delinquency (Washington, D.C.: U.S. Government Printing Office, 1976).

22. H. D. Kletschka, "Violent Behavior Associated with Brain Tumors," *Minnesota Medicine* 49 (1966): pp. 1835-1855.

23. See, for example, Andrea Dorfman, "The Criminal Mind: Body Chemistry and Nutrition May Lie at the Roots of Crime," *Science Digest* 92 (1984): pp. 44; Leonard J. Hippchen, ed., *Ecologic-Biochemical Approaches to Treatment of Delinquents and Criminals* (New York: Van Nostrand Reinhold, 1978).

Chapter 10. Psychological Propositions

1. Sigmund Freud, *New Introductory Lectures on Psychoanalysis* (New York: W. W. Norton, 1933).

2. August Aichorn, *Wayward Youth* (New York: Viking Press, 1935).

3. C. G. Schoenfeld, "A Psychoanalytic Theory of Juvenile Delinquency," in Edward E. Peoples, ed., *Readings in Correctional Casework and Counseling* (Pacific Palisades, Calif.: Goodyear, 1975), pp. 23-26.

4. Joseph F. Sheley, *America's "Crime Problem": An Introduction to Criminology* (Belmont, Calif.: Wadsworth, 1985), p. 202.

5. Cyril Burt, *The Young Delinquent* (London: University of London Press, 1938).

6. William Healy and Augusta F. Bronner, *New Light on Delinquency and Its Treatment* (New Haven: Yale University Press, 1936).

7. Gordon Waldo and Simon Dinitz, "Personality Attributes of the Criminal: An Analysis of Research Studies, 1950–1965," *Journal of Research in Crime and Delinquency* **4** (1967): pp. 185–202.

8. Michael Hakeem, "A Critique of the Psychiatric Approach," in Joseph S. Roucek, ed., *Juvenile Delinquency* (New York: Philosophical Library, 1958), pp. 89–95.

9. Clyde Sullivan, Marguerite Q. Grant, and J. Douglas Grant, "The Development of Interpersonal Maturity: Applications to Delinquency," *Psychiatry* **20** (1957): pp. 373–385.

10. William McCord and Joan McCord, *The Psychopath* (Princeton, N.J.: Van Nostrand, 1964).

11. Lee N. Robins, *Deviant Children Grown Up* (Baltimore: Williams and Wilkins, 1966).

12. Herbert C. Quay, "Crime Causation: Psychological Theories," in S. H. Kadish, ed., *Encyclopedia of Crime and Justice,* Vol. 1 (New York: Free Press, 1983), p. 340; Herbert C. Quay, "Patterns of Delinquent Behavior," in Herbert C. Quay, ed., *Handbook of Juvenile Delinquency* (New York: Wiley-Interscience, 1987), pp. 118–138.

13. Samuel Yochelson and Stanton E. Samenow, *The Criminal Personality,* Vol. 1 (New York: Jason Arsonson, 1976); Stanton E. Samenow, *Inside the Criminal Mind* (New York: Time Books, 1984).

14. See, for example, William Healy and Augusta F. Bronner, *Delinquency and Criminals: Their Making and Unmaking* (New York: Macmillan, 1926).

15. Travis Hirschi and Michael J. Hindelang, "Intelligence and Delinquency: A Revisionist Review," *American Sociological Review* **42** (1977): pp. 571–586.

16. R. Loeber and T. Dishion, "Early Predictors of Male Delinquency: A Review," *Psychological Bulletin* **94** (1983): pp. 68–99.

17. Martin R. Haskell and Lewis Yablonsky, *Juvenile Delinquency* (Chicago: Rand McNally, 1974), pp. 225–226.

18. President's Commission on Mental Health, *Report to the President,* Vol. 1 (Washington, D.C.: U.S. Government Printing Office, 1978), p. 9.

Chapter 11. Sociological Concepts

1. Robert E. Park and Ernest W. Burgess, *The City* (Chicago: University of Chicago Press, 1925).

2. Clifford R. Shaw and Henry D. McKay, *Juvenile Delinquency and Urban Areas* (Chicago: University of Chicago Press, 1969).

3. Frederic M. Thrasher, *The Gang* (Chicago: University of Chicago Press, 1927).

4. Travis Hirschi, *Causes of Delinquency* (Berkeley: University of California, 1969).

5. Walter C. Reckless, *The Crime Problem,* 5th ed. (Santa Monica: Goodyear, 1973); Walter C. Reckless, Simon Dinitz, and Ellen Murray, "Self-Concept as an Insulator Against Delinquency," in James E. Teele, ed., *Juvenile Delinquency: A Reader* (Itasca, Ill.: Peacock, 1970).

6. Gary F. Jensen, "Inner Containment and Delinquency," *Journal of Criminal Law and Criminology* **64** (1973): pp. 464–470.

7. Emile Durkheim, *The Division of Labor in Society,* George Simpson, trans. (New York: Free Press, 1933).

8. Robert K. Merton, *Social Theory and Social Structure* (Glencoe, Ill.: Free Press, 1957).

9. Albert K. Cohen, *Delinquent Boys* (New York: Free Press, 1955).

10. Walter B. Miller, *Violence by Youth Gangs and Youth Groups as a Crime Problem in Major American Cities* (Washington, D.C.: Law Enforcement Administration, 1975).

11. James F. Short, Jr., "Gang Delinquency and Anomie," in Marshall B. Clinard, ed., *Anomie and Deviant Behavior* (New York: Free Press, 1964), pp. 98–127.

12. Richard A. Cloward and Lloyd E. Ohlin, *Delinquency and Opportunity* (New York: Free Press, 1960).

13. See, for example, Merton, *Social Theory and Social Structure;* Cohen, *Delinquent Boys.*

14. Ronald B. Flowers, *Children and Criminality: The Child as Victim and Perpetrator* (Westport, Conn.: Greenwood Press, 1986), p. 151.

15. Ibid.

16. Walter E. Schafer and Kenneth Polk, "Delinquency and the Schools," in the President's Commission on Law Enforcement and Administration of Justice, *Task Force Report: Juvenile Delinquency and Youth Crime* (Washington, D.C.: U.S. Government Printing Office, 1972), pp. 222–277.

17. Edwin H. Sutherland, *Principles of Criminology* (Philadelphia: Lippincott, 1939).

18. Ronald L. Akers, *Deviant Behavior: A Social Learning Approach,* 3rd ed. (Belmont, Calif.: Wadsworth, 1985).

19. Edwin Schur, *Labeling Deviant Behavior* (New York: Harper & Row, 1972), p. 21.

20. Howard Becker, *Outsiders, Studies in the Sociology of Deviance* (New York: Macmillan, 1963), p. 9.

21. Marjorie Zatz, "Race, Ethnicity, and Determinate Sentencing," *Criminology* 22 (1984): pp. 141–171.

22. Flowers, *Children and Criminality,* pp. 166–167.

23. Ronald B. Flowers, *Minorities in Criminality,* (Westport Conn.: Greenwood Press, 1988), pp. 71–72.

24. David F. Greenberg, "Delinquency and the Age Structure of Society," *Contemporary Crises* 1 (1977): pp. 189–224.

Chapter 12. Familial Correlates

1. *See* Ronald B. Flowers, *Children and Criminality: The Child as Victim and Perpetrator* (Westport, Conn.: Greenwood Press, 1986).

2. Brandt F. Steele, "Violence Without the Family," in Ray E. Helfer and C. Henry Kempe, eds., *Child Abuse and Neglect: The Family and the Community* (Cambridge: Ballinger, 1976).

3. Martin R. Haskell and Lewis Yablonsky, *Crime and Delinquency,* 2nd ed. (Chicago: Rand McNally, 1974).

4. D. E. Adams, H. A. Ishizuka, and K. S. Ishizuka, *The Child Abuse Delinquent: An Exploratory/Descriptive Study.* Unpublished MSW thesis, University of South Carolina, South Carolina, 1977.

5. James Garbarino, "Child Abuse and Juvenile Delinquency: The Developmental Impact of Social Isolation," in Robert J. Hunner and Yvonne Elder Walker, eds., *Exploring the Relationship Between Child Abuse and Delinquency* (Montclair, N.J.: Allanheld, Osmun and Co., 1981), p. 117.

6. B. D. Schmitt and C. H. Kempe, "Neglect and Abuse in Children," in V. C. Vaugh and R. McKay, eds., *Nelson Textbook of Pediatrics,* 10th ed. (Philadelphia, W. B. Saunders, 1975), pp. 107–111.

7. Sparky Harlan, Luanna L. Rodgers, and Brian Slattery, *Male and Female Adolescent Prostitution: Huckleberry House Sexual Minority Youth Services Project* (Washington, D.C.: U.S. Department of Health and Human Services, 1981), p. 21.

8. Mimi H. Silbert, "Delancey Street Study: Prostitution and Sexual Assault," Summary of results (San Francisco: Delancey Street Foundation, 1982), p. 3.

9. Mayhall and Norgard, *Child Abuse and Neglect,* pp. 106-107.

10. H. E. Simmons, *Protective Services for Children,* 2nd ed. (Sacramento, Citadel Press, 1970).

11. Cited in Glenn Collins, "The Violent Child: Some Patterns Emerge," *New York Times* (September 27, 1982): p. B10(L).

12. Jeanne Cyriaque, "The Chronic Serious Offender: How Illinois Juveniles 'Match Up'," Illinois Department of Corrections, *Illinois* (February, 1982), pp. 4-5.

13. Karen S. Peterson, "The Nightmare of a Battered Parent," *USA Today* (March 18, 1983): p. A6.

14. See, for example, R. Campbell, "Violence in Adolescence," *Journal of Analytical Psychology* **12,** 2 (1967): pp. 161-173.

15. Cited in Cliff Yudell, "I'm Afraid of My Own Children," *Reader's Digest* (August, 1983): p. 79.

16. Sheldon Glueck and Eleanor Glueck, *Delinquents and Non-Delinquents in Perspective* (Cambridge: Harvard University Press, 1968); Richard J. Gelles and Murray A. Straus, "Determinants of Violence in the Family: Toward a Theoretical Integration," in Wesley R. Burr et al., eds., *Contemporary Theories About the Family* (New York: Free Press, 1979), pp. 549-581; D. P. Farrington, G. Grundy, and D. J. West, "The Familial Transmission of Criminality," *Medicine, Science, and the Law* **15** (1975): pp. 177-186.

17. Vincent J. Fontana, *The Maltreated Child: The Maltreatment Syndrome in Children* (Springfield, Ill.: Charles C Thomas, 1964).

18. Christopher Ounsted, Rhoda Oppenheimer, and Janet Lindsay, "The Psychopathology and Psychotherapy of the Families, Aspects Bounding Failure," in A. Franklin, ed., *Concerning Child Abuse* (London: Churchill Livingston, 1975).

19. Norman A. Polansky, Christine De Saix, and Shlomo A. Sharlin, *Child Neglect: Understanding and Reaching the Parents* (New York: Child Welfare League of America, 1972).

20. Robert W. Weinback et al., "Theoretical Linkages Between Child Abuse and Juvenile Delinquency," in Robert J. Hunner and Yvonne E. Walker, eds., *Exploring the Relationship Between Child Abuse and Delinquency* (Montclair, N.J.: Allanheld, Osmun and Co., 1981), p. 162.

21. D. J. West and D. P. Farrington, *Who Becomes Delinquent?* (London: Heinemann, 1973); D. Olweus, "Familial and Temperamental Determinants of Aggressive Behavior in Adolescents: A Causal Analysis," *Developmental Psychology* **14** (1980): pp. 644-660. *See also* James Snyder and Gerald Patterson, "Family Interaction and Delinquent Behavior," in Herbert C. Quay, ed., *Handbook of Juvenile Delinquency* (New York: Wiley-Interscience, 1987), pp. 220-223.

22. E. Y. Deykin, "Life Functioning in Families of Delinquent Boys: An Assessment Model," *Social Services Review* **46,** 1 (1971): pp. 90-91.

23. A. Buttons, "Some Antecedents of Felonious and Delinquent Behavior," *Journal of Child Clinical Psychology* **2** (1973): pp. 35-37.

24. M. F. Shore, "Psychological Theories of the Causes of Antisocial Behavior," *Crime and Delinquency* **17,** 4 (1971): pp. 456-458.

25. Flowers, *Children and Criminality,* pp. 56-57.

26. Walter Slocum and Carol L. Stone, "Family Culture Patterns and Delinquent-Type Behavior," *Marriage and Family Living* **25** (1963): pp. 202-208.

27. Sheldon Glueck and Eleanor T. Glueck, *Unraveling Juvenile Delinquency* (New York: Commonwealth Fund, 1950).

28. William McCord, Joan McCord, and Irving K. Zola, *Origins of Crime* (New York: Columbia University Press, 1959).

29. Glueck and Glueck, *Unraveling Juvenile Delinquency.*

30. Robert G. Andry, "Paternal Affection and Delinquency," in Marvin E.

Wolfgang, Leonard Savitz, and Norman Johnson, eds., *The Sociology of Crime and Delinquency* (New York: John Wiley & Sons, 1962), pp. 342–352.

31. Slocum and Stone, "Family Culture Patterns."

32. Leo Davids, "Delinquency Prevention through Father Training: Some Observations and Proposals," in Paul C. Friday and V. Lorne Stewart, eds., *Youth, Crime and Juvenile Justice: International Perspectives* (New York: Holt, Rinehart and Winston, 1977).

33. F. Ivan Nye, *Family Relations and Delinquent Behavior* (New York: John Wiley & Sons, 1958).

34. McCord, McCord, and Zola, *Origins of Crime.*

35. Joan McCord, W. McCord, and A. Howard, "Family Interaction as Antecedent to the Direction of Male Aggressiveness," *Journal of Abnormal Social Psychology* **66** (1963): pp. 239–242.

36. S. Kirson Weinberg, "Sociological Processes and Factors in Juvenile Delinquency," in Joseph S. Roucek, ed., *Juvenile Delinquency* (New York: Philosophical Library, 1958), pp. 113–132.

37. Albert Bandura and Richard H. Walters, "Dependency Conflicts in Aggressive Delinquents," *Journal of Social Issues* **4** (1958): pp. 52–65.

38. Wesley C. Becker, "Consequences of Different Kinds of Parental Discipline," in Martin L. Hoffman and Lois Hoffman, eds., *Review of Child Development Research* (New York: Russell Sage Foundation, 1964), pp. 169–208.

39. *See* Snyder and Patterson, "Family Interaction," pp. 223–225.

40. Ibid.; Olweus, "Familial and Temperamental Determinants;" M.E.J. Wadsworth, *Roots of Delinquency: Infancy, Adolescence and Crime* (Oxford, England: Robertson, 1979).

41. Clifford R. Shaw and Henry D. McKay, "Are Broken Homes a Causative Factor in Juvenile Delinquency?" *Social Forces* **10** (1932): pp. 514–524.

42. H. Ashley and Margaret G. Smith, "Juvenile Delinquency and Broken Homes in Spokane, Washington," *Social Forces* **18** (1939): pp. 48–49.

43. Sheldon Glueck and Eleanor T. Glueck, *Family Environments and Delinquency* (Boston: Houghton Mifflin, 1962).

44. *See* H. B. Gibson, "Early Delinquency in Relation to Broken Homes," *Journal of Child Psychology* **10** (1969): pp. 195–204; M. Rutter, "Parent-Child Separation: Psychological Effects on the Children," *Journal of Child Psychology and Psychiatry* **12** (1971): pp. 233–260.

45. Lawrence Rosen and Kathleen Neilson, The Broken Home and Delinquency," in Leonard D. Savitz and Norman Johnston, *Crime in Society* (New York: John Wiley & Sons, 1978), pp. 406–415.

46. William M. Wattenberg and Frank Saunders, "Sex Differences Among Juvenile Offenders," *Sociology and Social Research* **39** (1954): pp. 24–31.

47. Rochelle J. Canter, "Family Correlates of Male and Female Delinquency," *Criminology* **20** (1982): pp. 163–164.

48. Charles J. Browning, "Differential Impact of Family Disorganization on Male Adolescents," *Social Forces* **8** (1960): pp. 37–44.

49. Ibid.

50. Glueck and Glueck, *Unraveling Juvenile Delinquency.*

51. Lester D. Jaffe, "Delinquency Proneness and Family Anomie," *Journal of Criminal Law, Criminology and Police Science* **54** (1963): pp. 146–154.

52. Beatrice Freeman, George Savastano, and J. J. Tobias, "The Affluent Suburban Male Delinquent," *Crime and Delinquency* **16** (1970): pp. 264–272.

53. See, for example, S. Liverant, "MMPI Differences Between Parents of Disturbed and Non-Disturbed Children," *Journal of Consulting Psychology* **23** (1959): pp. 256–260.

54. Rutter, "Parent-Child Separation."

55. J. P. Lees and L. J. Newson, "Family or Sibship Position and Some Aspects of Juvenile Delinquency," *British Journal of Delinquency* 5 (1954): pp. 46–55.

56. Nye, *Family Relations and Delinquent Behavior.*

57. Glueck and Glueck, *Unraveling Juvenile Delinquency.*

58. Albert J. Reiss, Jr., "Social Correlates of Psychological Types of Delinquency," *American Sociological Review* 17 (1961): pp. 710–718.

59. Flowers, *Children and Criminality.*

Chapter 13. Law Enforcement

1. Donald J. Black and Albert J. Reiss, Jr., "Police Control of Juveniles," *American Sociological Review* 35 (1979): pp. 63–77.

2. Norval Morris and Gordon Hawkins, *The Honest Politician's Guide to Crime Control* (Chicago: University of Chicago Press, 1970), p. 91.

3. The two examples represent a composite of two typical police-juvenile encounters as based on studies and profiles of these contacts.

4. James Q. Wilson, "Dilemmas of Police Administration," *Public Administration Review* 28 (1968).

5. Black and Reiss, "Police Control of Juveniles."

6. Ibid.

7. See, for example, Robert M. Emerson, *Judging Delinquents: Context and Process in Juvenile Court* (Chicago: Aldine, 1969), p. 42.

8. Douglas A. Smith, Christy A. Visher, and Laura A. Davidson, "Equity and Discretionary Justice: The Influence of Race on Police Arrest Decisions," *Journal of Criminal Law and Criminology* 75 (1984): pp. 234–249.

9. Emerson, *Judging Delinquents;* Black and Reiss, "Police Control of Juveniles."

10. Media Chesney-Lind, "Juvenile Delinquency: The Sexualization of Female Crime," *Psychology Today* 8 (1974): pp. 43–46; Media Chesney-Lind, "Judicial Paternalism and the Female Status Offender," *Crime and Delinquency* 23 (1977): pp. 121–130.

11. Marvin E. Wolfgang, Robert M. Figlio, and Thorsten Sellin, *Delinquency in a Birth Cohort* (Chicago: University of Chicago Press, 1972), p. 252.

12. Dale Dannefer and Russell K. Schmitt, "Race and Juvenile Justice Processing in Court and Police Agencies," *American Journal of Sociology* 87 (1982): pp. 1113–1132.

13. Black and Reiss, "Police Control of Juveniles."

14. Ronald B. Flowers, *Minorities and Criminality* (Westport, Conn.: Greenwood Press, 1988), p. 151; Clemens Bartollas, *Juvenile Delinquency* (New York: John Wiley & Sons, 1985), p. 420.

15. Richard C. Hollinger, "Race, Occupational Status, and Pro-Active Police Arrests for Drinking and Driving," *Journal of Criminal Justice* 12 (1984): pp. 173–183.

16. Bartollas, *Juvenile Delinquency,* p. 420.

17. A. W. McEachern and Riva Bauzer, "Factors Related to Disposition in Juvenile-Police Contacts," in Malcolm W. Klein, *Juvenile Gangs in Context* (Englewood Cliffs, N.J.: Prentice-Hall, 1967), pp. 48–160; James T. Carey et al., *The Handling of Juveniles from Offense to Disposition* (Washington, D.C.: Government Printing Office, 1976), p. 419.

18. Irvin Piliavin and Scott Briar, "Police Encounters with Juveniles," *American Journal of Sociology* 70 (1964): pp. 206–214.

19. Carl Werthman and Irving Piliavin, "Gang Members and the Police," in David J. Bordual, ed., *The Police* (New York: John Wiley & Sons, 1967), pp. 56–98.

20. Richard J. Lundman, Richard E. Sykes, and John P. Clark, "Police Control of Juveniles: A Replication," in Richard J. Lundman, ed., *Police Behavior: A Sociological Perspective* (New York: Oxford Press, 1980), pp. 147–148.

21. Wilson, "Dilemmas of Police Administration," p. 19.

22. Nathan Goldman, "The Differential Selection of Juvenile Offenders for Court Appearance," in William Chambliss, ed., *Crime and the Legal Process* (New York: McGraw-Hill, 1969).

23. Study cited in Bartollas, *Juvenile Delinquency,* p. 421.

24. *Mapp v. Ohio,* 367 U.S. 643 (1961).

25. *In re Two Brothers and a Case of Liquor,* Juvenile Court of the District of Columbia, 1966, cited in *Washington Law Reporter* **95** (1967): p. 113.

26. *Miranda v. Arizona,* 384 U.S. 436 (1966).

27. *In re Gault,* 387 U.S. (1967).

28. National Advisory Committee for Juvenile Justice and Delinquency Prevention, *Standards for the Administration of Juvenile Justice* (Washington, D.C.: Government Printing Office, 1980), p. 213.

29. *Haley v. Ohio,* 332 U.S. 596, 68 S. Ct. 302 (1948).

30. *Gallegos v. Colorado,* 370 U.S. 49, 82 S. Ct. 1209 (1962).

31. Elyce Z. Ferster and Thomas F. Courtless, "The Beginning of Juvenile Justice, Police Practices, and the Juvenile Offender," *Vanderbilt Law Review* **22** (1969): pp. 598–601.

32. *Davis v. Mississippi,* 394 U.S. 721 (1969).

33. Paul H. Hahn, *The Juvenile Offender and the Law,* 3rd ed. (Cincinnati: W. H. Anderson Co., 1984), pp. 171–172.

34. Bartollas, *Juvenile Delinquency,* p. 425; Peter C. Kratcoski and Lucille Kratcoski, *Juvenile Delinquency,* 2nd ed. (Englewood Cliffs, N.J.: Prentice-Hall, 1986), pp. 225–226.

35. Cited in Hahn, *The Juvenile Offender,* p. 172.

36. *Wade v. U.S.,* 388 U.S. 218 (1967).

37. *Stovall v. Denno,* 388 U.S. 293, 203 (1967).

38. *Simmons v. U.S.,* 390 U.S. 377 (1968).

39. Robert Portune, *Changing Adolescent Attitudes Toward Police* (Cincinnati: W. H. Anderson Co., 1971).

40. Donald H. Bouma, *Kids and Cops* (Grand Rapids, Mich.: William E. Eerdman Publishing Co., 1969), pp. 69–70.

41. L. Thomas Winfree, Jr. and Curtis T. Griffiths, "Adolescents' Attitudes Toward the Police: A Survey of High School Students," in *Juvenile Delinquency: Little Brother Grows Up* (Beverly Hills: Sage, 1977), pp. 79–99.

42. Bouma, *Kids and Cops.*

43. Werthman and Piliavin, "Gang Members and the Police," p. 70.

Chapter 14. Juvenile Court

1. Peter C. Kratcoski and Lucille Dunn Kratcoski, *Juvenile Delinquency,* 2nd ed. (Englewood, N.J.: Prentice-Hall, 1986), p. 77.

2. Ronald B. Flowers, *Children and Criminality: The Child as Victim and Perpetrator* (Westport, Conn.: Greenwood Press, 1986), pp. 171–173.

3. Ibid.

4. Anthony Platt, *The Child-Savers: The Invention of Delinquency* (Chicago: University of Chicago Press, 1968).

5. Flowers, *Children and Criminality,* p. 172.

6. Ibid., p. 173.

7. Ibid.

8. *Kent v. United States,* 383 U.S. 541 (1966).

9. *In re Gault,* 387 U.S. 1 (1967).

10. *In re Winship,* 397 U.S. 358 (1970).

11. Clemens Bartollas, *Juvenile Delinquency* (New York: John Wiley & Sons, 1985), p. 444.

12. *McKeiver v. Pennsylvania,* 403 U.S. 528 (1971). *See also In re Barbara Burrus,* 275 N.C. 517, 169 S.E. 2d 879 (1969).

13. *Breed v. Jones* 421 U.S. 519, 95 S. Ct. 1779 (1975).

14. Donna Hamparian et al., *Youth in Adult Courts: Between Two Worlds* (Columbus, Ohio: Academy of Contemporary Problems, 1983), p. 24; U.S. Department of Justice, *Juvenile Justice: Before and After the Onset of Delinquency* (Washington, D.C.: Government Printing Office, 1981), p. 50.

Chapter 15. Institutionalization

1. Robert M. Carter, Richard A. McGee, and E. Kim Nelson, *Corrections in America* (Philadelphia: Lippincott, 1975), p. 33.

2. U.S. Department of Justice, Bureau of Justice Statistics, *Jail Inmates 1986* (Washington, D.C.: Government Printing Office, 1987), p. 1.

3. Rob Wilson, "Juvenile Inmates: The Long-Term Trend Is Down," *Corrections Magazine* 4 (1978): pp. 3–11; Rosemary Sarri, "The Use of Detention and Alternatives in the United States Since the Gault Decision," in Raymond R. Corrado, Marc LeBlanc, and Jean Trepanier, eds., *Current Issues in Juvenile Justice* (Toronto: Butterworth, 1983), p. 328.

4. President's Commission on Law Enforcement and Administration of Justice, *Task Force Report: Corrections* (Washington, D.C.: Government Printing Office, 1967), pp. 124–128; Mary Jordan, "More Juveniles Being Tried as Adults," *Washington Post* (December 30, 1984): p. A6.

5. Ronald B. Flowers, *Demographics and Criminality: The Characteristics of Crime in America* (Westport, Conn.: Greenwood Press, 1989).

6. Wisconsin Department of Health and Social Services, "Juvenile Detention in Wisconsin, 1976. Final Report." Madison, Wisconsin, 1976.

7. John J. Downey, "Why Children Are in Jail and How to Keep Them Out," *Children* 17 (1970): pp. 3–4.

8. Thomas J. Cottle, *Children in Jail: Seven Lessons in American Justice* (Boston: Beacon Press, 1977), pp. viii–ix.

9. "Juvenile Detention in Wisconsin."

10. Downey, "Why Children Are in Jail."

11. Governor's Commission on Crime, Prevention and Control, "A Study of the Local Secure Facilities in Minnesota," St. Paul, 1977.

12. "Jailing Youths with Adults—A National Catastrophe," *Justice Assistance News* 1 (1980): p. 3.

13. William G. Nagle, "Prison Architecture and Prison Violence," in Albert K. Cohen, George F. Cole, and Robert G. Bailey, eds., *Prison Violence* (Lexington, Mass.: D. C. Heath, 1976), p. 105.

14. "When Children Go To Jail," *Newsweek* (May 27, 1985): p. 87.

15. Clemens Bartollas, *Juvenile Delinquency* (New York: John Wiley & Sons, 1985), p. 503.

16. Jordan, "More Juveniles Being Tried as Adults."

17. Margaret Werner Calahan, *Historical Corrections Statistics in the United States, 1850–1984* (Washington, D.C.: Government Printing Office, 1986), p. 66.

18. Jordan, "More Juveniles Being Tried as Adults."

19. M. Kilfoyle and D. Lesser, *Juvenile Offenders in New York State 9/1/78–6/30/81* (New York: Division of Criminal Justice Services, 1981), p. 81.

20. Jails also are used as short-term detention facilities for adolescents and, in fact, confine more juveniles over the course of the year than any other type of correctional institution.

21. Mary Barbera-Hogan, "Teens Who Turn to Trouble: Inside Juvenile Hall," *Teen* (July, 1986): p. 44.

22. The story of Janice was adopted from Barbera-Hogan's article, pp. 42–45.

23. Eric D. Poole and Robert M. Regoli, "Violence in Juvenile Institutions," *Criminology* **21**, 2 (1983): p. 214.

24. Clemens Bartollas, Stuart J. Miller, and Simon Dinitz, *Juvenile Victimization: The Institutional Paradox* (New York: Halstead Press, 1976), pp. 131–150.

25. Christopher M. Sieverdes and Clemens Bartollas, "Modes of Adaptation and Game Behavior at Two Juvenile Institutions," in Paul C. Friday and V. Lorne Stewart, eds., *Youth Crime and Juvenile Justice: International Perspectives* (New York: Holt, Rinehart and Winston, 1977), pp. 27–35.

26. Howard Polsky, *Cottage Six* (New York: Russell Sage Foundation, 1962), pp. 69–88.

27. 125 F. Supp. 647 D.D.C. (1954).

28. 346 F. Supp. 1354 D.R.I. (1972).

29. *Nelson v. Heyne*, 491 F. 2d 352 (1974).

30. *Moralas v. Turman,* 383 F. Supp. 53 (1974).

31. Adrienne Volenik, "Right to Treatment: Case Developments in Juvenile Law," *Justice System Journal* **3** (1978): pp. 303–304.

32. 419 F. Supp. 203 S.D.N.Y. (1976).

33. 346 F. Supp. 1354 D.R.I. (1972).

34. See, for example, *Lollis v. N.Y. State Department of Social Services,* 322 F. Supp. 473 S.D.N.Y. (1970).

Chapter 16. Noninstitutional Approaches

1. Howard N. Snyder and Terrence A. Finnegan, *Delinquency in the United States 1983* (Pittsburgh: National Center for Juvenile Justice, 1987), p. 11.

2. Frank R. Scarpitti and Richard M. Stephenson, "Juvenile Court Dispositions: Factors in the Decision-Making Process," *Crime and Delinquency* **17**, 2 (1971): p. 190.

3. In some large probation departments, there may be separate intake units. In these, the intake officers may not function as probation officers.

4. In most states, intake screening is a function of the juvenile court. However, in some states, intake screening is handled by a state department of social services or a prosecutor.

5. Eloise C. Snyder, "The Impact of the Juvenile Court Hearing on the Child," *Crime and Delinquency* **17** (1971): p. 190.

6. Clifford Simonsen and Marshall S. Gordon III, *Juvenile Justice in America* (Encino, Calif.: Glencoe Publishing Co., 1979), p. 203.

7. R. M. Emerson, *Judging Delinquents: Context and Process in Juvenile Court* (Chicago: Aldine-Atherton, 1969), p. 219.

8. President's Commission on Law Enforcement and Administration of Justice, *Task Force Report on Juvenile Delinquency and Youth Crime* (Washington, D.C.: U.S. Government Printing Office, 1967).

9. U.S. Federal Bureau of Investigation, *Crime in the United States: Uniform Crime Reports 1986* (Washington, D.C.: Government Printing Office, 1987), p. 240.

10. Snyder and Finnegan, *Delinquency in the United States, 1983.*

11. Youth Development and Delinquency Prevention Administration, "The Challenge of Youth Service Bureaus," in Robert M. Carter and Malcolm W. Klein, eds., *Back on the Streets* (Englewood Cliffs, N.J.: Prentice-Hall, 1976); Sherwood Norman, *Youth Services Bureau: A Key to Prevention* (Paramus, N.J.: National Council on Crime and Delinquency, 1972).

12. T. Edwin Black and Charles P. Smith, *A Preliminary National Assessment of the Numbers and Characteristics of Juveniles Processed in the Juvenile Justice System* (Washington, D.C.: U.S. Government Printing Office, 1981), p. 184.

Chapter 17. Other Countries

1. See, for example, U.S. Department of Justice, *Victimization and Fear of Crime: World Perspectives* (Washington, D.C.: Government Printing Office); Peter M. Jones, "Juvenile Crime Is a Worldwide Problem," *Scholastic Update* (November 3, 1986): pp. 26–27; Ruth Shonle Cavan and Jordan T. Cavan, *Delinquency and Crime: Cross-Cultural Perspectives* (Philadelphia: Lippincott, 1968); Don C. Gibbons and Marvin D. Krohn, *Delinquent Behavior,* 4th ed. (Englewood Cliffs, N.J.: Prentice-Hall, 1986), pp. 194–210.
2. Cavan and Cavan, *Delinquency and Crime.*
3. T. C. N. Gibbens and R. H. Ahrenfeldt, *Cultural Factors in Delinquency* (Philadelphia: Lippincott, 1966).
4. Jackson Toby, "Affluence and Adolescent Crime," in The President's Commission on Law Enforcement and Administration of Justice, *Task Force Report: Juvenile Delinquency and Youth Crime* (Washington, D.C.: U.S. Government Printing Office, 1967), pp. 132–144; Jackson Toby, "Delinquency in Cross-Cultural Perspectives," in LaMar T. Empey, ed., *Juvenile Justice: The Progressive Legacy and Current Reforms* (Charlottesville, Va.: University Press of Virginia, 1979), pp. 105–149.
5. See, for example, Cavan and Cavan, *Delinquency and Crime;* C. P. Wallis and R. Maliphant, "Delinquent Areas in the County of London: Ecological Factors," *British Journal of Criminology* 7 (1967): pp. 250–284; David M. Downs, *The Delinquent Solution* (New York: Free Press, 1966).
6. Gibbons and Krohn, *Delinquent Behavior,* p. 208. *See also* Peter Willmott, *Adolescent Boys in East London* (London: Routledge and Kegan Paul, 1966).
7. Jones, "Juvenile Crime."
8. Ibid.
9. Mark G. Field, "Alcoholism, Crime, and Delinquency in Soviet Society," *Social Problems* 3 (1955): pp. 100–109.
10. Walter D. Connor, "Juvenile Delinquency in the U.S.S.R.: Some Quantitative and Qualitative Indicators," *American Sociological Review* 35 (1970): pp. 288–297.
11. Gibbons and Krohn, *Delinquent Behavior,* pp. 203–204; Cavan and Cavan, *Delinquency and Crime.*
12. Paul Hollander, "A Converging Social Problem: Juvenile Delinquency in the Soviet Union and the United States," *British Journal of Criminology* 9 (1969): pp. 148–166.
13. Jones, "Juvenile Crime."
14. Deborah Strigenz as quoted in Ibid.
15. Cited in Jones, "Juvenile Crime."
16. Ibid.
17. Ibid.
18. Jerry Sarnecki, quoted in Ibid.
19. Quoted in Ibid.
20. Carl-Gunnar Janson, "Juvenile Delinquency in Sweden," *Youth and Society* 2 (1970): pp. 207–231; Gibbons and Krohn, *Delinquent Behavior,* p. 204.
21. Edmund W. Vaz, "Juvenile Gang Delinquency in Paris," *Social Problems* 10 (1962): pp. 23–31.
22. Lois B. DeFleur, *Delinquency in Argentina—A Study of Cordoba's Youth* (Pullman, Wash.: Washington State University Press, 1970).
23. Pedro R. David and Joseph W. Scott, "A Cross-Cultural Comparison of

Juvenile Offenders, Offenses, Due Process, and Societies: The Cases of Toledo, Ohio, and Rosario, Argentina," *Criminology* 11 (1973): pp. 185-203.

24. See, for example, S. Kirson Weinberg, "Juvenile Delinquency in Ghana: A Comparative Analysis of Delinquents and Nondelinquents," *Journal of Criminal Law, Criminology and Police Science* 55 (1964): pp. 471-481; Clayton A. Hartjen and S. Priyadarsini, *Delinquency in India* (New Brunswick, N.J.: Rutgers University Press, 1984); Tsung-Vi Lin, "Two Types of Delinquent Youth in Chinese Society," in S. N. Eisenstadt, ed., *Comparative Social Problems* (New York: Free Press, 1964), pp. 169-176; Olufunmilayo Oloruntimehin, "A Study of Juvenile Delinquency in a Nigerian City," *British Journal of Criminology* (1973): pp. 157-169.

25. U.S. Department of Justice, *Victimization and Fear of Crime,* pp. 3-9.

Chapter 18. Directions

1. Dennis A. Romig, *Justice for Our Children* (Lexington, Mass.: Lexington Books, 1978), pp. 121-128; Anthony Rutherford and Robert McDermott, *National Evaluation Program Phase 1 Report: Juvenile Diversion* (Washington, D.C.: Government Printing Office, 1976).

2. Michael Sherill, "Jerome Miller: Does He Have the Answers...?" *Corrections Magazine* 2 (1975): pp. 24-28; U.S. Department of Justice, *Juvenile Correctional Reform in Massachusetts* (Washington, D.C.: Government Printing Office, 1977).

3. Robert D. Vinter, George Downs, and John Hall, *Juvenile Corrections in the States: Residential Programs and Deinstitutionalization: A Preliminary Report* (Ann Arbor, Mich.: National Assessment of Juvenile Corrections, 1975).

4. Ibid.; Clemens Bartollas, *Juvenile Delinquency* (New York: John Wiley & Sons, 1985), pp. 399, 405.

5. Bartollas, *Juvenile Delinquency,* pp. 493, 595.

6. Rob Wilson, "Corrections Magazine Survey of Juvenile Inmates," *Corrections Magazine* 4 (1978): p. 9.

7. Juvenile Justice and Delinquency Act of 1974, P.L. No. 93-415 (1974).

8. 42 U.S.C. §5101-5106 (1974); Child Abuse Prevention and Treatment and Adoption Reform Act of 1978, P.L. No. 95-266, 92 Stat. 205 (1978).

9. 18 U.S.C. §§2251, 2253-2254 (1978). *See also* Tina M. Beranbaum et al., "Child Pornography in the 1970s," in Ann Wolbert, ed., *Child Pornography and Sex Rings* (Lexington, Mass.: Lexington Books, 1984), p. 15.

10. Ronald B. Flowers, *Children and Criminality: The Child as Victim and Perpetrator* (Westport, Conn.: Greenwood Press, 1986), pp. 190-191.

11. The Runaway and Homeless Youth Act, U.S.C. 5701-5702 Supp. II (1978).

12. P.L. No. 96-509; 42 U.S.C. §5711 Supp. (1981).

13. Flowers, *Children and Criminality,* pp. 191-192; D. Kelly Weisberg, *Children of the Night: A Study of Adolescent Prostitution* (Lexington, Mass.: Lexington Books, 1985), pp. 197-201.

14. Flowers, *Children and Criminality,* p. 192; National Center for Missing and Exploited Children, Washington, D.C.

Bibliography

Adler, Freda. *Sisters in Crime: The Rise of the New Female Criminal.* New York: McGraw-Hill, 1975. A controversial perspective on a new, more violent and aggressive female criminal and its relationship to the women's liberation movement.

Ageton, Suzanne S. "The Dynamics of Female Delinquency, 1976–1980." *Criminology* **21** (1983): pp. 555–584. An analysis of the extent and nature of female delinquency based on a national probability sample of adolescents.

Allen, Harry E., and Simonsen, Clifford E. *Corrections in America: An Introduction,* 4th ed. New York: Macmillan, 1986. An exploration of the ramifications surrounding corrections in the United States.

Anderson, Etta A. "The Chivalrous Treatment of the Female Offender in the Arms of the Criminal Justice System: A Review of the Literature." *Social Problems* **23** (1976): pp. 350–357. Chivalry and discriminatory treatment by the system of juvenile justice are probed.

Barbera-Hogan, Mary. "Teens Who Turn to Trouble: Inside Juvenile Hall." *Teen* (July, 1986): pp. 42–44. The path from juvenile arrest to detention is traced through this focus on one adolescent delinquent.

Bartol, Curt R., and Bartol, Anne M. *Criminal Behavior: A Psychosocial Approach.* Englewood Cliffs, N.J.: Prentice-Hall, 1986. A psychological study of criminal behavior and trends in the discipline of psychological criminology.

Bartollas, Clemens. *Juvenile Delinquency.* New York: John Wiley & Sons, 1985. A multicontextual examination of juvenile delinquency, juvenile corrections, and delinquency prevention.

Block, Richard, ed. *Victimization and Fear of Crime: World Perspectives.* Washington, D.C.: U.S. Government Printing Office, 1984. An interesting collection of articles offering perspectives on crime and victimization in different parts of the world.

Bracey, Dorothy H. *"Baby-Pros": Preliminary Profiles of Juvenile Prostitutes.* New York: John Jay Press, 1979. An empirical examination of adolescent prostitution.

Calahan, Margaret Werner, and Parsons, Lee Anne. *Historical Corrections Statistics in the United States, 1850–1984.* Rockville, Md.: Westat, Inc., 1986. An interesting collection of statistical data on juvenile and adult corrections historically and their inmate populations.

Campbell, Anne. *Girl Delinquents.* New York: St. Martin's Press, 1981. An examination of aggression among female adolescents in Great Britain.

Carpenter, Cheryl, Glassner, Barry, Johnson, Bruce D., and Loughlin, Julia. *Kids, Drugs, and Crime.* Lexington, Mass.: Lexington Books, 1988. An enlightening investigation of the relationship between juvenile criminality and drug and alcohol use, with special emphasis on addressing this relationship from the adolescent's point of view.

Cavan, Ruth Shonle, and Cavan, Jordan T. *Delinquency and Crime: Cross-Cultural Perspectives.* Philadelphia: Lippincott, 1968. A detailed treatment of the dynamics of juvenile delinquency in other countries.

Cernkovich, Steve A., and Giordano, Peggy C. "A Comparative Analysis of Male and Female Delinquency." *Sociological Quarterly* **20** (1979): pp. 131–145. The characteristics of juvenile delinquency as related to gender are examined from self-report data.

Chesney-Lind, Media. "Juvenile Delinquency: The Sexualization of Female Crime." *Psychology Today* **8** (1974): pp. 43–46. An argument on a sexual double standard in juvenile court dispositions.

Clear, Todd R., and Cole, George F. *American Corrections*. Monterey: Brooks/Cole, 1986. Examination of crime and correctional system in the United States.

Cloward, Richard A., and Ohlin, Lloyd E. *Delinquency and Opportunity: A Theory of Delinquent Gangs*. New York: Free Press, 1960. An explanation of juvenile delinquency, focusing on differential opportunities.

Cohen, Albert K. *Delinquent Boys: The Culture of the Gang*. New York: Free Press, 1955. A strain theoretical perspective on juvenile delinquency, emphasizing the concept of status frustration.

"Crack: A Cheap and Deadly Cocaine Is a Spreading Menace." *Time* **127** (June 2, 1986): pp. 16–18. An informative discussion on the harmful effects of crack as a drug, crime, and in relation to other crimes.

Dalgaard, Odd S., and Kringlen, Einar. "A Norwegian Twin Study of Criminality." *British Journal of Criminology* **16** (1976): pp. 213–233. An examination into the relative relationship between delinquency, heredity and environment.

Danna, Alfred. "Juvenile Male Prostitution: How Can We Reduce the Problem?" *USA Today* **113** (May, 1985): pp. 86–88. A detective's first person account of the dynamics of adolescent male prostitution.

Enablers. *Juvenile Prostitution in Minnesota: The Report of a Research Project*. St. Paul: The Enablers, 1978. An empirical study of adolescent prostitution in Minnesota.

Field, Mark G. "Alcoholism, Crime, and Delinquency in Soviet Society." *Social Problems* **3** (1955): pp. 100–109. A fascinating study of the problem of delinquency in the Soviet Union.

Flowers, Ronald Barri. *Children and Criminality: The Child as Victim and Perpetrator*. Westport, Conn.: Greenwood Press, 1986. An in-depth examination of children as victims of crime, juvenile delinquents, and how these phenomena relate to each other.

_____. *Demographics and Criminality: The Characteristics of Crime in America*. Westport, Conn.: Greenwood Press, 1989. A comprehensive statistical analysis of the demographic characteristics of criminality in the United States.

_____. *Minorities and Criminality*. Westport, Conn.: Greenwood Press, 1988. An important exploration of the interrelationship between minority victimization and minority criminality in America with respect to Blacks, Hispanics, Native Americans, and Asians.

Freud, Sigmund. *New Introductory Lectures on Psychoanalysis*. New York: W.W. Norton, 1933. Psychoanalysis as a concept is outlined in this treatise.

Gibbons, Don C., and Krohn, Marvin D. *Delinquent Behavior*, 4th ed. Englewood Cliffs, N.J.: Prentice-Hall, 1986. A sociological exploration into the factors and influences of delinquent behavior.

Hahn, Paul H. *The Juvenile Offender and the Law*, 3rd ed. Cincinnati: Anderson Publishing Co., 1984. A study of various facets of youthful misbehavior and the juvenile justice system.

Hardman, Dale G. "Small Town Gangs." *Journal of Criminal Law, Criminology and Police Science* **60**, 2 (1969): pp. 176–177. An examination of the characteristics of youth gangs in small towns.

Harlan, Sparky, Rodgers, Luanne L., and Slattery, Brian. *Male and Female Adolescent Prostitution: Huckleberry House Sexual Minority Youth Services Project*.

Washington, D.C.: U.S. Department of Health and Human Services, 1981. An empirical treatise on adolescent prostitution in San Francisco.

Hersch, Patricia. "Coming of Age on City Streets." *Psychology Today* (January, 1988): pp. 28-37. A disturbing treatise on the relationship between AIDS, runaways, and adolescence.

Hollander, Paul. "A Converging Social Problem: Juvenile Delinquency in the Soviet Union and the United States." *British Journal of Criminology* **9** (1969): pp. 148-166. A comparison study of delinquent behavior in the U.S.S.R. and U.S.

"How to Stop Teen Drug Use." *Consumer's Research* **70** (January, 1987): pp. 27-31. Advice to parents on the realities of adolescent drug use and how to recognize symptoms and prevent drug use.

Hunner, Robert J., and Walker, Yvonne E., eds. *Exploring the Relationship Between Child Abuse and Delinquency*. Montclair, N.J.: Allanheld, Osmun and Co., 1981. A multifaceted collection of articles on the linkage between child abuse and juvenile delinquency.

James, Jennifer. *Entrance into Juvenile Prostitution*. Washington, D.C.: National Institute of Mental Health, 1980. A detailed examination of the characteristics and features of juvenile female prostitution.

Johnson, Lloyd D., Bachman, Jerald G., and O'Malley, Patrick M. *Student Drug Use, Attitudes and Beliefs, National Trends, 1975-1982*. Washington, D.C.: U.S. Government Printing Office, 1983. A nationwide survey of drug use among high school seniors.

Jones, Peter M. "Juvenile Crime Is a Worldwide Problem." *Scholastic Update* (November 3, 1986): pp. 26-27. Juvenile delinquency as a problem in the Soviet Union, United Kingdom, and Sweden is addressed.

Jordan, Mary. "More Juveniles Being Tried as Adults." *Washington Post* (December 30, 1984): p. A12. An essay presenting different views on trying juvenile offenders in adult criminal courts.

"Juvenile Justice Under Fire." *Scholastic Update* (November 3, 1986): pp. 3-20. Several articles exploring various issues related to juvenile crime historically and currently.

Konopka, Gisela. *The Adolescent Girl in Conflict*. Englewood Cliffs, N.J.: Prentice-Hall, 1966. A comprehensive study of the factors that are involved in female adolescents becoming delinquent.

Kratcoski, Peter C., and Kratcoski, Lucille Dunn. *Juvenile Delinquency,* 2nd ed. Englewood Cliffs, N.J.: Prentice-Hall, 1986. An investigation of juvenile delinquency and juvenile justice.

Lloyd, Robin. *For Money or Love: Boy Prostitution in America*. New York: Ballantine, 1976. The dynamics of male adolescent prostitution are probed in this comprehensive exploration.

Miller, Walter B. *Violence by Youth Gangs and Youth Groups as a Crime Problem in Major American Cities*. Washington, D.C.: U.S. Government Printing Office, 1975. A nationwide investigation of the problem of juvenile gangs in major U.S. cities.

Morris, Jim. "Gangs at War in L.A. Streets." *Sacramento Bee* (October 19, 1986): p. A1. An examination of Los Angeles' problem with youth gangs.

National Center for Missing & Exploited Children. *Directory: Support Services and Resources for Missing and Exploited Children*. Washington, D.C.: National Center for Missing and Exploited Children, 1985. A directory of programs, organizations, and resources pertaining to missing and exploited juveniles.

O'Brien, Shirley. *Child Pornography*. Dubuque, Iowa: Kendall/Hunt, 1983. An in-depth exploration of child pornography and sexual exploitation.

Platt, Anthony M. *The Child Savers: The Invention of Delinquency,* 2nd ed. Chicago: University of Chicago Press, 1977. A chronicle of the child-saving movement and the system of juvenile justice.

Quay, Herbert C., ed. *Handbook of Juvenile Delinquency.* New York: Wiley-Interscience, 1987. A series of articles addressing the research and theories of juvenile delinquency, primarily from a psychological perspective.

Radar, Dotson. "I Want to Die So I Won't Hurt No More." *Parade Magazine* (August 18, 1985: pp. 4–6. A first person exploration of the problems of runaways in America.

"A 'Rite of Passage' More Young People Avoid." *Scholastic Update* 117 (May 10, 1985): pp. 14–15. A treatment of adolescent drug use and abuse.

Rooney, Rita. "Children for Sale: Pornography's Dark New World." *Reader's Digest* (July, 1983): pp. 52–56. An examination of child pornography and the battle against it.

"'Runaways,' 'Throwaways,' 'Bag Kids'—An Army of Drifter Teens." *U.S. News & World Report* (March 11, 1985): p. 53. An examination of the country's homeless youth.

Satchell, Michael. "Kids for Sale: A Shocking Report on Child Prostitution Across America." *Parade Magazine* (July 20, 1986): pp. 4–6. The sad reality of adolescent prostitution in the United States is uncovered in this treatment.

Siegel, Barry. "Justice: The Cases of Two Young Killers." *Los Angeles Times* (May 8, 1983): Part 1, p. 1. An interesting examination of the common and differential factors associated with two juveniles convicted of parricide.

Snyder, Howard N., and Finnegan, Terrence A. *Delinquency in the United States 1983.* Pittsburgh: National Center for Juvenile Justice, 1987. A report on the volume and characteristics of delinquency and status offense cases disposed by the nation's juvenile courts in 1983.

Straus, Murray, A., Gelles, Richard J., Steinmetz, Suzanne K. *Behind Closed Doors: Violence in the American Family.* Garden City, N.Y.: Doubleday/Anchor, 1979. A revealing look at the dimensions of familial violence.

Thrasher, Frederick. *The Gang.* Chicago: University of Chicago Press, 1927. A pioneering study of juvenile gangs and gang formation.

U.S. Department of Health and Human Services. *A Drug Retrospective: 1961–1980.* Washington, D.C.: Government Printing Office, 1980. A national self-report survey of nearly 7,000 subjects concerning drug use and abuse.

U.S. Department of Justice. Bureau of Justice Statistics Bulletin. *Jail Inmates 1986.* Washington, D.C.: Government Printing Office, 1987. Findings from the fourth annual Survey of Jails on the country's jail inmate population.

U.S. Department of Justice. Bureau of Justice Statistics Bulletin. *Public Juvenile Facilities, 1985: Children in Custody.* Washington, D.C.: Government Printing Office, 1986. Biennial data on public and private juvenile detention, correctional, and shelter facilities nationwide and characteristics of the juveniles they contain.

U.S. Department of Justice. Bureau of Justice Statistics Bulletin. *Report to the Nation on Crime and Justice: The Data.* Washington, D.C.: Government Printing Office, 1983. A comprehensive report on crime and victims across the United States.

U.S. Department of Justice. *Children in Custody: 1982/83 Census of Juvenile Detention and Correctional Facilities.* Washington, D.C.: Government Printing Office, 1986. Statistical information on the characteristics of public and private juvenile custody facilities and juveniles in custody.

U.S. Department of Justice. Bureau of Justice Statistics. *Criminal Victimization in the United States, 1985: A National Crime Survey Report.* Washington, D.C.: Government Printing Office, 1987. An annual statistical report on criminal victimization in the United States involving victims age 12 and over.

U.S. Federal Bureau of Investigation. *Crime in the United States: Uniform Crime Reports 1986.* Washington, D.C.: Government Printing Office, 1987. An annual statistical analysis of crime in America as reported by law enforcement agencies.

Weisberg, D. Kelly. *Children of the Night: A Study of Adolescent Prostitution.*

Lexington, Mass.: Lexington Books, 1985. A comprehensive examination of the dynamics of adolescent prostitution.

Wolfgang, Marvin E.; Figlio, Robert M.; and Sellin, Thorsten. *Delinquency in a Birth Cohort*. Chicago: University of Chicago Press, 1972. A prospective study of a cohort of Philadelphia male youths, following their delinquent and nondelinquent careers from adolescence into young adulthood.

Index

A

Adams, D. E., 133
Adler, Freda, 73–74, 81, 101
Adolescent criminality: characteristics of, 3–21; defining, 3–6; dimensions of, 3–109; of females, 66–82; of gangs, 98–109; measurement of, 3–21; of minority youths, 17–20 (*see also* Minorities; Race); official statistics, 7–12; pornography, 64–65; property, 32–41; prostitution, 54–65; self-reported, 12–13; by sex, 16–17; short-comings of crime data, 20–21; trends, in, 14–20; and victimization surveys, 13–14; violent, 22–31; *see also* Crime; Delinquency; Gangs, adolescent
Adoption and fosterling studies, 114–115
Adult courts, 31; *see also* Criminal court
Aftercare, 189–190
Ageton, Suzanne S., 73
Ahrenfeldt, R. H., 192
Aichorn, August, 118
AIDS (Acquired Immune Deficiency Syndrome), 54, 60, 63–64, 65, 95; and pornography, 54; and prostitution, 54, 60, 63–64; and runaways, 51; and substance abuse, 95
Akers, Ronald L., 131
Alcohol use/abuse, 88–90, 94–97; gender and adolescent, 89; legal ramifications of adolescent, 89–90; and traffic fatalities, 90; *see also* Substance use/abuse
American Corrections Association, 169
American Journal of Psychiatry, 28
Andry, Robert G., 136
Annual Survey of Jails, 167–168
Argentina, 196–197
Arson, 41
Asians, 56, 71, 87, 103–104
Atavistic theories, 111–112

B

Bandura, Albert, 137
Bartollas, Clemens, 147, 182
Becker, Howard, 131
Becker, Wesley C., 137
Bender, L., 29
Biogenic theories, 111–113
Biological theories, 79, 111–117
Black, Donald J., 145–146
Blacks, 17–18, 24, 36, 47, 56, 71, 86, 101–104, 144, 174, 182; *see also* Minorities; Race
Bloods, 103; *see also* Gangs, adolescent
Body type theories, 112–113
Bouma, Donald H., 151
Bracey, Dorothy J., 57–59
Brain disorder studies, 116–117
Breed v. Jones, 156, 159
Briar, Scott, 147
Broken homes, 137–138
Bronner, Augusta F., 119
Brown, Waln K., 101
Browning, Charles J., 138
Bucy, June, 51
Bureau of Justice Statistics, 12, 26
Burgess, Ernest W., 125
Burglary, 40
Burkett, Stephen R., 96
Burt, Cyril, 119
Buttons, A., 136

C

California State Youth Authority, 18, 159
Campbell, Anne, 79, 101
Canter, Rochelle J., 138
Carpenter, Cheryl, 39–40, 93, 94
Causes of Delinquency (Hirschi), 125
Cavan, Jordan T., 192, 194
Cavan, Ruth, 192, 194